KEY FACTS KEY CASES

Criminal Law

KEY FACTS KEY CASES

The Key Facts Key Cases revision series is designed to give you a clear understanding and concise overview of the fundamental principles of your law course. The books' chapters reflect the most commonly taught topics, breaking the law down into bite-size sections with descriptive headings. Diagrams, tables and bullet points are used throughout to make the law easy to understand and memorise, and comprehensive case checklists are provided that show the principles and application of case law for your subject.

Titles in the series:

Contract Law

Criminal Law

English Legal System

Equity & Trusts

EU Law

Family Law

Human Rights

Land Law

Tort Law

For a full listing of the Routledge Revision range of titles, visit www.routledge.com/law

KEY FACTS KEY CASES

Criminal Law

Jacqueline Martin

Routledge
Taylor & Francis Group

LONDON AND NEW YORK

First published 2014
by Routledge
2 Park Square, Milton Park, Abingdon, Oxon OX14 4RN

and by Routledge
711 Third Avenue, New York, NY 10017

Routledge is an imprint of the Taylor & Francis Group, an informa business

© 2014 Jacqueline Martin

British Library Cataloguing in Publication Data
A catalogue record for this book is available from the British Library

Library of Congress Cataloging in Publication Data
A catalog record for this book has been requested.

ISBN: 978–0–415–83325–7 (pbk)
ISBN: 978–1–315–87167–7 (ebk)

Typeset in Helvetica
by RefineCatch Limited, Bungay, Suffolk

Contents

Preface

This new series of Key Facts Key Cases is built on the two well-known series, Key Facts and Key Cases. Each title in the Key Facts series now incorporates a Key Cases section at the end of most chapters, which is designed to give a clear understanding of important cases. This is useful when studying a new topic and invaluable as a revision aid. Each case is broken down into fact and law. In addition, many cases are extended by the use of important extracts from the judgment or by comment or by highlighting problems. In some instances, students are reminded that there is a link to other cases or material. If the link case is in another part of the book, the reference will be clearly shown. Some links will be to additional cases or materials that do not feature in the book.

The basic Key Facts sections are a practical and complete revision aid that can be used by students of law courses at all levels from A-level to degree and beyond, and in professional and vocational courses.

They are designed to give a clear view of each subject. This will be useful to students when tackling new topics and is invaluable as a revision aid.

Most chapters open with an outline in diagram form of the points covered in that chapter. The points are then developed in a structured list form to make learning easier. Supporting cases are given throughout by name and for some complex areas facts are given to reinforce the point being made. The most important cases are then given in more detail. The cases that feature in the Key Cases sections are given in blue in the ordinary text to alert students to that fact.

The Key Facts Key Cases series aims to accommodate the syllabus content of most qualifications in a subject area, using many visual learning aids.

Some areas of criminal law are very complex and this book helps students by breaking down each topic into key points. This is done for the general principles such as *actus reus* and *mens rea* and also for the specific offences. The topics covered make it a useful resource for criminal law components of degree courses, ILEX courses and A-level specifications.

Chapter 1 starts with an introduction to basic principles in criminal law. The general principles are covered in Chapters 2 to 9. Chapters 10 to 17 cover substantive areas of law.

In the Key Cases sections in order to give a clear layout, symbols have been used at the start of each component of the case. The symbols are:

Key Facts – These are the basic facts of the case.

Key Law – This is the major principle of law in the case, the *ratio decidendi*.

Key Judgment – This is an actual extract from a judgment made on the case.

Key Comment – Influential or appropriate comments made on the case.

Key Problem – Apparent inconsistencies or difficulties in the law.

Key Link – This indicates other cases which should be considered with this case.

The Key Link symbol alerts readers to links within the book and also to cases and other material especially statutory provisions that are not included.

The court abbreviations used in the key case sections of this book are shown below.

Ass	Assize Court	CA	Court of Appeal
CC	County Court	CCA	Court of Criminal Appeal
CCR	Crown Cases Reserved	CH	Court of Chancery
ChDiv	Chancery Division	CJEU	Court of Justice of the European Union

C-MAC	Court Martial Appeal Court	CP	Court of Probate
DC	Divisional Court	EAT	Employment Appeal Tribunal
ECHR	European Court of Human Rights	ECJ	European Court of Justice
ET/IT	Employment tribunal/ Industrial tribunal	Exch	Court of the Exchequer
HC	High Court	HL	House of Lords
KBD	King's Bench Division	NIRC	National Industrial Relations Court
PC	Privy Council	QBD	Queen's Bench Division
RC	Rolls Court	SC	Supreme Court

The law is as I believe it to be at June 2013.

Table of Cases

1 Introduction to criminal law

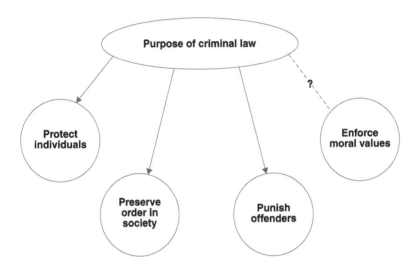

▶ 1.1 The purpose of criminal law

The main purposes are to:

1 Protect individuals and their property from harm.

2 Preserve order in society.

3 Punish those who deserve punishment. (N.B. There are also other aims when sentencing offenders, including incapacitation, deterrence, reformation and reparation.)

1.1.1 Should the law enforce moral values?

This area is controversial. It is argued that it is not the function of criminal law to interfere in the private lives of citizens unless it is necessary to try to impose certain standards of behaviour. The Wolfenden Committee (1957) felt that intervention in private lives should only be:

- to preserve public order and decency;
- to protect the citizen from what is offensive or injurious; and
- to provide sufficient safeguards against exploitation and corruption of others, particularly those who are especially vulnerable

Lord Devlin in the *Enforcement of Morals* (1965) disagreed. He felt that 'there are acts so gross and outrageous that they must be prevented at any cost'.

1.1.2 Conflicting cases

The courts are not always consistent in their approach to this area of law. *Brown* (1993): The House of Lords upheld convictions for assault causing actual bodily harm (s 47 Offences against the Person Act 1861) and malicious wounding (s 20 Offences against the Person Act 1861) for acts done in private by a group of consenting adult sado-masochists. *Wilson* (1996): The Court of Appeal quashed a conviction for assault causing actual bodily harm (s 47 Offences against the Person Act 1861) where a husband had branded his initials on his wife's buttocks, at her request.

1.2 Defining a crime

1. A crime is conduct forbidden by the State and to which a punishment has been attached because the conduct is regarded by the State as being criminal.
2. The statement above is the only definition which covers all crimes.
3. What conduct is criminal will, therefore, vary from country to country and from one time to another. The law is likely to change when there is a change in the values of government and society.

1.2.1 Example of the changing nature of criminal law

- The Criminal Law Amendment Act 1885 criminalised consensual homosexual acts between adults in private.
- The Sexual Offences Act 1967 decriminalised such behaviour between those aged 21 and over.
- The Criminal Justice and Public Order Act 1994 decriminalised such behaviour for those aged 18 and over.

- In 2000, the government reduced the age of consent for homosexual acts to 16, though the Parliament Acts had to be used as the House of Lords voted against the change in the law.

1.2.2 Judicial law-making

1   Some conduct is criminalised not by the State but by judges.

2   This happened in *Shaw v DPP* (1962) where the offence of conspiracy to corrupt public morals was created. The creation of the offence was confirmed in *Knuller (Publishing, Printing and Promotions) Ltd v DPP* (1973).

3   Another example is the offence of outraging public decency which has never been enacted by Parliament. It is an invention of the judges, yet people can be convicted of it (*Gibson* (1991)).

4   Marital rape has also been criminalised by the decisions of judges (*R v R* (1991)).

5   See also the cases of *Brown* (1993) and *Wilson* (1996) in 1.1.2.

▶ 1.3 Classification of offences

There are many ways of classifying offences depending on the purpose of the classification.

1.3.1 Classification by where a case will be tried

One of the most important ways of classifying offences is by the categories that affect where and how a case will be tried. For this purpose offences are classified as:

1   Indictable only offences, which must be tried on indictment at the Crown Court (e.g. murder, manslaughter, rape).

2   Triable either way offences which can be tried either on indictment at the Crown Court or summarily at the magistrates' court (e.g. theft, burglary, assault occasioning actual bodily harm).

3   Summary offences which can only be tried at the magistrates' court (e.g. assaulting a policeman in the execution of his duty, common assault).

1.3.2 Categories for police powers of detention

1   Police powers to detain a suspect who has been arrested depend on the category of offence. There are three categories:

● summary offences;

● indictable offences; and

● terrorism offences.

2   For summary offences, the police can only detain an arrested person for a maximum of 24 hours.

3   For indictable offences the suspect can be detained for 24 hours but this can be extended to 36 hours by an officer of the rank of superintendent or above. The police then have the right to apply to a magistrate for permission to detain the suspect for up to a maximum of 96 hours.

4   A person arrested on suspicion of terrorism offences can be detained for 48 hours. After this an application can be made to a judge to extend the detention up to a maximum of 14 days.

1.3.3 Classifying law by its source

Law comes from different sources. This is important from an academic point of view. These sources are:

● common law (judge-made);

● statutory (defined in an Act of Parliament);

● regulatory (set out in delegated legislation).

1.3.4 Classifying by the type of harm caused by the crime

When studying criminal law it is usual to study offences according to the type of harm caused. The main categories here are:

● offences against the person;

● offences against property;

● offences against public order.

▶ 1.4 Elements of a crime

1   For all crimes, except crimes of strict liability (see Chapter 4), there are two elements that must be proved by the prosecution. These are:

● *actus reus*;

● *mens rea*.

2   These terms come from a Latin maxim *actus non facit reum nisi mens sit rea* which means the act itself does not constitute guilt unless done with a guilty mind.

3   *Actus reus* has a wider meaning than an act as it can cover omissions or a state of affairs.

4   The term *actus reus* has been criticised as misleading. Lord Diplock in *Miller* (1983) preferred the term 'prohibited conduct'. The Law Commission in the Draft Criminal Code (1989) used the term 'external element'.

5   *Mens rea* translates as 'guilty mind' but this is also misleading. The levels of 'guilty mind' vary (see Chapter 3). The Law Commission in the Draft Criminal Code (1989) used the term 'fault element'.

6   The *actus reus* and *mens rea* will be different for different crimes.

7   The *actus reus* and the *mens rea* must be present together, but if there is an ongoing act, then the existence of the necessary mens rea at any point during that act is sufficient (*Fagan v Metropolitan Police Commissioner* (1969)). This also applies where there is a sequence of events or acts (*Thabo Meli* (1954), *Le Brun* (1991)).

8   For crimes of strict liability the prosecution need only prove the *actus reus*; no mental element is needed for guilt. (See Chapter 4 for strict liability.)

9   Even where the *actus reus* and *mens rea* are present, the defendant may be not guilty if he has a defence (see Chapters 8 and 9 for defences).

▶ 1.5 Burden and standard of proof

1   The burden is on the prosecution to prove the case. This means that they must prove both the required *actus reus* and the required *mens rea* (*Woolmington v DPP* (1935)). An accused person is presumed innocent until proven guilty.

2   The standard of proof is 'beyond reasonable doubt'.

3   If the defendant raises a defence then it is for the prosecution to negate that defence. In *Woolmington*, the defendant stated that the gun had gone off accidentally, thus raising the defence of accident. The prosecution were obliged to disprove this if the defendant was to be found guilty.

4   For certain defences, the burden of proof is on the defendant. For example, for the defence of insanity the defendant has to prove he was insane at the time of the offence. Placing the burden of proof on the defence may breach Art 6(2) of the European Convention on Human Rights (see 1.6.2).

5   Where the defendant has to prove a defence, the standard is the civil one of balance of probabilities.

▶ 1.6 Criminal law and human rights

1   The Human Rights Act 1998 incorporated the European Convention on Human Rights into our law. All Articles have to be considered in English law.

2   In criminal law the most relevant rights under the Convention are:
●   the right to a fair trial (Art 6(1));
●   the presumption of innocence (Art 6(2));
●   no punishment without law (Art 7(1)).

3   Other Convention rights relevant to criminal law include:
●   the right not to be subjected to inhuman or degrading treatment (Art 3(1));
●   the right of respect for a person's private life (Art 8);
●   that, in the application of the Convention rights and freedoms, there should be no discrimination on the grounds of sex, race, colour, religion or political opinion (Art 14).

1.6.1 The right to a fair trial

1   This right is contained in Article 6(1).

2   In G (2008), the House of Lords held that the fact that the offence was one of strict liability did not render the trial unfair.

1.6.2 Burden of proof

1   Article 6(2) states that: 'Everyone charged with a criminal offence shall be presumed innocent until proven guilty.' This places the burden of proof on the prosecution.

2   Defences which place the burden of proving the defence on the defendant may be in breach of this Article (*Lambert* (2001)).

3   However, the courts have held that in some statutes the reverse burden of proof may be interpreted as evidential only (*A-G Reference (No 4 of 2002)* (2004)).

4   In addition, the House of Lords has held that a full reverse burden of proof may be acceptable if it is not unfair or disproportionate (*Sheldrake v DPP* (2005)).

1.6.3 No punishment without law

1   Article 7(1) states that: 'No one shall be held guilty of any criminal offence on account of any act or omission which did not constitute a criminal offence under national law or international law at the time it was committed.'

2   If the offence is one which conforms to the fundamental objectives of the Convention, then it will not be in breach of this Article: *CR v UK* (1996) where the conviction of a husband for the rape of his wife was approved by the European Court of Human Rights.

3   In other cases there have been challenges under Art 7 on the basis that the offence is too uncertain or lacks clarity, e.g. gross negligence manslaughter (*R v Misra; R v Srivastava* (2004)) (see 10.4.3) and public nuisance (*Goldstein* (2005)). To date, no challenge on the basis of lack of clarity has been successful.

1.6.4 Other human rights

1   There have been challenges to the criminal law on the basis of other rights in the Convention.

2   In *Altham* (2006), the defendant claimed that the refusal to allow him the defence of necessity in respect of his use of cannabis for extreme physical pain was a breach of Art 3 which provides that no one shall be subjected to 'inhuman or degrading treatment'. This challenge failed.

3   Similarly, in *Quayle* (2005), the defendant argued that the refusal to allow him the defence of necessity in respect of his use of cannabis for extreme physical pain was a breach of Art 8. This Article gives a right to respect for a person's private life. This challenge also failed.

4   In G (2008), a minority of the Law Lords held that prosecuting D, aged 15, under s 5 Sexual Offences Act 2003 (rape of a child) was disproportionate and a breach of Art 8 when the sexual intercourse was consensual and D could have been charged under s 13 of the Act.

5   In *Dehal* (2005), it was held that D's right to freedom of expression (Art 10) had been infringed when he was prosecuted under s 4 Public Order Act 1986 for placing a notice in a temple stating that the preacher was a hypocrite.

1.6.5 Human rights and criminal procedure

1   The procedure in a case where the defendant is thought to be unfit to plead was amended after it was held in H (2003) that s 4A Criminal Procedure (Insanity) Act 1964 was not compatible with the European Convention on Human Rights.

2   Procedure for trying child defendants was altered after the European Court of Human Rights held there was a breach of Art 6 on the right to a fair trial in *T v UK: V v UK* (2000).

Key Cases Checklist

Purpose of Law

Brown (1993)
The law <u>should protect society from a cult of violence</u>

Wilson (1996)
Consensual marital behaviour was not criminal BUT the law should develop on a case-by-case basis

Judicial Law-Making

Shaw v DPP (1961)
Created the offence of corrupting public morals

Knuller v DPP (1973)
Recognised that *Shaw* had created the offence of corrupting public morals: majority also thought an offence of outraging public decency existed

R (1991)
Law should change with society

Introductory Points

Elements of a Crime

Fagan v MPC (1968)
Actus reus can be a continuing act, so that if *mens rea* is superimposed on it at any point, it completes the offence

Thabo Meli v R (1954)
Where *mens rea* and *actus reus* are present in a series of acts then there is sufficient coincidence for D to be guilty

Burden of Proof

Woolmington (1935)
Where D raises a defence it is for the prosecution to negate that defence.
This applies to nearly all defences

Lambert (2001)
It is normally a breach of human rights for D to have to prove innocence

Sheldrake (2004)
BUT imposing a legal burden of proof on D is not objectionable where the offence carries risk of death and the relevant information is within D's knowledge

1.1.2

Brown [1993] 2 All ER 75, (1993) 97 Cr App R 44

 HL

Key Facts

Five men in a group of consenting adult sado-masochists were convicted of offences of assault causing actual bodily harm (s 47 Offences Against the Person Act 1861) and malicious wounding (s 20 Offences Against the Person Act 1861). They had carried out acts which included applying stinging nettles to the genital area and inserting map pins or fish hooks into each other's penises. All the victims had consented and none had needed medical attention.

Key Law

Consent could not be used as a defence to charges of assault, even though the acts were between adults in private and did not result in serious bodily injury.

Key Judgment: Lord Templeman

'Society is entitled and bound to protect itself against a cult of violence. Pleasure derived from the infliction of pain is an evil thing. Cruelty is uncivilized.'

Key Problem

Two of the judges in the House of Lords dissented in this case. Lord Mustill thought that the case raised 'questions of private morality' and that the standards by which the defendants should be judged were not those of the criminal law. This dissent among the judges shows the difficulty of deciding just when the judges should intervene. Compare the decision with that in the next case.

1.1.2

Wilson [1996] 3 WLR 125, [1996] 2 Cr App R 241

CA

Key Facts

A husband had used a heated butter knife to brand his initials on his wife's buttocks, at her request. The wife's burns became infected and she needed medical treatment. He was convicted of assault causing actual bodily harm (s 47 Offences Against the Person Act 1861) but on appeal, the Court of Appeal quashed the conviction.

Key Law

Consent was a defence in such a case. However, the law should develop on a case-by-case basis.

Key Judgment: Russell LJ

'It is not in the public interest that activities such as the appellant's in this appeal should amount to a criminal behaviour. Consensual activity between husband and wife, in the privacy of the matrimonial home, is not, in our judgment, a proper matter for criminal investigation, let alone criminal prosecution.'

Key Link

Attorney-General's Reference (No 6 of 1980) [1981] 2 All ER 1057. See 8.6.

1.2.2   ***Shaw v DPP* [1962] AC 220, (1961) 45 Cr App R 113**   (HL)

Key Facts

D published a directory of prostitutes. It included photographs of some of the prostitutes and information on the type of conduct in which they were prepared to participate.

Key Law

The House of Lords created the offence of conspiracy to corrupt public morals as there did not appear to be an offence which covered the situation.

Key Judgment: Viscount Simmonds

'I entertain no doubt that there remains in the courts a residual power to enforce the supreme and fundamental purpose of the law, to conserve not only the safety and order but also the moral welfare of the state . . .'

Key Problem

This case highlights whether unelected judges should make law. It can be argued that if Parliament has chosen not to prohibit certain conduct then it is not for judges to fill the gaps.

1.2.2

Knuller (Publishing, Printing and Promotions) Ltd v DPP [1973] AC 435, (1972) 56 Cr App R 633

HL

Key Facts

The appellants published a magazine which contained, on inside pages, a number of advertisements headed 'Males'. Most of these were put in by homosexuals with the intention of meeting other men for homosexual purposes. At the time, the age of consent for homosexual behaviour was 21. The appellants accepted that many males under the age of 21 would see the advertisements and that some of them might reply.

The appellants were charged with 1) conspiracy to corrupt public morals and 2) conspiracy to outrage public decency. They were convicted of both charges and appealed.

Key Law

The offence of corrupting public morals existed. It had been created in *Shaw v DPP* (1962) and it was for Parliament, not the courts, to abolish it. The appellants' conviction for 1) was upheld. However, the appellants' conviction for 2) was quashed.

Key Problem

The judges were divided as to whether an offence of outraging public decency existed. Two of them held that it did not and that the courts could not create such an offence. The other three held that such an offence did exist, but quashed the conviction because the trial judge had not directed the jury adequately on what was meant by 'outrage'.

Key Comment

The existence of the offences of corrupting public morals and outraging public decency has been recognised by Parliament in the Criminal Law Act 1977. Section 5(1) of this Act abolished common law conspiracy, but s 5(3)(a) specifically provides that the offences of conspiracy to corrupt public morals with conspiracy to outrage public decency were not abolished.

1.2.2 *R v R* [1991] 4 All ER 481, (1991) 94 Cr App R 216

(HL)

Key Facts

D and his wife had separated and agreed to seek a divorce. Three weeks later, D broke into the wife's parents' home, where she was staying, and attempted to rape her.

Key Law

Although old authorities stated that a man could not be guilty of raping his wife, the law had to evolve to suit modern society. D could be guilty.

Key Judgment: Lord Keith of Kinkel

'[The] question is whether . . . this is an area where the court should step aside to leave the matter to the parliamentary process. This is not the creation of a new offence, it is the removal of a common law fiction which has become anachronistic and offensive and we consider that it is our duty, having reached that conclusion, to act upon it.'

Key Comment

D took the case to the European Court of Human Rights, claiming that the retrospective recognition of marital rape was a breach of Article 7 of the European Convention on Human Rights. It was held that there was no breach of Article 7. In fact, abandoning the idea that a husband could not be prosecuted for rape of his wife conformed with the fundamental objective of respect for human dignity.

1.4

Fagan v Metropolitan Police Commissioner [1968] 3 All ER 442, (1968) 52 Cr App R 700   (DC)

Key Facts

D accidentally drove his car onto a police officer's foot. When D was asked to move the car, he refused to do so for some time. He was convicted of assaulting a police officer in the execution of his duty. This involved proving an assault.

Key Law

The *actus reus* of assault could be a continuing act so that if D developed the necessary *mens rea* at any time during that period, he could be guilty of battery.

Key Judgment: James J

'For an assault to be committed, both the elements of actus reus *and* mens rea *must be present at the same time . . . It is not necessary that mens rea should be present at the inception of the* actus reus, *it can be superimposed on an existing act. On the other hand, the subsequent inception of* mens rea *cannot convert an act which has been completed without* mens rea *into an assault.'*

Key Problem

Would the failure of D to remove his car from the police officer's foot now be recognised as the *actus reus* of assault? This would be in line with the decision in *DPP v Santana-Bermudez* [2003] EWHC 2908, where D's failure to tell a police woman that there was a needle in his pocket which she was about to search was held to be sufficient for the *actus reus* of assault.

1.4

Thabo Meli v R [1954] 1 All ER 373   (PC)

Key Facts

Ds attacked a man and believed they had killed him. They then pushed his body over a low cliff. In fact, the man had survived the attack and died of exposure while unconscious at the foot of the cliff.

Key Law

Provided that the required *mens rea* and *actus reus* were combined in a series of acts, a defendant could be guilty.

Key Links

- *Church* [1965] 2 All ER 72, (1965) 49 Cr App R 206 (see 10.4.1);
- *Le Brun* [1991] 4 All ER 673, (1991) 94 Cr App R 101.

1.5

Woolmington v DPP [1935] AC 462, (1935) 25 Cr App R 72   (HL)

Key Facts

D went to ask his wife to return to him. He took with him a loaded sawn-off shotgun with which, he claimed, he intended to commit suicide if she refused to return to him. Following her refusal, he brought the gun out from under his coat, to show her he meant to commit suicide. As he brought it across his waist it somehow went off, killing his wife. He claimed that this was a pure accident.

Key Law

When D raises a defence, it is for the prosecution to negate that defence. This is part of the prosecution's duty to prove D's guilt.

Key Judgment: Lord Sankey

'Throughout the web of the English criminal law one golden thread is always to be seen – that it is the duty of the prosecution to prove the prisoner's guilt . . . No matter what the charge or where the trial, the principle that the prosecution must prove the guilt of the prisoner is part of the common law of England and no attempt to whittle it down can be entertained.'

1.6.2

Lambert [2001] UKHL 37, [2001] 2 Cr App R 511   (HL)

Key Facts

This concerned s 28(2) Misuse of Drugs Act 1971 which states that a defendant shall be acquitted if he 'proves that he neither believed nor suspected nor had any reasons to suspect that the substance or product in question was a controlled drug'. D claimed that this subsection meant he had to prove his innocence and this was a breach of Article 6(2) European Convention on Human Rights (the presumption of innocence). The appeal failed because a majority of the Lords held that the Human Rights Act 1998 was not retrospective.

Key Law

A majority of the Law Lords held that if s 28(2) of the Misuse of Drugs Act 1971 was read as imposing a legal burden on the defendant to prove lack of knowledge, then this under-mined the presumption of innocence to an impermissible extent. However, they thought it could be read down as imposing only an evidential burden. They did this by interpreting the subsection as meaning not 'prove' but 'introduce evidence of'.

Key Problem

Is this interpretation of the subsection really viable? The word used in it is 'prove'. This idea of 'reading down' so as to impose an evidential burden rather than a legal one was also used in *Attorney-General's Reference (No 4 of 2002)* (2004), which was heard together with the appeal in *Sheldrake* (2004) (see below).

 1.6.2   *Sheldrake v DPP* [2004] UKHL 43   HL

Key Facts

Sheldrake was convicted of being in charge of a motor car in a public place after consuming so much alcohol that he exceeded the prescribed limit, contrary to s 5(1)(b) Road Traffic Act 1988. He appealed to the Divisional Court who allowed his appeal. The prosecution appealed to the House of Lords.

The defence argued that s 5(2) infringed the presumption of innocence guaranteed by Article 6(2) as it imposed on the defendant a legal burden of proving innocence by proving a defence. The House of Lords allowed the prosecution's appeal and reinstated the conviction.

Key Law

The House of Lords held that s 5(2) did impose a legal burden of proof on the defendant but it was justified.

Key Judgment: Lord Bingham

'It is not objectionable to criminalise a defendant's conduct in these circumstances without requiring a prosecutor to prove criminal intent. The defendant has a full opportunity to show that there was no likelihood of his driving, a matter so closely conditioned by his own knowledge ... as to make it much more appropriate for him to prove, on the balance of probabilities, that he would not have been likely to drive than for the prosecutor to prove beyond reasonable doubt that he would.'

2 Actus reus

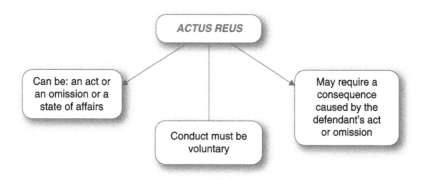

▶ 2.1 The physical element

1   The *actus reus* is the physical element of a crime. It can be:

- an act;
- a failure to act (an omission); or
- a state of affairs (very rare).

2   For some crimes the act or omission must also result in a consequence.

2.1.1 Examples

1   **An act** – picking up an item in a shop (one way of committing the physical element for theft); or punching a victim which could be part of the physical element of an assault occasioning actual bodily harm (s 47 Offences against the Person Act 1861).

2   **An omission** – failing to provide a specimen of breath; or wilful neglect of a child (i.e. failing to provide one's child with food, clothing or medical care under s 1 Children and Young Persons Act 1933).

3   **A state of affairs** – being found drunk in a public place. Merely being drunk and in a public place is sufficient (*Winzar v Chief Constable of Kent* (1983)). Also *Larsonneur* (1933), in which an individual considered to

be alien under the law was brought back to the United Kingdom by Irish police. On her arrival she was arrested and charged with 'being an alien, to whom leave to land had been refused, was found in the UK'. Being in the UK was enough to make her guilty.

4 **A consequence** – in murder there may be a stabbing, but there must also be the consequence of death resulting from that stab wound; or, for example, a broken nose for the consequence of actual bodily harm in s 47 Offences against the Person Act 1861; if the assault did not cause any injury then there is no s 47 offence.

▶ 2.2 Voluntary conduct

1 The act or omission must be voluntary on the part of the defendant.

2 If the defendant has no control over his actions, then he has not committed the *actus reus*.

3 In *Hill v Baxter* (1958) the court gave examples where a driver of a vehicle could not be said to be to doing the act of driving voluntarily. These included where a driver lost control of his vehicle because he:

● was stung by a swarm of bees; or

● was struck on the head by a stone; or

● had a heart attack while driving.

4 Other examples of involuntary conduct include:

● another person pushing the defendant so that the defendant falls on to the victim;

● a reflex action; or

● a muscle spasm.

5 If the defendant knew that he was liable to lose control of his movements because of an existing health problem, then his actions would be considered as voluntary (*Broome v Perkins* (1987)).

6 Where the defendant's act occurs while he is asleep or his consciousness is impaired, or it is because of a reflex, spasm or convulsion, the defendant may have the defence of automatism (see Chapter 9).

▶ 2.3 Liability for omissions

1 At common law there are five situations where there is a duty to act and a failure to act (omission) creates liability.

2 Acts of Parliament can create liability for an omission.

2.3.1 Omissions as *actus reus* of common law offences

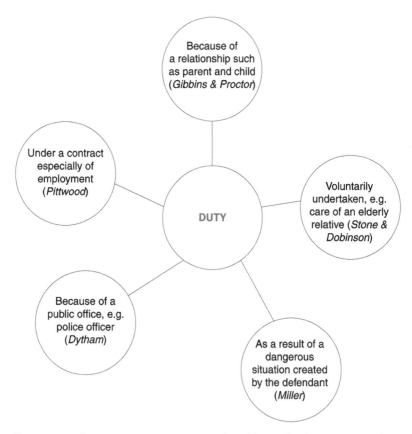

For common law crimes an omission is only sufficient for the *actus reus* where there is a duty to act. This can be:

- A contractual duty; in *Pittwood* (1902) a railway crossing keeper omitted to shut the gates so that a person crossing the line was struck and killed by a train. The keeper was guilty of manslaughter.

- A duty by virtue of a relationship, usually parent and child; in *Gibbins and Proctor* (1918), a child's father and his mistress failed to feed the child, so that it died of starvation; they were guilty of murder. In *Evans* (2009), a mother was convicted of gross negligence manslaughter when she failed to take any action although she knew that V had taken drugs and was ill.

● A duty by virtue of voluntarily undertaking it; in *Stone and Dobinson* (1977) the defendants had undertaken the care of Stone's elderly sister; they were guilty of manslaughter in failing to care for her or summon help when she became helpless.

● A duty through one's official position; in *Dytham* (1979) a police officer witnessed a violent attack on the victim, but took no steps to intervene or summon help; instead he drove away from the scene. The officer was guilty of wilfully and without reasonable excuse of neglecting to perform his duty.

● A duty which arises because the defendant has set in motion a chain of events; in *Miller* (1983) a squatter accidentally started a fire. When he realised this he left the room and did not attempt to put it out or summon help. He was guilty of arson. In *Evans* (2009) (see above) the sister of the victim was guilty of manslaughter on the same basis as *Miller*.

Note that in *DPP v Santana-Bermudez* (2003) it was held the defendant's failure to tell a police woman, who was going to search his pockets, that he had a hypodermic needle in one of them could amount to the *actus reus* for the purposes of an assault causing actual bodily harm when she was injured by the needle.

Note that discontinuance of medical treatment where it is in the best interests of the patient is not an omission that can form the *actus reus* (*Airedale NHS Trust v Bland* (1993)).

2.3.2 Omissions as *actus reus* for statutory crimes

1 Where an offence is defined in an Act of Parliament or statutory instrument, the wording determines whether it can be committed by omission.

2 Failing to report a road traffic accident is a clear example of a statutory offence of omission.

3 Wording of other offences is not always so clear; for example, s 17 Theft Act 1968, where the offence is committed if the defendant '. . . destroys, defaces, conceals or falsifies any . . . document made or required for any accountancy purpose' has been held to be an offence of omission (*Shama* (1990)).

4 A more recently created offence which can be committed by omission is causing or allowing the death of a child or vulnerable adult (s 5 Domestic Violence and Victims Act 2004).

▶ 2.4 Causation

Where a consequence must be proved, then the prosecution has to show that the defendant's conduct was:

- the factual cause of that consequence; and
- the legal cause of that consequence; and
- that there was no intervening act which broke the chain of causation.

2.4.1 Factual cause

The consequence would not have happened 'but for' the defendant's conduct. In *White* (1910) the defendant put cyanide in his mother's drink intending to kill her. She died of a heart attack before she could drink it. The defendant did not cause her death; he was not guilty of murder, though he was guilty of attempted murder.

2.4.2 Legal cause

1   The defendant's conduct must be more than a 'minimal' cause of the consequence (*Cato* (1976)), but it need not be a substantial cause.

2   The defendant's conduct need not be the only cause; another's act may have contributed to the consequence.

2.4.3 Intervening act

1   The chain of causation can be broken by:
    - an act of a third party;
    - the victim's own act; or
    - a natural but unpredictable event.

2   In order to break the chain of causation so that the defendant is not responsible for the consequence, the intervening act must be sufficiently independent of the defendant's conduct and sufficiently serious.

3   Where V's death was caused by the deliberate independent act of a third party, then D did not cause the death even though he took part in an earlier assault on V (*Rafferty* (2007)).

4   Where the defendant's conduct causes foreseeable action by a third party, then the defendant is likely to be held to have caused the consequence (*Pagett* (1983)).

5   Where D has prepared an injection for V, but V self-injects, then V's act breaks the chain of causation (*Kennedy* (2007)).

6   Medical treatment is unlikely to break the chain of causation unless it is so independent of the defendant's acts and 'in itself so potent in causing death' that the defendant's acts are insignificant (*Cheshire* (1991), *Jordan* (1956)).

7   The defendant must take the victim as he finds him as in *Blaue* (1975) where a Jehovah's witness died because she refused a blood transfusion.

8   Switching off a life support machine does not break the chain of causation (*Malcherek* (1981)).

9   If the defendant causes the victim to react in a foreseeable way, then any injury to the victim will have been caused by the defendant (*Roberts* (1971), *Marjoram* (2000)).

10 If the victim's reaction is unreasonable, then this may break the chain of causation (*Williams and Davis* (1992)).

Key Cases Checklist

Omissions as *actus reus*
This can occur where D owes a duty of care

***Gibbins and Proctor* (1918)**
Parents and anyone who has undertaken the care of a child

***Stone and Dobinson* (1977)**
D may owe a duty to vulnerable family members. Anyone undertaking care of an elderly person may owe a duty

***Dytham* (1979)**
There may be a duty because of a public office

***Miller* (1983)**
Where D sets in motion a chain of events which might cause harm, he has a duty of care

***Evans* (2009)**
A person who has created or contributed to a life-threatening state of affairs is under a duty to act

Causation

***White* (1910)**
The act must be the factual cause

***Pagett* (1983)**
A reasonable response in self-defence does not break the chain of causation

***Kennedy No 2* (2007)**
Self-injection of a drug breaks the chain of causation

***Malcherek* (1981)**
Switching off a life-support machine does not break the chain of causation

***Cheshire* (1991)**
Negligent treatment by medical staff does not normally break the chain of causation

Actus reus

Intervening acts

***Roberts* (1972)**
Where V's intervening act is reasonably foreseeable then it does not break the chain of causation

***Williams and Davis* (1992)**
If V's conduct is not reasonably foreseeable then it will break the chain of causation

2.3.1   *Gibbins and Proctor* (1918) 13 Cr App R 134   CCA

Key Facts

Gibbins and his partner starved his seven-year-old daughter to death. The other children of the family were well cared for and fed.

Key Law

An omission can be the *actus reus* of murder where a duty exists. In this case Gibbins, as the child's father, had a duty towards her. His partner had undertaken care of the children and so also owed a duty to the child.

2.3.1   *Stone and Dobinson* [1977] QB 354, (1977) 64 Cr App R 186   HL

Key Facts

Stone's sister, Fanny, came to live with the defendants. Fanny was eccentric and often stayed in her room for several days. She also failed to eat. She eventually became bed-ridden and incapable of caring for herself. On at least one occasion Dobinson helped to wash Fanny and also occasionally prepared food for her. Fanny died from malnutrition. Both Ds were found guilty of her manslaughter.

As Fanny was Stone's sister he owed a duty of care to her. Dobinson had undertaken some care of Fanny and so also owed a duty of care. The duty was to either help her themselves or to summon help from other sources. Their failure to do either of these meant that they were in breach of their duty.

2.3.1   *Dytham* [1979] QB 722   CA

Key Facts

D was a police officer who was on duty. V was ejected from a nightclub about 30 yards from where D was standing. There was a fight and three men kicked V to death. D took no steps to intervene or summon help. When the fight was over, D told a bystander he was going off duty and left the scene. He was convicted of misconduct in a public office.

Key Law

An omission (a wilful failure to act) was sufficient for the *actus reus*. D had a duty to protect V or to arrest the attackers or otherwise bring them to justice.

2.3.1   *Miller* [1983] 1 All ER 978, (1983) 77 Cr App R 17   HL

Key Facts

D was living in a squat. He fell asleep while smoking a cigarette. He awoke to find his mattress on fire. He went into another room and went back to sleep. The house caught fire. He was convicted of arson.

Where D had set a chain of events in motion that might cause harm, a failure to take reasonable steps to deal with the fire when he discovered his mattress was on fire meant that he had committed the *actus reus* for arson.

Key Link

DPP v Santana-Bermudez [2003] EWHC 2908. See 12.1.

2.3.1   *Evans* [2009] EWCA Crim 650   CA

Key Facts

D bought heroin for V, her 16-year-old half-sister, who was an addict. V self-injected and it became obvious she had overdosed. D and their mother put V to bed but did not call the emergency services. V died. D (and the mother) were convicted of gross negligence manslaughter.

Key Judgment: Lord Judge CJ

'The duty necessary to found gross negligence manslaughter is plainly not confined to cases of familial or professional relationship between D and V ... [W]here a person has created or contributed to the creation of a state of affairs which he knows, or ought reasonably to know, has become life-threatening, a consequent duty to act by taking reasonable steps to save the other's life will normally arise.'

2.4.1

White [1910] 2 KB 124, (1910) 4 Cr App R 257

Key Facts

D added poison to his mother's drink, with the intention of killing her. The evidence showed she died of a heart attack but there was no evidence to show she had drunk any of the poison. Also, the amount of poison was insufficient to kill her in any event.

Key Law

Although D had the intention to kill and did the act of putting poison into his mother's drink, his act was not the cause of her death so he could not be guilty of murder.

Key Link

Attempts – see 6.4.

2.4.3

Pagett [1983] Crim LR 393, (1983) 76 Cr App R 279

Key Facts

D took his girlfriend, who was pregnant by him, from her home by force. He then held the girl hostage. Police called on him to surrender. D came out, holding the girl in front of him and firing at the police. The police returned fire and the girl was killed by police bullets. D was convicted of manslaughter.

Key Law

1) D's act need not be the sole cause, nor need it be the main cause. It is enough if his act contributed significantly to the death.
2) A reasonable act in self-defence caused by D's own acts is not an intervening act for the purpose of breaking the chain of causation.

Key Judgment: Goff LJ

'There can, we consider, be no doubt that a reasonable act performed for the purpose of self-preservation, being of

course an act caused by the accused's own act, does not operate as a novus actus interveniens.'

2.4.3

Kennedy [2007] UKHL 38, [2008] 1 AC 269

Key Facts

D and V lived in a hostel. D, at V's request, prepared a dose of heroin and gave V the syringe with it in. V then self-injected. He later died as a result. D's conviction for unlawful act manslaughter was quashed by the House of Lords.

Key Law

A voluntary and informed act by V will break the chain of causation.

Key Judgment: Lord Bingham:

'The criminal law assumes the existence of free will. Thus [D] is not to be treated as causing [V] to act in a certain way if [V] makes a voluntary and informed decision to act in that way rather than another. The finding that [V] freely and voluntarily administered the injection to himself, knowing what it was, is fatal to any contention that [D] caused the heroin to be administered to [V] or taken by him.'

2.4.3

Cheshire [1991] 3 All ER 670, [1991] Crim LR 709

Key Facts

D shot V in the stomach. V was treated in hospital where a tracheotomy tube was inserted to help him breathe. Two months later, when his wounds were virtually healed, V died of a rare complication caused by the tracheotomy.

Key Law

D's acts need not be the sole cause or even the main cause of death. It is suffcient if his acts contributed significantly to the death. Negligent treatment by medical staff will not normally exclude D's responsibility for the death.

Key Judgment: Beldam LJ

'Even though negligence in the treatment of the victim was the immediate cause of death, the jury should not regard it as excluding the responsibility of the accused unless the negligent treatment was so independent of his acts, and in itself so potent in causing death, that they regard the contribution made by his acts as insignificant.'

Key Problem

The level of negligence in medical treatment required to break the chain of causation is very high – 'so potent in causing death'. It will only be in an exceptional case that medical treatment will break the chain of causation. The courts are likely to hold the original attacker liable for the death even where the medical treatment is 'thoroughly bad' (*Smith* (1959)).

Key Link

- *Smith* [1959] 2 QB 35 Courts Martial Appeal Court.
- *Jordan* (1956) 40 Cr App R 152 CA.
- *Mellor* [1996] 2 Cr App R 245 CA.

2.4.3

Malcherek [1981] 2 All ER 422, (1981) 73 Cr App R 173

CA

Key Facts

D stabbed his wife in the stomach. In hospital, she was put on a life-support machine. After a number of tests showed that she was brain dead, the machine was switched off. D was charged with her murder. The trial judge refused to allow the issue of causation to go to the jury. D was convicted. He appealed.

Key Law

Discontinuance of treatment by switching off a life-support machine does not break the chain of causation. The original attacker is still liable for the death.

2.4.3

Roberts [1972] Crim LR 27, (1971) 56 Cr App R 95

CA

Key Facts

V was a passenger in D's car. While driving along, D made sexual advances to V and attempted to pull her coat off. She jumped from the car and was injured. D was convicted of an assault occasioning actual bodily harm.

Key Law

A foreseeable act by V does not break the chain of causation.

Key Judgment: Stephenson LJ

'The test is: Was it a natural result of what the alleged assailant said and did, in the sense that it was something that could reasonably have been foreseen as the consequence of what he was saying or doing?'

2.4.3

Williams and Davis [1992] 2 All ER 183, (1992) 95 Cr App R 1

CA

Key Facts

Ds gave a lift to a hitch-hiker. He (V) jumped from Ds' car when it was travelling at about 30 mph, allegedly because Ds had tried to rob him. V died from head injuries. Both Ds were convicted of manslaughter. The Court of Appeal quashed their convictions.

Key Law

V's conduct must be something which could be reasonably foreseen. If it is not reasonably foreseeable then the chain of causation is broken.

Key Judgment: Stuart-Smith LJ

'There must be some proportionality between the gravity of the threat and the action of the deceased in seeking to escape from it . . . [T]he deceased's conduct . . . [must] be *something that a reasonable and responsible man in the assailant's shoes would have foreseen . . . [T]he nature of the threat is of importance in considering both the foreseeability of harm to the victim from the threat and the question whether the deceased's conduct was proportionate to the threat, that is to say that it was within the ambit of reasonableness and not so daft as to make it his own voluntary act which amounted to a* novus actus interveniens *and consequently broke the chain of causation.'*

3 Mens rea

The different levels of intention are shown in the chart below.

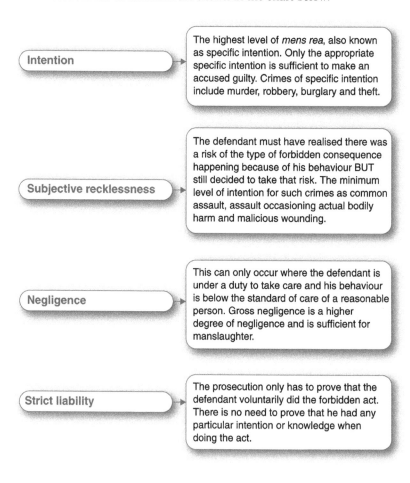

Intention → The highest level of *mens rea*, also known as specific intention. Only the appropriate specific intention is sufficient to make an accused guilty. Crimes of specific intention include murder, robbery, burglary and theft.

Subjective recklessness → The defendant must have realised there was a risk of the type of forbidden consequence happening because of his behaviour BUT still decided to take that risk. The minimum level of intention for such crimes as common assault, assault occasioning actual bodily harm and malicious wounding.

Negligence → This can only occur where the defendant is under a duty to take care and his behaviour is below the standard of care of a reasonable person. Gross negligence is a higher degree of negligence and is sufficient for manslaughter.

Strict liability → The prosecution only has to prove that the defendant voluntarily did the forbidden act. There is no need to prove that he had any particular intention or knowledge when doing the act.

▶ 3.1 Mental element

Mens rea means the mental element of an offence. Each offence has its own *mens rea*. The prosecution must prove that the accused had the relevant *mens rea* for the offence charged. There are different levels of *mens rea*.

To be guilty the accused must have at least the minimum level of *mens rea* required by the offence. As there are different levels of *mens rea*, it is difficult to define. It is easier to say what *mens rea* is not.

1   *Mens rea* is not the same as motive.

2   It does not mean an 'evil' mind.

3   It does not require knowledge that the act was forbidden by law.

▶ 3.2 Intention

1   Intention is the highest level of *mens rea*. It is also referred to as specific intention.

2   Intention has never been defined by Parliament, but the Draft Criminal Code suggested the following definition:

> '. . . a person acts intentionally with respect to a result when he acts either in order to bring it about or being aware that it will occur in the ordinary course of events'.

3   One judicial definition is 'a decision to bring about, in so far as it lies within the accused's power (the prohibited consequence), no matter whether the accused desired that consequence of his act or not' (*Mohan* (1976)).

4   Intention can be divided into:

● direct intent; and

● oblique intent (foresight of consequences).

5   Direct intent is also known as purposive intent. The defendant has a certain aim or result in mind and intends to achieve that result.

6   Oblique intent is where the defendant has one purpose in mind but in achieving that purpose also causes other consequences. This area of intention has caused many problems.

3.2.1 Oblique intent/foresight of consequences

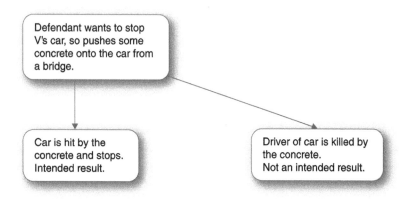

1   Section 8 of the Criminal Justice Act 1967 states:

> 'A court or jury, in determining whether a person has committed an Offence:
>
> (a) shall not be bound in law to infer that he intended or foresaw a result of his actions by reason only of it being a natural and probable consequence of those actions; but
> (b) shall decide whether he did intend or foresee that result by referring to all the evidence, drawing such inferences from the evidence as appear proper in the circumstances.'

2   Foresight of consequences is not intention; it is only evidence from which intention can be inferred (or found) (*Moloney (1985)*, *Hancock and Shankland (1986)*).

3   Intention cannot be inferred unless the harm caused was a virtual certainty as a result of the defendant's actions and the defendant realised that this was so (*Nedrick (1986)*, *Woollin (1998)*).

3.2.2 Key cases

1   *Moloney (1985)* – the defendant shot and killed his stepfather in a drunken challenge to see who was quicker on the draw. The House of Lords decided that foresight of consequences was only evidence of intention. The House of Lords also gave guidelines, which referred to the natural consequence of the defendant's act, but omitted to mention probability. This was overruled in the next case.

2   *Hancock and Shankland* (1986) – the defendants wanted to frighten a fellow worker so that he would not break a strike by going into work. They pushed two concrete blocks from a bridge onto the road below where he was travelling to work by taxi. The taxi driver was killed. The House of Lords pointed out that the probability of the result occurring was something to take into account in deciding whether there was sufficient evidence from which intention could be inferred.

3   *Nedrick* (1986) – the defendant poured paraffin through the letterbox of a house in order to frighten the woman who lived there. A child died in the fire. The Court of Appeal suggested that juries ask themselves two questions:

   ● How probable was the consequence which resulted from the defendant's voluntary act?

   ● Did the defendant foresee the consequence?

   The jury should be directed that they are not entitled to infer the necessary intention unless they feel sure that the consequence was a virtual certainty as a result of the defendant's actions and that the defendant appreciated that such was the case.

4   *Woollin* (1998) – the defendant threw his three-month-old baby towards his pram which was against a wall some three or four feet away. The baby suffered head injuries and died. The House of Lords approved the direction given in *Nedrick*, provided the word 'find' was used instead of 'infer'. However, the House of Lords disapproved of the use of the two questions in *Nedrick*.

▶ 3.3 Recklessness

1   Recklessness is the taking of an unjustifiable risk.

2   The test now is a subjective one: that is, the defendant must realise the risk, but decides to take it. This is known as *Cunningham* recklessness.

3   Where a statute uses the word 'maliciously' to indicate the *mens rea* required, this word means doing something intentionally or being subjectively reckless about the risk involved (*Cunningham* (1957)).

4   Between 1982 and 2003 the criminal law also recognised an objective test for recklessness. This was where an ordinary prudent person would have realised the risk; the defendant could then be guilty even if he did not realise the risk. This was known as *Caldwell* recklessness.

5   This interpretation of recklessness in criminal damage was overruled by the House of Lords in *G and another* (2003). This case laid down that the test for recklessness in criminal damage is the subjective test.

3.3.1 *Cunningham* recklessness

1   This is subjective recklessness. The defendant realised that there was a risk of the consequence happening, but decided to take that risk.

2   In *Cunningham* (1957) the defendant tore a gas meter from the wall of an empty house in order to steal money in it. This caused gas to seep into the house next door affecting a woman there. Cunningham was not guilty of an offence against s 23 of the Offences against the Person Act 1861 of maliciously administering a noxious thing, as he did not realise the risk of gas escaping into the next-door house. He had not intended to cause the harm, nor had he been subjectively reckless.

3   The case of *Savage* (1992) confirmed that *Cunningham* recklessness applies to all offences in which the statutory definition uses the word 'maliciously'.

3.3.2 *Caldwell* recklessness

1   This was a wider test covering both subjective and objective recklessness.

2   *Caldwell* (1982), who was drunk, set fire to a hotel. The fire was put out and no serious damage was done. Caldwell was charged with arson with intent to endanger life or being reckless as to whether life was endangered. In s 1(2) Criminal Damage Act 1971, the House of Lords ruled that a person was reckless if he did an act which created an obvious risk; and when he did the act he either:

●   had not given any thought to the possibility of there being any such risk; or

●   had recognised that there was some risk involved but had gone on to take the risk.

3   In *Lawrence* (1982) it was stated that, in order for the defendant to be reckless, there must be something in the circumstances that would have drawn the attention of an ordinary prudent individual to the possibility that his act might cause the consequences.

4   This test was applied to criminal damage cases until *Caldwell* was overruled by **G and another** (2003). The test of objective recklessness is no longer used in the criminal law.

▶ 3.4 Negligence

1 Negligence is failing to meet the standards of the reasonable man.

2 Some statutory offences of strict liability have no-negligence defences, i.e. the defendant will be not guilty if he can prove he was not negligent.

3 Gross negligence is where the 'negligence of the accused went beyond a mere matter of compensation between subjects and showed such disregard for the life and safety of others as to amount to a crime against the State and conduct deserving of punishment' (*Bateman* (1925)).

4 Gross negligence is one of the ways in which manslaughter can be committed (*Adomako* (1994)).

▶ 3.5 Knowledge

1 Some statutory offences use the word 'knowingly'. This indicates that *mens rea* is required for the offence.

2 Knowingly includes:

● actually having knowledge of a particular fact;

● being virtually certain that a particular fact is true; and

● being wilfully blind to the truth.

▶ 3.6 Transferred malice

1 This is the principle that the defendant is guilty if he intended to commit a similar crime but against a different victim.

2 An example is aiming a blow at one person with the necessary *mens rea* for some kind of assault. This will be sufficient to make the defendant guilty even though the blow strikes another person (*Latimer* (1886)).

3 *A-G's reference No 3 of 1997* confirmed that the doctrine of transferred malice was still good law (see also *Gnango* (2011)).

4 In some cases, the defendant may have no specific victim in mind, e.g. a terrorist planting a bomb in a pub. The defendant's *mens rea* is imputed so as to apply to the actual victim.

5 If the *mens rea* is for a completely different type of offence then the defendant may not be guilty (*Pembliton* (1874)).

Key Cases Checklist

Intention

Mohan (1975)
Intention is a decision to bring about a certain consequence

Moloney (1985)
Foresight of consequences is evidence of intention

Hancock and Shankland (1986)
Probability is important in foresight of consequences

Nedrick (1986)
The consequence has to be a virtual certainty and D must realise this

Woollin (1998)
Where the consequence is a virtual certainty and D realises this, the jury can find intention

Recklessness

Cunningham (1957)
Maliciously means either intention or subjective recklessness

G and another (2003)
Recklessness means that D must realise there is risk and take that risk

Mens Rea

Gross Negligence

Bateman (1925)
The negligence must be higher than for a civil case. D's conduct must show such disregard for the life and safety of others as to amount to a crime

Adomako (1994)
The three elements of negligence must be present AND the breach must be sufficiently serious to make it criminal

Transferred Malice

Latimer (1886)
An intention can be transferred to an unintended victim

Pembliton (1874)
Malice cannot be transferred if D intended a completely different offence

A-G's ref (No 3 of 1994) (1997)
Confirmed that the doctrine of transferred malice is good law

3.2

Mohan [1975] 2 All ER 193, (1975) 60 Cr App R 272   (PC)

Key Facts

In order to get away, D drove his car at a police officer. The officer jumped out of the way and was not injured. D was convicted of attempting to cause bodily harm to a police officer by wanton driving.

Key Law

Intention is not the same as motive. Intention is a decision to bring about a certain consequence.

3.2.1

Moloney [1985] 1 All ER 1025, (1985) 81 Cr App R 93   (HL)

Key Facts

D and his stepfather had drunk a considerable amount at a family party. After the party they were heard talking and laughing. Then there was a shot. D phoned the police, saying he had just murdered his father. D said that they had been seeing who was the fastest at loading and firing a shotgun. He had loaded his gun the fastest. His stepfather then said he hadn't 'got the guts' to pull the trigger. D said: 'I didn't aim the gun. I just pulled the trigger and he was dead.'

Key Law

Foresight of consequences is evidence of intention.

Key Judgment: Lord Bridge

'I am firmly of the opinion that foresight of consequences, as an element bearing on the issue of intention in murder, or indeed any other crime of specific intent, belongs not to the substantive law but to the law of evidence.'

Key Comment

Lord Bridge in his judgment in *Moloney* discussed s 8 of the Criminal Justice Act 1967 but finished by giving guidelines on the question of foresight of consequences that did not use the word 'probable' which is used in the section. He referred only to a natural result. This omission of the word 'probable' was held in *Hancock and Shankland* (1986) (see below) to make the guidelines defective.

3.2.1 *Hancock and Shankland* [1986] 1 All ER 641, (1986) 82 Cr App R 264

HL

Key Facts

Ds were miners who were on strike. They tried to prevent another miner from going to work by pushing a concrete block from a bridge onto the road along which he was being driven to work in a taxi. The block struck the windscreen of the taxi and killed the driver. The trial judge used the *Moloney* guidelines to direct the jury and Ds were convicted of murder. On appeal, the Court of Appeal quashed their conviction.

This was upheld by the House of Lords.

Key Law

The *Moloney* guidelines were defective as they omitted the word 'probable'. Probability is important in deciding whether a consequence was intended.

Key Judgment: Lord Scarman

'*In my judgment, therefore, the* Moloney *guidelines as they stand are unsafe and misleading. They require a reference to probability. They also require an explanation that the greater the probability of a consequence, the more likely it is that the consequence was foreseen and that if that consequence was foreseen the greater the probability is that that consequence was also intended.*'

3.2.1 *Nedrick* [1986] 3 All ER 1, (1986) 83 Cr App R 267

CA

Key Facts

D had a grudge against a woman. He poured paraffin through the letterbox of her house and set it alight. A child died in the fire. D was convicted of murder, but the Court of Appeal quashed the conviction and substituted one of manslaughter.

Key Law

It was helpful for a jury to ask themselves two questions:

1) How probable was the consequence which resulted from D's voluntary act? and

2) Did D foresee that consequence?

The consequence had to be a virtual certainty and D must have realised that for there to be evidence on which to infer that D had the necessary intention.

Key Judgment: Lord Lane CJ

'The jury should be directed that they are not entitled to infer the necessary intention unless they feel sure that death or serious bodily harm was a virtual certainty (barring some unforeseen intervention) as a result of the defendant's actions and that the defendant appreciated that such was the case.'

3.2.1   *Woollin* [1998] UKHL 28, [1999] 1 Cr App R 8 (HL)

Key Facts

D lost his temper with his three-month-old son and threw him towards his pram. The child struck his head on a hard surface and died from a fractured skull.

Key Law

The two questions in *Nedrick* were not helpful. The model direction from *Nedrick* should be used, but the word 'find' should be used rather than the word 'infer'.

The model direction should now be: 'the jury should be directed that they are not entitled to *find* the necessary intention unless they feel sure that death or serious bodily harm was a virtual certainty (barring some unforeseen intervention) as a result of the defendant's actions and that the defendant appreciated that such was the case'.

Key Problem

The word 'infer' is used in s 8 Criminal Justice Act 1967 and this is presumably why it was used in *Nedrick*. Does the substitution of the word 'find' improve the clarity of the direction to the jury? Also, does the use of the word 'find' mean that foresight of consequence is intention and not merely evidence of it?

In the civil case of *Re A* (2000) doctors asked the courts whether they could operate to separate conjoined twins when they foresaw that this would kill the weaker twin. The Court of Appeal (Civil Division) clearly thought that *Woollin* laid down the rule that foresight of consequences **is** intention.

Key Link

Matthews and Alleyne [2003] EWCA Crim 192.

 3.3

Cunningham [1957] 2 All ER 412, (1957) 41 Cr App R 155

 CCA

Key Facts

D broke into a gas meter to steal money. In doing this, he fractured a gas pipe. Gas then leaked into the next-door house where V was sleeping. D was charged under s 23 of the Offences Against the Person Act 1861 with 'unlawfully and maliciously' administering a noxious substance to V endangering her life.

Key Law

'Maliciously' in a statute has the meaning of either intention or subjective recklessness, i.e. D must have had intention OR realised there was a risk of the consequence occurring and gone on to take that risk.

Key Judgment: Byrne J

'In any statutory definition of a crime, "malice" must be taken not in the old vague sense of wickedness in general, but as requiring either (1) an actual intention to do the particular kind of harm that in fact was done, or (2) reckless-ness as to whether such harm should occur or not (i.e. the

accused has foreseen the risk that the particular kind of harm might be done, and yet has gone on to take the risk).'

Key Comment

There need only be realisation of a risk for recklessness: whereas for specifc intent D must realise that the consequence is a virtual certainty.

3.3.2   ***G and another* [2003] UKHL 50**

Key Facts

The defendants were two boys aged 11 and 12 years. During a night out camping, they went into the yard of a shop and set fire to some bundles of newspapers that they threw under a large wheelie bin. They then left the yard. They expected that as there was a concrete floor under the wheelie bin the fire would extinguish itself. In fact, the bin caught fire and this spread to the shop and other buildings, causing about £1 million worth of damage. The boys were convicted under both s 1 and s 3 Criminal Damage Act 1971. On appeal, the House of Lords quashed their conviction

Key Law

A defendant could not be guilty unless he had realised the risk and decided to take it. The House of Lords overruled an earlier decision in *Caldwell* (see Key Comment below), holding that in that case the Law Lords had 'adopted an interpretation of section 1 of the 1971 Act which was beyond the range of feasible meanings'.

Key Comment

In the case of *Metropolitan Police Commissioner v Caldwell* [1981] 1 All ER 961, the House of Lords had held that reckless covered two situations. The first was where D had realised the risk and the second where D had not thought about the possibility of any risk. The second meaning of reckless caused problems in cases where D was not capable of appreciating the risk involved in his conduct, even though a reasonable person would have realised there was a risk. This occurred in *Elliott v C* [1983] 2 All ER 1005 where D was a 14-year-old girl with learning difficulties.

Despite the fact that she did not appreciate the risk of her act, she was held to be guilty. This has now been overruled by *G and another*.

3.4

Bateman (1925) 19 Cr App R 8

CA

Key Facts

D was a doctor who attended a woman who was due to give birth. His supervision of her labour was negligent and she died.

Key Law

The standard of negligence that has to be proved in manslaughter cases is considerably higher than the level which is sufficient for civil claims in negligence.

Key Judgment: Lord Hewitt CJ

'In order to establish criminal liability, the facts must be such that, in the opinion of the jury, the negligence of the accused went beyond a mere matter of compensation between subjects and showed such disregard for the life and safety of others as to amount to a crime against the state and conduct deserving of punishment.'

Key Link

Andrews v DPP [1937] AC 576.

3.4

Adomako [1994] 3 All ER 79, [1994] Crim LR 757

HL

Key Facts

D was an anaesthetist who failed to notice that, during an operation, a tube supplying oxygen to a patient had become disconnected. As a result, the patient died.

Key Law

To establish gross negligent manslaughter, the elements of the civil tort of negligence must be present. These are:

- D must owe V a duty of care;
- D must be in breach of that duty; and
- the breach must cause the death.

In addition, to impose criminal liability, the breach must be sufficiently serious to make it criminal behaviour.

Key Judgment: Lord Mackay LC

'The ordinary principles of the law of negligence apply to ascertain whether or not the defendant has been in breach of a duty of care towards the victim who had died. If such a breach of duty is established the next question is whether that breach of duty caused the death of the victim. If so, the jury must go on to consider whether that breach of duty should be characterised as gross negligence and therefore a crime. This will depend on the seriousness of the breach of duty committed by the defendant in all the circumstances in which the defendant was placed when it occurred. The jury will have to consider whether the extent to which the defendant's conduct departed from the proper standard of care incumbent upon him, involving as it must have done a risk of death to the patient, was such that it should be judged criminal.'

Key Comment

This places the decision as to whether the breach is criminal negligence on the jury. It has been argued that different juries may well apply different standards in making this decision.

It can also be argued that the test is circular – the jury must decide that the breach is criminal and they do this by deciding that D's conduct should be judged as criminal.

3.6 *Latimer* (1886) 17 QBD 359

Key Facts

D quarrelled with a man. During the quarrel, D aimed a blow with his belt at the man. The blow glanced off the man and struck and cut a woman on the face. D was found guilty under s 20 of the Offences against the Person Act 1861.

Key Law

An intention aimed at one person can be transferred to an unintended victim.

Key Judgment: Coleridge CJ

'It is common knowledge that a man who has an unlawful and malicious intent against another, and, in attempting to carry it out, injures a third person, is guilty of what the law deems malice against the person injured, because the offender is doing an unlawful act, and has that which the judges call general malice, and that is enough.'

3.6

Attorney-General's Reference (No 3 of 1994) [1997] 3 All ER 936, [1998] 1 Cr App R 91   (HL)

Key Facts

D stabbed his pregnant girlfriend. The girl recovered but the wound caused her baby to be born prematurely. As a result of the premature birth the child died at four months old. D was charged with the murder of the baby, but the judge directed an acquittal, ruling that a foetus is not a person in law and so no conviction for either murder or manslaughter was possible in law.

Key Law

The doctrine of transferred malice existed and was good law. However, in these circumstances it could not be used as a foetus was not a person. D could not be guilty of unlawful act manslaughter (see Chapter 10).

Pembliton (1874) LR 2 CCR 119

Key Facts

In the course of a fight with other men, D threw a stone at some of them. The stone missed the men, but struck and broke a window.

Key Law

Where the type of crime is completely different to that intended, then there cannot be transferred malice.

4 Strict liability

Absolute liability
- No *mens rea*
- No need for voluntary act (*Winzar, Larsonneur*)

Strict liability
Mens rea does not need to be proved in respect of at least part of the *actus reus*

Two levels of strict liability
STRICT LIABILITY
Two levels of strict liability

Common law
Very rare; only:
- Public nuisance
- Criminal libel
- Outraging public decency

Statutory offences
Numerous
- Definition has no words for *mens rea*
- Presumption that *mens rea* is required
- This presumption can be displaced

▶ 4.1 Absolute liability

1   This is very rare.

2   The offence requires no *mens rea*.

3   The defendant's *actus reus* need not be voluntary (**Winzar (1983)**, *Larsonneur* (1933)).

▶ 4.2 Strict liability

1 Neither *mens rea* nor negligence need be proved in respect of one or more elements of the *actus reus*.

2 The *actus reus* must be proved.

3 The defence of mistake is not available.

▶ 4.3 Common law strict liability offences

1 Strict liability is very rare in common law offences.

2 Public nuisance and criminal libel probably do not require *mens rea*, but there are no modern cases.

3 Outraging public decency is a strict liability common law offence (*Gibson and Sylveire* (1990)).

4 Criminal contempt of court was a strict liability offence at common law.

5 It is now a statutory offence and Parliament has continued it as a strict liability offence.

▶ 4.4 Statutory strict liability offences

1 About half of all statutory offences are strict liability (i.e. over 3,500 offences).

2 The courts start by assuming that *mens rea* is required, but are prepared to interpret the offence as one of strict liability if Parliament has expressly, or by implication, indicated this in the relevant statute.

3 The modern judicial attitude is to avoid interpreting offences as strict liability (*Sweet v Parsley* (1970), B *(a minor) v DPP* (2000), K (2001), *Kumar* (2004), *DPP v Collins* (2006)).

4 The necessary implication may be found by the courts from 'the language used, the nature of the offence, the mischief sought to be prevented and other circumstances that might assist' (Lord Nicholls in B *v DPP*).

4.4.1 The *Gammon* tests

In *Gammon (Hong Kong) Ltd v A-G of Hong Kong* (1985), the Privy Council set out five factors to be considered.

1 There is a presumption that *mens rea* is required before a person can be guilty of a criminal offence.

2   The presumption is particularly strong where the offence is 'truly criminal' in character.

3   The presumption applies to statutory offences and can be displaced only if this is clearly or by necessary implication the effect of the statute.

4   The only situation in which the presumption can be displaced is where the statute is concerned with an issue of social concern; public safety is such an issue.

5   Even where the statute is concerned with such an issue, the presumption of *mens rea* stands unless it can be shown that the creation of strict liability will be effective to promote the objects of the statute by encouraging greater vigilance to prevent the commission of the prohibited act.

4.4.2 Looking at the wording of an Act

1   Where words indicating *mens rea* are used (e.g. knowingly, intentionally, maliciously or permitting), the offence requires *mens rea* and is not one of strict liability.

2   Where the particular offence has no words of intention, but other sections in the Act do, then it is likely that this offence is a strict liability offence (*Storkwain* (1986)).

3   But even this is not a conclusive test as in *Sherras v de Rutzen* (1895), where it was held that *mens rea* was still required.

4   Where other sections allow for a defence of no negligence, but another section does not, then this indicates that it is an offence of strict liability (*Harrow London Borough Council v Shah* (1999)).

5   Where one section allows a defence when D reasonably believed that V was older than the relevant age for an offence, but another section has no such defence, then the latter section may be regarded as creating strict liability (G (2008), where D reasonably believed that V was over 13, D was still guilty under s 5 Sexual Offences Act 2003).

4.4.3 Quasi-criminal offences

1   Regulatory offences which are not considered truly criminal matters are more likely to be interpreted as strict liability.

2   This includes offences such as breaches of regulations for selling food (*Callow v Tillstone* (1900)) and causing pollution (*Alphacel Ltd v Woodward* (1972)).

3   Where an offence carries a penalty of imprisonment it is less likely to be an offence of strict liability (*B v DPP* (2000)).

4   But some offences carrying imprisonment have been made strict liability offences (*Champ* (1981), *Gammon* (1985)).

4.4.4 Regulatory, Enforcement and Sanctions Act 2008

1   This Act is a move towards civil sanctions for minor breaches of some regulations.

2   The Act provides a range of civil sanctions:
    ● a variable monetary penalty;
    ● a requirement that certain steps be taken to ensure that the offence does not occur again;
    ● a restoration order; and
    ● a stop notice prohibiting certain activities until specified steps have been taken.

3   Criminal proceedings will still be used for serious breaches.

▶ 4.5 Justification for strict liability

1   It protects society by:
    ● promoting greater care over matters of public safety; and
    ● encouraging higher standards, e.g. of hygiene in processing and selling food.

2   It is easier to enforce as there is no need to prove *mens rea*.

3   It saves court time as people are more likely to plead guilty.

4   Parliament can provide a no-negligence defence where this is thought appropriate.

5   Lack of blameworthiness can be taken into account when sentencing.

4.5.1 Arguments against strict liability

1   Liability should not be imposed on people who are not blameworthy.

2   Those who have taken all possible care should not be penalised (*Harrow London Borough Council v Shah* (1999)).

3   There is no evidence that it improves standards.

4   It is contrary to the principles of human rights although the courts have held that strict liability offences do not breach human rights (G (2008), *Deyemi and Edwards* (2008)).

Key Cases Checklist

Absolute Liability

Larsonneur (1933)
An absolute offence can be committed through a state of affairs.
Not only need D have no *mens rea*, but D's act need not be voluntary.

Strict Liability

Strict Liability and Human Rights

G (2008)
The concept of strict liability offences does not breach human rights

Statutory Offences

Sweet v Parsley (1969)
There is a presumption that *mens rea* is required

Gammon (Hong Kong) Ltd (1984)
The presumption that *mens rea* is required can only be displaced if it is clearly the effect of the statute

B (a minor) (2000)
The starting point is that *mens rea* is required

Sherras v de Rutzen (1895)
A genuine mistake can be a defence only if the offence is not one of strict liability

Larsonneur (1933) 24 Cr App R 74

Key Facts

D was an alien under the law who had been ordered to leave the UK. She went to Eire, but the Irish police deported her and took her in police custody back to the UK where she was put in a cell. She was found guilty under the Aliens Order 1920 of 'being an alien to whom leave to land in the United Kingdom has been refused' who was found in the United Kingdom.

Key Law

An absolute offence can be committed through a state of affairs. D's act in returning was not voluntary. She had no *mens rea*.

Key Comment

Should a state of affairs give rise to criminal liability? Not only did D not have any intention of returning to the UK, but her act was involuntary. She did not want to return to the UK, but was brought back by the Irish police. Is it just that there should be criminal liability in such a situation?

Key Link

Winzar v Chief Constable of Kent, The Times, 28 March 1983; Co/1111/82 (Lexis) Queen's Bench Division.

Sweet v Parsley [1969] 1 All ER 347, (1969) 53 Cr App R 221

Key Facts

D rented a farmhouse out to students. The police found cannabis at the farmhouse and D was charged with 'being concerned in the management of premises used for the purpose of smoking cannabis resin'. D did not know that cannabis was being smoked there.

Key Law

There was a presumption that the offence required *mens rea*. D was not guilty as she had no knowledge of the cannabis smoking.

Key Judgment: Lord Reid

'*[T]here has for centuries been a presumption that Parliament did not intend to make criminals of persons who were in no way blameworthy in what they did. That means that, whenever a section is silent as to mens rea, there is a presumption that, in order to give effect to the will of Parliament, we must read in words appropriate to require* mens rea.'

4.4   ### *B (a minor) v DPP* [2000] 1 All ER 833, [2000] 2 Cr App R 65   (HL)

Key Facts

D, a 15-year-old boy, asked a 13-year-old girl on a bus to give him a 'shiner' (i.e. have oral sex with him). He believed she was over the age of 14. He was charged with inciting a child under the age of 14 to commit an act of gross indecency under s 1(1) of the Indecency with Children Act 1960.

Key Law

The starting point for the courts was the presumption that *mens rea* was intended. The judgment in *Sweet v Parsley* (1969) was approved.

Key Comment

The case identified the major elements that have to be considered in deciding whether the offence is one of strict liability as:

- the presumption of *mens rea*;
- the lack of words of intention;
- whether that presumption was negatived by necessary implication;
- the severity of the punishment;
- the purpose of the section;
- evidential problems; and
- effectiveness of strict liability.

4.4.1

Gammon (Hong Kong) Ltd v Attorney-General of Hong Kong [1984] 2 All ER 503, (1984) 80 Cr App R 194   PC

Key Facts

The appellants were charged with deviating from building work in a material way from the approved plan, contrary to the Hong Kong Building Ordinances. It had to be decided whether it was necessary to prove that they knew their deviation was material. It was held that it was not necessary: it was a strict liability offence and they were found guilty.

Key Law

The presumption in favour of *mens rea* being required before D can be convicted applies to statutory offences and can be displaced only if this is clearly or by necessary implication the effect of the statute.

4.4.2

Sherras v de Rutzen [1895] 1 QB 918   DC

Key Facts

D was convicted of supplying liquor to a constable on duty, under s 16(2) of the Licensing Act 1872. Normally, local police who were on duty wore an armband on their uniform. An on-duty police officer removed his armband before entering D's public house. He was served by D's daughter in the presence of D. Neither D nor his daughter made any enquiry as to whether the policeman was on duty. D thought that the constable was off duty because he was not wearing his armband. D appealed.

Key Law

Held that the offence was not one of strict liability and therefore a genuine mistake provided the defendant with a defence.

4.4.2 *Harrow LBC v Shah and Shah* [1999] 3 All ER 302

Key Facts

Ds owned a newsagent's business where lottery tickets were sold. They told their staff not to sell to anyone under 16 and to ask for proof of age if there was any doubt. A member of staff sold a lottery ticket to a 13-year-old boy without asking for proof of age. The magistrates acquitted Ds of selling a lottery ticket to a person under 16, but the prosecution appealed to the Divisional Court which held the offence was one of strict liability and convicted Ds.

Key Comment

Even where D has acted with due diligence, he can be guilty of a strict liability offence. There have been proposals for a general due diligence defence.

4.5.1 *G* [2008] UKHL 37

Key Facts

D, a boy aged 15, had consensual sexual intercourse with a girl aged 12. D believed on reasonable grounds that she was 15. He was charged under s 5 Sexual Offences Act 2003 with the rape of a child under 13. D was held to be guilty under s 5 as it is an offence of strict liability. He appealed on the basis that this was a breach of Articles 6 and 8 of the European Convention on Human Rights.

Key Law

Having offences of strict liability does not breach the Convention. Article 6(1) guarantees fair procedure. Article 6(2) requires that D be presumed innocent until proved guilty. Neither part of Article 6 makes any requirement about the substantive content of the law, nor says anything about the mental elements of an offence.

The majority of the judges in the House of Lords also held that there was no breach of Article 8 (the right of respect for D's private life).

Key Problem

In regard to Article 8, two of the judges in the House of Lords dissented and stated that they thought there was a breach of Article 8. The use of s 5 was disproportionate as it labelled the offence committed by D as rape. The prosecution should have substituted a charge under s 13(1) Sexual Offences Act 2003 (sexual activity with a child).

5 Participation

Principal offender
- Directly causes the *actus reus*
- Has *mens rea* for offence
- Can have two or more joint principals (*Tyler v Whatmore*)

Innocent agent
Where the principal acts through another, who is not guilty, because:
- no capacity; or
- no *mens rea*; or
- has defence (*Bourne*)

PARTICIPATION

Secondary party

Actus reus
- Aids
- Abets
- Counsels
- Procures

Accessories and Abettors Act 1861 (*Attorney-General's Ref (No 1 of 1975)*)

Mens rea
Intends to assist principal
Knowledge of type of offence (*Bainbridge* (1959))
or
Contemplation of what principal might do (*Powell: English* (1997))

▶ 5.1 Principal offenders

1   This is the person whose act is the immediate cause of the *actus reus*.

2   A principal offender must also have the necessary *mens rea* to be guilty of the offence.

3   There can be two or more joint or co-principals.

5.1.1 Joint principals

1   Where two or more people do the *actus reus* with the required *mens rea* (e.g. two burglars enter a house to steal) then they are all principals (*Tyler v Whatmore* (1976)).

2   Where an offence is committed by one of two people but it is not possible to prove which of them did the *actus reus*:

● if they had a joint purpose, one is the principal and the other(s) are accessories: all will be guilty of the offence (*Mohan v R* (1967), *Russell and Russell* (1987)); or

● if there was no joint purpose or agreement between them, then neither can be convicted (*Strudwick* (1993)).

3   A few offences require two or more principals for the offence to be committed, e.g. riot, affray.

▶ 5.2 Innocent agents

1   An innocent agent is someone whom the principal uses to do the act; one who acts as a 'puppet'.

2   The agent may be innocent because:

● they do not have the capacity to commit the offence, e.g. where a child under the age of ten is used by an adult to enter a house and steal; or

● they do not have the necessary *mens rea* (*Cogan and Leak* (1976)); or

● they have a defence such as insanity or automatism.

▶ 5.3 Secondary parties

1   A secondary party is also called an accessory.

2   A secondary party is guilty of the main crime and liable to the same punishment as the principal (s 8 Accessories and Abettors Act 1861, s 44 Magistrates' Courts Act 1980).

3   A secondary party can only be convicted if there was an *actus reus* for the main offence (*Thornton v Mitchell* (1940)).

4   The Serious Crime Act 2007 creates an offence of assisting or encouraging the commission of an offence, even though the offence is not actually committed (see 6.2).

5   A secondary party can be convicted even though the principal is acquitted, if the *actus reus* was committed, but the principal:

●   lacked the required *mens rea*; or

●   has a defence not available to the secondary party (*Bourne* (1952)).

6   If the principal has attempted the main crime then the secondary party can be guilty as an accessory to the attempt (*Donnington* (1984)).

7   D can be a secondary party even though he is the intended victim of the main crime. The fact that he was to have been the victim does not give him a defence under accessorial liability (*Gnango* (2011)).

5.3.1 The *actus reus* for secondary participation

1   The *actus reus* is that the secondary party must 'aid, abet, counsel or procure' the commission of an offence (s 8 Accessories and Abettors Act 1861).

2   *Attorney-General's Reference No 1 of 1975* (1975) stated that each of these four words (aid, abet, counsel or procure) had a separate meaning.

3   Aiding is giving help, support or assistance. This can be before the offence is committed, e.g. providing tools to carry out a burglary (*Bainbridge* (1959)) or during the time it is being committed, e.g. acting as look-out (*Betts and Ridley* (1930)).

4   Abetting is any involvement from 'mere encouragement' upwards (*Giannetto* (1997)):

●   This can be immediately before the offence is committed or during its commission, e.g. shouting encouragement or paying for a ticket for an illegal performance (*Wilcox v Jeffery* (1951)).

●   But mere presence is not usually enough for secondary participation, there must be an intention to encourage (*Clarkson* (1971), *Bland* (1988)).

●   However, if there is a duty to control then passive presence may be enough (*Tuck v Robson* (1970)).

5   Counselling is advising or encouraging. It takes place before the commission of the offence (*Calhaem* (1985)).

6   In *Luffman* (2008), the Court of Appeal accepted for the purposes of that case that there should be some causal link between the counselling and the commission of the offence.

7   Procuring means 'to produce by endeavour', that is, setting out to see that it happens and taking the appropriate steps to produce that happening (*Attorney-General's Reference No 1 of 1975* (1975)).

8   There must be a causal link between the procuring and the offence done by the principal (*Attorney-General's Reference No 1 of 1975* (1975)).

5.3.2 The *mens rea* for secondary participation

1   There must be an intention to do the act that aids or, abets, the main offence. It does not matter that D is indifferent whether the offence is committed or not (*National Coal Board v Gamble* (1958)).

2   The secondary party need only have knowledge of the type of crime and not the details of where and when, etc. (*Bainbridge* (1959)).

3   Knowledge that one of a range of offences is going to be committed may be sufficient (*DPP for Northern Ireland v Maxwell* (1979)).

4   Contemplation or foresight that the principal might commit a certain type of offence is sufficient (*Chan Wing Sui* (1985), *Powell: English* (1997)).

5   This rule on foresight is criticised as its effect is to put the *mens rea* for an accomplice at a lower level than that for the principal in crimes of specific intent. This can be seen as unjust, particularly in murder cases where the penalty is a mandatory life sentence for the accomplice.

6   In *Rahman* (2008), the House of Lords held that the principal's intention is irrelevant both to:

    ● whether the killing was within the scope of a common purpose, and

    ● whether P's act was fundamentally different from the act which D foresaw.

7   Where the principal does a completely different act, then the secondary party is not liable. As in *Powell: English* (1997), where there was an agreement to assault a policeman with wooden posts, but one of the defendants killed him by stabbing him with a knife. English was not a secondary party to the murder.

5.3.3 Withdrawal from a joint enterprise

1   If the secondary party is to be not guilty, then the withdrawal from the enterprise must be clear and effective.

2   Repentance alone unsupported by action demonstrating withdrawal is insufficient (*Bryce* (2004)).

3   The more the secondary party has done towards assisting the main crime, the more effective his withdrawal must be (*Becerra and Cooper* (1976), *Rook* ((1993)).

4   Where spontaneous violence has occurred then it is possible for the secondary party to withdraw effectively by walking away. There is no need for him to communicate his withdrawal to the principal (*Mitchell and King* (1998)).

▶ 5.4 Proposals for reform

1   The Law Commission, in their report *Participating in Crime* (2007), recommended abolishing s 8 of the Accessories and Abettors Act 1861.

2   Instead they recommended that secondary liability would be defined by two basic rules:

● D would be liable for an offence committed by P where D assisted or encouraged that offence and intended it to be committed.

● Where D and P have formed a joint criminal venture, D would be liable for any offence (agreed or collateral) that he foresaw might be committed as a result of the joint venture.

3   In 2006, in their report *Murder, Manslaughter and Infanticide*, the Law Commission included proposals for the reform of participation in the offence of murder.

4   That report recommended that there should be two degrees of murder and D should be liable to be convicted of P's offence of first- or second-degree murder if:

● D intended to assist or encourage P to commit the relevant offence; or

● D was engaged in a joint criminal venture with P, and realised that P, or another party to the joint venture, might commit the relevant offence.

5   The report also recommended that D should be liable as a secondary party for manslaughter if:

- D and P were parties to a joint venture to commit an offence;

- P committed the offence of first-degree murder or second-degree murder in relation to the fulfilment of that venture;

- D intended or foresaw that (non-serious) harm or the fear of harm might be caused by a party to the venture; and

- a reasonable person in D's position, with D's knowledge of the relevant facts, would have foreseen an obvious risk of death or serious injury being caused by a party to the venture.

▶ 5.5 Assistance or concealment after a crime

1   Acts done after the crime has been committed are not done as a secondary party but may be a separate substantive offence.

2   The main substantive offences are:

- s 4 Criminal Law Act 1967, which makes it an offence for a person who, knowing or believing that another person is guilty of an arrestable offence, does 'any act with intent to impede his apprehension or prosecution';

- s 5 Criminal Law Act 1967, which makes it an offence for any person to accept money (or other bargain) in return for withholding information about an arrestable offence;

- s 1 of the Perjury Act 1911, which makes it an offence for a witness to lie on oath in court proceedings.

Key Cases Checklist

Actus Reus

Gnango (2011)
D can be a secondary party even though he is the intended victim

Attorney-General's Reference (No 1 of 1975) (1975)
Aid, abet, counsel and procure have different meanings

Giannetto (1997)
Abetting can be 'mere encouragement upwards'

Wilcox v Jeffery (1951)
Presence at a public performance can be sufficient

Clarkson and others (1971)
Mere presence at the scene of a crime is not enough

Calhaem (1985)
There is no need for a causal link between counselling and the offence

Mens Rea

National Coal Board v Gamble (1958)
Intention to do the act which aids and abets, but there can be indifference to the offence

Bainbridge (1959)
There is no need to know the details of the offence the principal will commit

DPP for Northern Ireland v Maxwell (1978)
It is enough for D to know that it is one of a number of possible crimes

Attorney-General's Reference (No 1 of 1975) (1975)
For procuring there is no need to prove a shared intention

Secondary Participation

Joint Enterprise

Powell: English (1997)
There need only be foresight or contemplation that the principal might commit the offence

Stewart and Schofield (1995)
If a secondary party does not foresee or contemplate serious injury or death, they cannot be liable for murder

Uddin (1998)
If all intend serious injury or death, they are all liable for murder. If a very different weapon is used, D is not liable for the death

Rahman (2008)
Confirmed decision in *Powell: English*

Withdrawal from a Joint Enterprise

Becerra and Cooper (1975)
D must effectively communicate his withdrawal

Mitchell and King (1999)
Where there is spontaneous violence then walking away is sufficient for withdrawal

5.3

Gnango [2011] UKSC 59, [2012] 2 WLR 17   SC

Key Facts

D and another man known only as 'Bandana Man' had a gun battle, each trying to kill the other. 'Bandana Man' shot and killed V, a passer-by. D was convicted of the murder of V on the basis of joint enterprise. The Court of Appeal quashed this conviction but it was re-instated by the Supreme Court by six judges to one.

Key Law

A majority of the Supreme Court held that D was guilty on the basis of accessorial liability. D was aiding and abetting the attempted murder of himself.

Key Judgment: Lord Phillips

'(i) Bandana Man attempted to kill [D]. (ii) By agreeing to the shoot-out, [D] aided and abetted Bandana Man in this attempted murder. (iii) Bandana Man accidentally killed [V] instead of Gnango. Under the doctrine of transferred malice he was guilty of her murder. (iv) The doctrine of transferred malice applied equally to [D] as aider and abetter of Bandana Man's attempted murder. [D] was also guilty of [V's] murder.'

Key Law

For participatory liability there must be a joint enterprise. In this case D and his opponent were firing at each other. This did not amount to a joint enterprise.

5.3.1

Attorney-General's Reference (No 1 of 1975) [1975] 2 All ER 684, (1975) 61 Cr App R 118   CA

Key Facts

D, who knew that a friend was going to drive home, laced his non-alcoholic drink with alcohol. When the friend was charged with driving while over the limit for alcohol (s 6(1) Road Traffic Act 1972), D was charged with aiding, abetting, counselling and procuring that offence. The trial judge ruled that there was no case to answer as there was no meeting of minds.

Key Law

(1) Each of the words 'aid', 'abet', 'counsel' and 'procure' has a different meaning.

(2) To 'procure' means to produce by endeavour.

(3) There must be a causal link between the procuring and the commission of the offence.

Key Judgment: Lord Widgery CJ

'(1) We approach s 8 of the [Accessories and Abettors] Act of 1861 on the basis that the words should be given their ordinary meaning, if possible. We approach the section on the basis also that if four words are employed here, 'aid, abet, counsel or procure,' the probability is that there is a difference between each of those four words and the other three, because if there were no such difference, then Parliament would be wasting time in using four words when two or three would do.

(2) To procure means to produce by endeavour. You procure a thing by setting out to see that it happens and taking the appropriate steps to produce that happening.

(3) Causation here is important. You cannot procure an offence unless there is a causal link between what you do and the commission of the offence.'

Key Comment

Later cases do not show a need to set out to produce a result by endeavour. The causal link is the important factor. In *Millward* [1994] Crim LR 527, a farmer gave instructions for a poorly maintained tractor and trailer to be driven on a public road. The trailer became detached, hit a car and killed the driver. D was convicted of procuring the offence of causing death by reckless driving, even though he certainly did not set out to produce that result through endeavour. *Millward* also illustrates that a secondary party may be guilty, even though the principal is acquitted.

5.3.1   *Giannetto* [1997] 1 Cr App R 1   CA

Key Facts

D was convicted of the murder of his wife. The prosecution relied on the fact that the wife had been murdered either by

D himself or by a hired killer on D's behalf. D appealed on the basis that, as the prosecution could not prove whether he or another person had killed the wife, he should have been acquitted. The Court of Appeal held that as he had the intention to murder and the act had been carried out, it did not matter whether he was the principal or a secondary party.

Key Law

For abetting, any involvement from 'mere encouragement upwards' is sufficient. Encouragement can be as little as patting on the back, nodding, or saying 'Oh goody' when told of the principal's intention to commit a particular crime.

5.3.1 · *Wilcox v Jeffery* [1951] 1 All ER 464 · (KBD)

Key Facts

Wilcox knew that an American saxophonist was not allowed to enter the United Kingdom. Despite this, Wilcox met him at the airport and attended a concert at which the American played. D was convicted of aiding and abetting the contravention of the Aliens Order 1920.

Key Law

Where presence at a public performance encourages that performance, then the presence is sufficient for aiding and abetting.

5.3.1 · *Clarkson and others* [1971] 3 All ER 344, (1971) 55 Cr App R 445 · (C-MAC)

Key Facts

D and another soldier entered a room within an army barracks where a woman was being raped. They remained in the room while the rape continued but did nothing.

Key Law

Being present but doing nothing is not sufficient to make D a secondary party. Non-interference to prevent a crime is not itself a crime.

5.3.1 *Calhaem* [1985] 2 All ER 266, (1985) 81 Cr App R 131 (CA)

Key Facts

D was infatuated with her solicitor. She hired a 'hitman' to kill a woman with whom the solicitor had been having an affair. The hitman claimed that he had decided not to go through with the plan to kill the woman, but when he saw her, he went berserk and killed her. D argued that the causal connection between her acts and the killing was broken when the hitman decided of his own accord to kill V.

Key Law

There is no need for any causal connection between the counselling and the offence.

Key Judgment: Parker LJ

'We must therefore approach the question raised on the basis that we should give to the word "counsel" its ordinary meaning, which is, as the judge said, "advise", "solicit" or something of that sort. There is no implication in the word itself that there should be any causal connection between the counselling and the offence.'

5.3.2 *National Coal Board v Gamble* [1958] 3 All ER 203, (1958) 42 Cr App R 240 (QBD)

Key Facts

A weighbridge operator employed by the National Coal Board issued a ticket to a lorry driver, although the operator knew that the lorry was overloaded. The Board was convicted as a secondary party to the offence of using a motor lorry on a road with a load weighing more than that permitted.

Key Law

The *mens rea* for secondary participation is the intention to do the act which aids or abets. D can be guilty as a secondary party even if he does not care whether the offence is committed or not.

Key Judgment: Lord Devlin

'An indifference to the result of the crime does not of itself negative abetting. If one man deliberately sells to another man a gun to be used for murdering a third, he may be indifferent about whether the third man lives or dies and interested only in the cash profit to be made out of the sale, but he can still be an aider and abetter.'

5.3.2

Bainbridge [1959] 3 All ER 200, (1959) 43 Cr App R 194

 CCA

Key Facts

D bought oxygen cutting equipment on behalf of others. He knew that the others were going to use the equipment for criminal purposes, though he did not know the exact details.

Key Law

A secondary party can be guilty where he knows the type of offence that the principal is going to commit. It does not matter that he does not know the details.

5.3.2

DPP for Northern Ireland v Maxwell [1978] 3 All ER 1140, (1979) 68 Cr App R 128

 HL

Key Facts

D guided terrorists in Northern Ireland to a pub. He knew that some sort of attack was to be carried out there, but he did not know exactly what.

Key Law

Bainbridge was correctly decided. It was not necessary to prove that D knew the exact offence, or even the exact type of offence.

Key Judgment: Lord Scarman

'[In Bainbridge, *the Court of Appeal] refused to limit criminal responsibility by reference to knowledge by the accused*

of the type or class of crime intended by those whom he assisted . . . The guilt of an accessory springs from the fact that he contemplates the commission of one (or more) of a number of crimes by the principal and he intentionally lends his assistance in order that such a crime will be committed.'

5.3.2

Attorney-General's Reference (No 1 of 1975) [1975] 2 All ER 684, (1975) 61 Cr App R 118

Key Facts

See 5.3.1.

Key Law

Where the prosecution relies on the secondary party procuring the offence, there is no need to prove a shared intention.

5.3.2

Powell: English [1997] 4 All ER 545, [1998] 1 Cr App R 261

These two cases were heard in a joined appeal.

Key Facts

(Powell)

D and two other men went to buy drugs at the house of a drug dealer. When the dealer opened the door, one of the other men shot him.

(English)

D took part with another man in a joint enterprise to attack and injure a police officer with wooden posts. During the attack the other man stabbed and killed the officer. English did not know that the other man was carrying a knife.

Key Law

Foresight or contemplation that the principal may commit the offence is sufficient for the *mens rea* of an accomplice.

Key Comment

This decision means that in order to be convicted, a lower level of intention is sufficient for a secondary party to be convicted of murder than for a principal. This was acknowledged by the House of Lords when Lord Steyn said: 'Recklessness may suffice in the case of the secondary party but it does not in the case of the primary offender. The answer to this supposed anomaly is to be found in practical and policy considerations.'

This causes particular problems in murder cases as the judge has no discretion in sentencing. Is it just that a secondary party, who did not personally carry out the killing, can be convicted on a lower level of intention and so face a mandatory life sentence?

Key Link

Chan Wing-Siu v R [1984] 3 All ER 877, (1984) 80 Cr App R 117.

5.3.2   *Rahman* **[2008] UKHL 45**   HL

Key Facts

A number of persons made a planned attack on V. Many of the attackers were armed with blunt instruments. V was stabbed to death. It was not known which of the attackers had stabbed him. D argued that he did not carry a knife and was unaware that any of the group had one. The House of Lords confirmed D's conviction.

Key Law

It was held that *Powell: English* was correct.

Key Judgment: Lord Bingham

'[The] significance of [English] lies in the emphasis it laid (a) on the overriding importance in this context of what the particular defendant subjectively foresaw, and (b) on the nature of the acts or behaviour said to be a radical departure from what was intended or foreseen.'

5.3.3

Becerra and Cooper (1975) 62 Cr App R 212   (CA)

Key Facts

B and C broke into a house in order to steal. B gave C a knife to use if anyone interrupted them. When they were interrupted by V, B said 'There's a bloke coming. Let's go,' and jumped out of a window. C stabbed and killed V. Both B and C were convicted of murder.

Key Law

To withdraw from a joint enterprise effectively, B must communicate his withdrawal. Merely saying 'Let's go' was not sufficient for communicating withdrawal where B had already given C the knife.

Key Link

Rook [1993] 2 All ER 955, (1993) 97 Cr App R 327.

5.3.3

Mitchell and King [1998] EWCA Crim 2375 [1999] Crim LR 496   (CA)

Key Facts

An unplanned fight broke out in a restaurant and continued into the street. D1 and D2 were involved in the fight during which V was badly beaten. D1 then dropped a stick, stopped fighting and walked away. D2 picked up the stick and renewed the attack on V who later died.

Key Law

Where spontaneous violence occurs, D can withdraw without communicating his withdrawal to others involved in the attack.

6 Inchoate offences

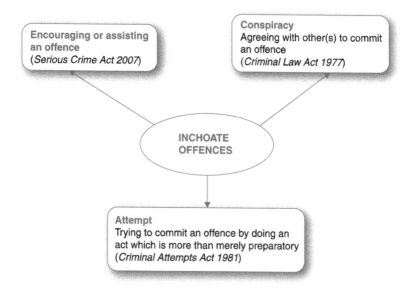

Encouraging or assisting an offence (*Serious Crime Act 2007*)

Conspiracy
Agreeing with other(s) to commit an offence (*Criminal Law Act 1977*)

INCHOATE OFFENCES

Attempt
Trying to commit an offence by doing an act which is more than merely preparatory (*Criminal Attempts Act 1981*)

▶ 6.1 Inchoate offences

1 An inchoate offence is an incomplete offence; one that is just begun or is undeveloped. The main offence has yet to be committed.

2 There are three types of inchoate offence:

- encouraging or assisting an offence;
- conspiracy; and
- attempt.

3 For an inchoate offence the defendant is charged with inciting or conspiring or attempting to do the substantive crime involved. For example, conspiring to murder or attempting to steal.

▶ 6.2 Encouraging or assisting an offence

1 The Serious Crime Act 2007 abolished the common law offence of incitement.

2   In its place the Act creates three offences. These are:

- doing an act capable of encouraging or assisting the commission of an offence intending to encourage or assist its commission (s 44);

- doing an act capable of encouraging or assisting the commission of an offence, and believing that the offence will be committed and that his act will encourage or assist its commission (s 45); or

- doing an act capable of encouraging or assisting the commission of one or more of a number of offences, believing that one or more of those offences will be committed and that his act will encourage or assist the commission of one or more of them (s 46).

3   Placing inciting material on Facebook or other social media can be an offence under the Serious Crime Act 2007 (*Blackshaw: Sutcliff* (2011)).

4   Section 46 should only be used where D believes that one or more different offences may be committed but does not know which (*Sadique and Hussain* (2011)).

6.2.1 *Mens rea* of encouraging or assisting an offence

1   Section 47 Serious Crime Act 2007 gives additional explanation of the *mens rea* required.

2   If the offence is one requiring proof of fault, it must be proved that:

- D believed that, were the act to be done, it would be done with that fault; or

- D was reckless as to whether or not it would be done with that fault; or

- D's state of mind was such that, were he to do it, it would be done with that fault.

3   Where the offence is one requiring proof of particular circumstances or consequences then it must be proved that:

- D believed that, were the act to be done, it would be done in those circumstances or with those consequences; or

- D was reckless as to whether or not it would be done in those circumstances or with those consequences.

▶ 6.3 Conspiracy

1   Nearly all conspiracies are charged as statutory conspiracy under the Criminal Law Act 1977 as amended.

2   Only three types of common law conspiracy still exist (s 5 Criminal Law Act 1977). These are:

- conspiracy to defraud;
- conspiracy to corrupt public morals; and
- conspiracy to outrage public decency.

6.3.1 Statutory conspiracy

1   This is defined by s 1 Criminal Law Act 1977 (as amended by s 5 Criminal Attempts Act 1981) as:

> '... if a person agrees with any other person or persons that a course of conduct shall be pursued which, if the agreement is carried out in accordance with their intentions, either:
>
> a)   will necessarily amount to or involve the commission of any offence or offences by one or more of the parties to the agreement; or
>
> b)   would do so but for the existence of facts which render the commission of the offence or any of the offences impossible, he is guilty of conspiracy to commit the offence or offences in question.'

2   The *actus reus* is the agreement of at least two persons on a course of conduct which will necessarily amount to or involve the commission of at least one offence.

3   The parties to the conspiracy need not have agreed all the details, but must have gone beyond merely talking about the possibility of committing an offence (*O'Brien* (1974)).

4   The course of conduct must necessarily 'involve the commission of an offence' (*Reed* (1982)).

5   Where there is a plan for a contingency which necessarily involves the commission of an offence, the defendant is guilty, even though the main plan may not necessarily involve the commission of an offence (*Jackson* (1985)).

6   Although it must be proved that there was an agreement between the defendant and at least one other person, the other(s) need not be identified (*Phillips* (1987)).

7   The defendant need not know all the other conspirators, provided he
     has agreed with one of them (*Chrastny* (1992)).

8   This means that there can be a 'chain' conspiracy where:

     ●   A agrees with B and B then agrees with C, but A and C do not know
         about each other; or

     ●   there can be a 'wheel' or 'spoke' conspiracy where one central person
         agrees with several others.

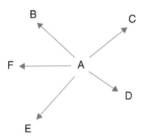

Spoke or wheel conspiracy

6.3.2 *Mens rea* of statutory conspiracy

1   The defendant must intend to agree to the plan; if he considers it to be
     a joke, then he is not agreeing to it.

2   The defendant must intend the course of conduct to be carried out and
     be aware that it will necessarily involve committing an offence.

3   In *Anderson* (1986) the House of Lords stated *obiter* that the *mens rea*
     included an intention to play some part in the agreed course of conduct.
     This does not accord with the wording of s 1 of the Criminal Law Act
     1977. In *Siracusa* (1989) the Court of Appeal said the House of Lords
     only meant that the defendant had to continue to agree to the other(s)
     criminal conduct.

4   In *Yip Chiu-Cheung v R* (1994) the Privy Council stressed that the
     necessary *mens rea* is the intention that the offence be carried out.

6.3.3 Conspiracy to do the impossible

1   Section 1(b) Criminal Law Act 1977 was inserted by s 5 Criminal
     Attempts Act 1981

2   This was in order to make it clear that a conspiracy to do an offence that
     was in fact impossible to commit was a criminal conspiracy.

3   Section 1(b) overturns the decision in *Nock v DPP* (1978), where it was ruled that factual or physical impossibility meant that the defendants were not guilty of conspiracy.

4   Defendants are now guilty even though there are facts which make the commission of the offence impossible, for example:

   ● where the items agreed to be stolen do not exist; or

   ● the person they agree to murder has already, unknown to them, died; or

   ● the substance they are planning to sell is not an illegal drug; or

   ● the means chosen to commit the offence will not work.

   In all these situations there can now be liability for a conspiracy.

6.3.4 Exemption from liability for conspiracy

1   An intended victim cannot be guilty of conspiracy (s 2(1) Criminal Law Act 1977).

2   Under s 2(2) Criminal Law Act 1977 a person cannot be guilty if the only other person(s) he has conspired with is:

   ● his/her spouse;

   ● a child under the age of 10; and

   ● an intended victim.

6.3.5 Proposals for reform

1   In 2007, the Law Commission published a consultation paper, *Conspiracy and Attempts*, in which they proposed possible reforms to the law of conspiracy.

2   In this they suggested:

   ● recklessness should be sufficient for the *mens rea* of conspiracy;

   ● where knowledge or belief is sufficient for the full offence then it should also be sufficient *mens rea* for conspiracy to commit that offence;

   ● the rule that D must intend to play some part in the agreed course (as decided in *Anderson* (1986)) should be abolished;

   ● the rule that D is guilty even if he did not intend the agreement to be carried through to completion should be abolished;

- the immunity of spouses to be abolished so that spouses would be guilty of conspiracy even if no other person was involved in the conspiracy;

- the rule that D cannot be guilty of conspiracy if the only other person to the conspiracy is the victim: V would have a defence to a charge of conspiracy in such circumstances; and

- create a defence of acting reasonably: this would reverse the decision in *Yip Chui-Cheung* (1994) and allow undercover agents a defence.

6.3.6 Common law conspiracy

1   These are:

   a) conspiracy to defraud;

   b) conspiracy to corrupt public morals; and

   c) conspiracy to outrage public decency.

2   A defendant can be charged with both a common law conspiracy and a statutory conspiracy.

3   a) A conspiracy to defraud is an agreement to practise a fraud on somebody.

   b) Fraud covers conduct which may not be a substantive criminal offence (*Scott v Metropolitan Police Commissioner* (1975)).

   c) The defendant must be dishonest (*Wai Yu-tsang* (1991)).

4   a) Conspiracy to corrupt public morals covers conduct which would not involve the commission of an offence if carried out by one person on their own (s 5(3)(b) Criminal Law Act 1977).

   b) In *Knuller v DPP* (1972), 'corrupt' was considered as being synonymous with 'depraved' and being 'conduct which a jury might find to be destructive of the very fabric of society'.

5   a) Conspiracy to outrage public decency also covers conduct which would not involve the commission of an offence if carried out by one person on their own (s 5(3)(b) Criminal Law Act 1977).

   b) In *Knuller v DPP* (1972), 'outrage' was considered to be something which goes beyond offending or shocking reasonable people.

   c) The case of *Gibson* (1990) confirms that there is a substantive offence of outraging public decency. It can therefore be argued that a conspiracy to outrage public decency can be charged as a statutory conspiracy.

▶ 6.4 Attempt

1   Attempting to commit an offence was made a statutory offence by the Criminal Attempts Act 1981.

2   A criminal attempt is defined by s 1(1) Criminal Attempts Act 1981 as: 'If, with intent to commit an offence . . ., a person does an act which is more than merely preparatory to the commission of the offence, he is guilty of attempting to commit the offence.'

3   Previous common law cases had evolved a number of tests (e.g. the last act test, the proximity test) to decide if the acts of the defendant amounted to an attempt. These tests have now been held to be irrelevant.

6.4.1 *Actus reus* of attempt

1   This is an act which is more than merely preparatory to the commission of the offence (s 1(1) Criminal Attempts Act 1981).

2   More than merely preparatory means the defendant must have gone beyond purely preparatory acts and be 'embarked on the crime proper' (*Gullefer* (1987)).

3   The dividing line between merely preparatory and an attempt can be explained by asking 'has the defendant done an act which shows that he has actually tried to commit the offence in question, or . . . has he only got ready or put himself in a position or equipped to do so?' (*Geddes* (1996)).

4   The defendant need not have performed the last act before the crime proper, nor reached the point of no return. (*A-G's Reference No 1 of 1992* (1993)).

5   This area between mere preparation and an attempt is difficult to define as the following cases show.

   a) *Cases which are mere preparation*

      Gullefer (1987) – the defendant jumped onto a race track in order to have the race declared void and enable him to reclaim money he had bet on the race. Not guilty of attempted theft.

      Campbell (1990) – the defendant had an imitation gun, sunglasses and a threatening note in his pocket and was in the street outside a post office. Not guilty of attempted robbery.

      Geddes (1996) – the defendant was found in the boys' lavatory block of a school in possession of a large kitchen knife, some rope and masking tape. He had no right to be in the school. He had not contacted any of the pupils. Not guilty of attempted false imprisonment.

b) *Cases in which there was an attempt*

Boyle and Boyle (1987) – the defendants were found standing by a door which had the lock and one hinge broken. Guilty of attempted burglary.

Jones (1990) – the defendant had bought a shotgun, shortened the barrel, disguised himself, got into the back of the victim's car and pointed the gun at him. The gun was loaded but the safety catch was still on. Guilty of attempted murder.

6.4.2 *Mens rea* of attempt

1   The *mens rea* of an attempt is essentially that of the completed crime.

2   The defendant has to intend to commit the substantive offence (*Easom* (1971)).

3   In some offences it is necessary to prove a higher level of *mens rea* than will suffice for the completed offence. For example, for attempted murder it is necessary to prove an intention to kill; an intention to cause grievous bodily harm is not enough (*Whybrow* (1951)).

4   For the purposes of attempt, intention has the same meaning as at common law (*Pearman* (1984)). This means there has to be proof of a decision to bring about (the offence) no matter whether the accused desired that consequence of his act or not (*Mohan* (1976)).

5   Intention can be inferred from foresight of consequences where the consequence is virtually certain to occur a result of the defendant's actions and he is aware that this is so (*Walker and Hayles* (1990)).

6   Recklessness with regard to a consequence is not sufficient, even though it would be sufficient for the completed offence. To be guilty of an attempt the defendant must intend the consequences (*O'Toole* (1978), *Millard and Vernon* (1987)).

7   However, recklessness as to one aspect may be sufficient, such as where the defendant intends to damage property by fire and is reckless as to whether life will be endangered thereby (*A-G's Reference (No 3 of 1992)* (1993)).

8   Where the defendant intends the consequence, recklessness in respect of a circumstance may be sufficient.

6.4.3 Attempts to do the impossible

1   A person may be guilty of attempting to commit an offence even though the facts are such that the commission of the offence is impossible (s 1(2) Criminal Attempts Act 1981).

2   If a person's intention would not be regarded as having amounted to an intent to commit an offence, but, if the facts of the case had been as the defendant believed them to be, his intention would be so regarded, then he shall be regarded as having had an intent to commit that offence (s 1(3) Criminal Attempts Act 1981).

3   In *Shivpuri* (1987) the House of Lords confirmed that these subsections of the Criminal Attempts Act 1981 meant that it is possible to be guilty of attempting to commit an offence even though commission of the actual offence is impossible. This overruled their earlier decision in *Anderton v Ryan* (1986).

6.4.4 Proposals for reform

1   In 2007, the Law Commission published a consultation paper, *Conspiracy and Attempts*, in which they put forward possible reforms to the law of attempts.

2   They pointed out that the courts have struggled to draw the line between acts that are 'merely preparatory' and acts that are more than merely preparatory.

3   The most radical proposal suggested that s 1(1) Criminal Attempts Act 1981 should be abolished and replaced with offences:

   ● attempt – limited to D's last acts; and

   ● criminal preparation – behaviour that was part of the execution of the plan.

4   Criminal preparation would include gaining entry to a building with a view to committing an offence there: this would cover the situation in *Geddes* (1996) (see 6.4.1).

5   The paper also suggested that where recklessness is sufficient for the *mens rea*, it should be sufficient for attempt.

6   Another suggestion was to extend attempt to omissions where the completed offence is capable of being committed by omission.

Key Cases Checklist

Attempts

A-G's Reference (No 1 of 1992) (1993)
Need not have performed the last act before the crime proper, nor reached the point of no return

Gullefer (1987)
Must have gone beyond purely preparatory acts and be 'embarked on the crime proper'

Millard and Vernon (1987)
Recklessness as to a consequence is not sufficient *mens rea* for an attempt

Shivpuri (1987)
Even when the complete offence is impossible to commit, there can be an attempt

Encouraging and Assisting
ss 44, 45 and 46 Serious Crime Act 2007

Blackshaw: Sutcliffe (2011)
Using Facebook to encourage people to meet at panto during riots is an offence under s 46

Sadique and Hussain (2011)
s 46 should only be used where D believes that one or more of different offences may be committed

Inchoate Offences

Statutory Conspiracy

Reed (1982)
There is a statutory conspiracy when an offence will 'necessarily' be committed if the plan is carried out as intended

Jackson (1985)
A plan for a contingency which necessarily involved the commission of an offence is sufficient

Yip Chiu-Cheung v R (1994)
D and at least one other must intend that the offence be committed

Kenning (2008)
Cannot conspire to aid and abet

Conspiracy to Defraud

Scott v MPC (1975)
(1) Not necessary to prove that economic loss was suffered, but V's economic interests must be put at risk.
(2) Deception is not a required element of the offence

Wai Yu-tsang (1991)
It is enough if anyone may be prejudiced in any way by the fraud

6.2

Blackshaw: Sutcliffe [2011] EWCA Crim 2312

Key Facts

Both Ds had posted material on Facebook calling for people to meet at specific places durng a period of rioting. Both pleaded guilty to an offence under s 46 Serious Crime Act 2007.

Key Judgment: Lord Judge

'. . . [t]he abuse of modern technology for criminal purposes extends to and includes incitement of very many people by a single step. Indeed it is a sinister feature of these cases that modern technology almost certainly assisted rioters in other places to organise the rapid movement and congregation of disorderly groups'.

6.2

Sadique and Hussain [2011] EWCA Crim 2872, [2012] 1 WLR 1700

Key Facts

Section 46 should only be used when there are different offences which D believes may be committed.

Key Law

Section 46 is not so vague and uncertain as to be contrary to Art 7 of the European Convention on Human Rights. Section 46 should only be used when it may be that D, at the time of doing the act, believes that one or more of either offence X or offence Y or offence Z will be committed but has no belief as to which one or ones of the three will be committed.

6.3.1

Reed [1982] Crim LR 819

Key Facts

D and another man agreed that the other man should visit individuals who were contemplating suicide and, depending on his assessment of the situation, either discourage them or actively help them to commit suicide. They were charged with conspiracy to murder.

Key Law

Provided an offence will 'necessarily' be committed if the plan is carried out as intended, D will be guilty of statutory conspiracy.

Key Judgment: Donaldson LJ

'(1) A and B agree to drive from London to Edinburgh in a time which can be achieved without exceeding the speed limit but only if the traffic is exceptionally light. Their agreement will not necessarily involve the commission of any offence.

(2) A and B agree to rob a bank if, when they arrive at the bank, it is safe to do so. Their agreement will necessarily involve the commission of the offence of robbery if it is carried out in accordance with their intentions.'

6.3.1   *Jackson* [1985] Crim LR 442

Key Facts

Three men agreed to shoot another in the leg if he was convicted, so that there would be mitigating circumstances when he was sentenced. They were convicted of conspiring to pervert the course of justice.

Key Law

Where the plan was for a contingency taking place, then provided that plan necessarily involved the commission of an offence, D was guilty of conspiracy.

Key Link

Anderson [1986] AC 27, (1985) 81 Cr App R 253.

6.3.2

Yip Chiu-Cheung v R [1994] 2 All ER 924, (1994) 99 Cr App R 406

 PC

Key Facts

D conspired with N to traffic in heroin. N was, in fact, an undercover drugs enforcement agent. D appealed against his conviction on the basis that N did not intend to carry out the offence and so could not be a conspirator.

Key Law

D and at least one other must intend that the offence be committed. In this case N was intending to take the drugs into Australia and so had the intention to commit the offence, although he knew he would not be prosecuted.

6.3.6

Scott v Metropolitan Police Commissioner [1975] AC 818, (1974) 60 Cr App R 124

 HL

Key Facts

D agreed with employees in cinemas that they would temporarily remove films so that D could make pirate copies. The cinema owners were unaware of the plan so there was no deception, nor did the owners suffer economic loss.

Key Law

1) It is not necessary to prove that economic loss was suffered. It is enough that V's economic interests are put at risk.

2) Deception is not a required element of the offence.

6.3.6

Wai Yu-tsang v R [1991] 4 All ER 664, (1994) 94 Cr App R 264

 PC

Key Facts

D and employees of a bank agreed to conceal the fact that cheques which the bank had purchased had been dishonoured. D had done this in order to prevent a 'run' on the bank.

Key Law

Conspiracy to defraud is not limited to economic loss, nor to the idea of depriving someone of something of value. It is enough if anyone may be prejudiced in any way by the fraud.

6.4.1

Attorney-General's Reference (No 1 of 1992) [1993] 2 All ER 190, (1993) 96 Cr App R 298

Key Facts

D dragged a girl up some steps to a shed. He lowered his trousers and interfered with her private parts. His penis remained flaccid. He argued that he could not therefore attempt to commit rape.

Key Law

D need not have performed the last act before the crime proper, nor need he have reached the point of no return.

6.4.1

Gullefer [1987] Crim LR 195, [1990] 3 All ER 882

Key Facts

D jumped onto a race track in order to have the race declared void and so enable him to reclaim money he had bet on it. His conviction for attempting to steal was quashed because his action was merely preparatory to committing the offence.

Key Law

'More than merely preparatory' means that the defendant must have gone beyond purely preparatory acts and be 'embarked on the crime proper'.

Key Links

- *Geddes* [1996] Crim LR 894;
- *Campbell* (1990) 93 Cr App R 350.

6.4.1   *Boyle and Boyle* [1987] Crim LR 574

Key Facts

The defendants were found standing by a door of which the lock and one hinge were broken. Their conviction for attempted burglary was upheld.

Embarking on the crime proper is the test. In this case, once Ds had entered they would be committing burglary, so trying to gain entry was an attempt.

Key Link

Jones [1990] 3 All ER 886, (1990) 91 Cr App R 351.

6.4.2   *Easom* [1971] 2 All ER 945, (1971) 55 Cr App R 410

Key Facts

D picked up a woman's handbag in a cinema, rummaged through it, then put it back on the floor without removing anything from it. His conviction for theft of the bag and its contents was quashed. The Court of Appeal also refused to substitute a conviction for attempted theft of the bag and named contents (including a purse and a pen) as there was no evidence that D intended to steal the items.

Key Law

To prove attempted theft, the *mens rea* for theft must be proved.

Key Comment

Where there is a conditional intent, that is D intended stealing if there was anything worth stealing, D could be charged with an attempt to steal some or all of the contents.

6.4.2 *Millard and Vernon* [1987] Crim LR 393   CA

Key Facts

Ds repeatedly pushed against a wooden fence on a stand at a football ground. The prosecution alleged that they were trying to break it and they were convicted of attempted criminal damage. The Court of Appeal quashed their convictions.

Key Law

Recklessness as to a consequence is not sufficient *mens rea* for an attempt. This is so even where recklessness would suffice for the completed offence.

6.4.3 *Shivpuri* [1987] AC 1, (1986) 83 Cr App R 178   HL

Key Facts

D thought he was dealing in prohibited drugs. In fact, it was snuff and harmless vegetable matter. He was convicted of attempting to be knowingly concerned in dealing with prohibited drugs.

Key Law

Subsections 1(2) and 1(3) of the Criminal Attempts Act 1981 meant that a person could be guilty of an attempt even if the commission of the full offence was impossible.

Key Comment

The decision in *Shivpuri* overruled the case of *Anderton v Ryan* [1985] 2 All ER 355, (1985) 81 Cr App R 166, which had been decided a year earlier. The House of Lords accepted that its decision in *Anderton v Ryan* had been wrong and used the Practice Statement to overrule it.

7 Capacity

Children
- Under age of ten *doli incapax*
- Ten and over fully liable for actions

BUT
- Different method of trial
- Different sentencing powers

Mentally ill
- May be ruled unfit to plead
- If tried may be found not guilty by reason of insanity (M'Naghten Rules)
- Diminished responsibility – partial defence to murder – reduces it to manslaughter

LIMITATIONS ON CAPACITY

Corporations
- Have legal personality so can be guilty of criminal offences
- Cannot be convicted of some physical crimes, e.g. rape
- Liable under one of three principles:
    Identification
    Vicarous liability
    Breach of statutory duty

There are some circumstances in which the law rules that a person is not capable of committing a crime. The main limitations are on:

- children under the age of ten;
- mentally ill persons;
- corporations.

On the other hand, there are some circumstances in which a person may be liable for the actions of another under the principle of vicarious liability.

▶ 7.1 Children

7.1.1 Children under the age of ten

1   Section 50 of the Children and Young Persons Act 1933 (as amended) states that 'it shall be conclusively presumed that no child under the age of ten can be guilty of any offence'.

2   This is known as the *doli incapax* presumption. Children under the age of ten cannot be criminally liable for their acts.

3   However, s 11 of the Crime and Disorder Act 1998 allows a 'child safety order' to be made where a child under ten has committed an act which would have been an offence had he been aged ten or over.

7.1.2 Children aged ten and over

1   Section 34 of the Crime and Disorder Act 1998 abolished the rebuttable presumption that a child aged 10 to 13 is incapable of committing an offence.

2   This means that a child aged 10 and over is considered to be 'as responsible for his actions as if he were 40'. This was confirmed by the case of *JTB* (2009).

3   For all but the most serious offences, children (10–13) and young persons (14–17) are tried in the Youth Court.

4   Where a child or young person is being tried in the Crown Court, special arrangements must be made to allow him to participate effectively in the trial. If this is not done there may be a breach of Article 6 of the European Convention on Human Rights (*T v UK; V v UK* (2000)).

5   Sentencing powers are different to those for adults.

▶ 7.2 Mentally ill persons

7.2.1 Unfitness to plead

1   Where, because of his mental state, the defendant is unable to understand the charge against him so as to be able to make a proper defence, he may be found unfit to plead (Criminal Procedure (Insanity) Act 1964 (as amended)).

2   Section 24 Domestic Violence, Crime and Victims Act 2004 amended the Criminal Procedure (Insanity) Act 1964, so that the decision as to whether the defendant is fit to plead is now made by a judge and not a jury.

3   If the defendant is found unfit to plead, a jury must then decide whether the defendant 'did the act or made the omission charged against him'.

4   In deciding this it is not necessary for the jury to consider the mental element of the crime (*Antoine* (2000)).

5   When a defendant is found unfit to plead and that he did the act or omission, the judge has the power to make:

● a hospital order; or

● a supervision order (which may include a treatment requirement); or

● an absolute discharge.

7.2.2 Insanity at time of offence

1   Where a person is fit to plead, but is found to be insane at the time he committed the offence, a special verdict of 'Not guilty by reason of insanity' is given by the jury.

2   The rules on insanity come from the *M'Naghten* Rules (see 9.1).

3   Where the verdict is 'Not guilty by reason of insanity', the judge has the same powers of disposal as in 7.2.1 (Criminal Procedure (Insanity and Unfitness to Plead) Act 1964).

7.2.3 Diminished responsibility

1   This is a partial defence which is only available on a charge of murder.

2   It operates where a person suffers from an abnormality of mental functioning which substantially impaired D's ability to:

● understand the nature of his conduct; and/or

● form a rational judgment; and/or

● exercise self-control.

(s 2 Homicide Act 1957 as amended by the Coroners and Justice Act 2009) (see 10.3.1).

3   If the defence is successful, the charge of murder is reduced to manslaughter.

▶ 7.3 Corporate liability

1   A corporation is a legal person (*Salomon v Salomon* (1897)). Corporations include limited companies and public corporations.

2   As a corporation is a legal person, it can be criminally liable even though it has no physical existence.

3   The Interpretation Act 1978 provides that unless the contrary intention appears, 'person' includes a corporation.

4   However, a corporation cannot be convicted of an offence where the only punishment available is physical, e.g. life imprisonment for murder.

5   A corporation cannot commit crimes of a physical nature, such as bigamy, rape or perjury, though it may be possible for a corporation to be liable as an accessory.

6   A corporation can be liable for manslaughter (*P & O European Ferries (Dover) Ltd* (1991))(common law) and under the Corporate Manslaughter and Corporate Homicide Act 2007.

7   There are three different principles by which a corporation may be liable. These are:

● the principle of identification;

● vicarious liability; and

● breach of statutory duty.

7.3.1 The principle of identification

1   As a corporation has no physical existence it is necessary to identify those people within the corporation who can be considered as the 'directing mind and will of the company' (*HL Bolton (Engineering) v TJ Graham & Sons Ltd* (1957)).

2   The acts and intentions of those who are identified as the 'embodiment of the company' are considered the acts and intention of that company (*Tesco Supermarkets Ltd v Natrass* (1972)). Only those in senior positions can be considered as the 'controlling mind' of a corporation.

3   This was a narrow test which made it difficult to establish corporate liability in a large company.

4   A corporation could be convicted of manslaughter by gross negligence if there was no evidence establishing the guilt of an identified human individual for the same crime (*A-G's Reference (No 2 of 1999)* (2000)).

5   In view of the difficulty of establishing liability, the Law Commission recommended a new offence of corporate killing.

6   The Corporate Manslaughter and Corporate Homicide Act was enacted in 2007 (see 7.3.4 for details).

7.3.2 Vicarious liability

1   Corporations may be vicariously liable for the acts of their employees in the same way as a natural person.

2   For this the principles of vicarious liability are set out in 7.4 apply.

3   The distinction between vicarious liability and the identification principle is that, under the identification principle, 'it is required that *mens rea* and *actus reus* should be established not against those who acted for or in the name of the company, but against those who were identified as the embodiment of the company' (*R v HM Coroner for East Kent, ex p Spooner* (1989)).

7.3.3 Breach of statutory duty

1   This occurs where a statute or regulation makes the corporation liable e.g. the Health and Safety at Work etc. Act 1974.

2   In *A-G's Reference (No 2 of 1999)* (2000), even though the company was held not guilty of manslaughter, the company pleaded guilty to a breach of statutory duty under the Health and Safety at Work etc. Act 1974.

7.3.4 Corporate manslaughter

1   During the last two decades of the twentieth century there were a number of high-profile disasters in which people died as a result of poor practice by a corporation.

2   None of the prosecutions for manslaughter for these was successful.

3   The only successful prosecutions of a corporation involved very small companies.

4   The Corporate Manslaughter and Corporate Homicide Act 2007 was passed to make larger corporations more accountable for poor practices.

5   The Act applies to:

● corporations;

- government departments;
- police forces; and
- partnerships, trade unions or employers' associations.

6   To prove the offence it is necessary to show that the way in which any of its activities were managed amounted to gross negligence of a duty of care and caused a death (s 1(1)).

7   An organisation is guilty of an offence if the way in which its activities are managed or organised by its senior management is a substantial element in the breach of the duty of care.

8   Senior management 'comprises' persons who play significant roles in the making of decisions about how the whole or a substantial part of its activities are to be managed or organised, or the actual managing or organising of the whole or a substantial part of those activities.

9   The duty of care is based on the civil law of negligence. Once a relevant duty of care has been established, then, under s 8(1)(b), the jury decide if there has been a gross breach.

10 To decide this, the jury must consider whether the evidence shows that the organisation failed to comply with any health and safety legislation that relates to the alleged breach, and if so:

- how serious that failure was; and
- how much of a risk of death it posed.

11 The jury may also consider the extent to which the evidence shows that there were attitudes, policies, systems or accepted practices within the organisation that were likely to have encouraged any such failure, or to have produced tolerance of it.

▶ 7.4 Vicarious liability

1   The normal rule is that one person is not liable for crimes committed by another (*Huggins* (1730)).

2   However, there are some situations in which one person can be liable for the acts or omission of another. This is the principle of vicarious liability.

3   Vicarious liability for common law crimes is very rare and only occurs in offences of public nuisance and criminal libel.

4   Vicarious liability can make employers liable for the actions of their employees; principals for the actions of their agents (*Duke of Leinster* (1924)); and licensees for the actions of those to whom they delegate control of their business.

5   In statutory offences vicarious liability can exist through the extended meanings of words or under the principle of delegation.

7.4.1 Authorised acts

1   Words such as 'sell' and 'use' are usually taken to include the employer (or principal or licensee) even though the actual sale or use is by an employee.

2   Vicarious liability has been held to exist even where the employer has taken steps to ensure that such an offence is not committed (*Coppen v Moore (No 2)* (1898)). This can only occur where an employee carries out an authorised act in an unauthorised way, as in *Coppen v Moore (No 2)* where a sales assistant sold ham that she wrongly described as 'Scotch ham' against instruction of the employer. The employer was liable because the assistant was authorised to sell the item.

3   Where the employee is not authorised to carry out the act then the employer is not liable (*Adams v Camfoni* (1929)).

7.4.2 Delegation principle

1   Where an offence requires proof of *mens rea* then vicarious liability can only exist if the principal has delegated responsibility.

2   In such instances the acts and intention of the person to whom responsibility has been delegated are imputed to the principal (*Allen v Whitehead* (1930)).

3   There must be complete delegation for the principal to be vicariously liable (*Vane v Yiannopoullos* (1965)).

7.4.3 Reasons for vicarious liability

1   It ensures that employers train and control staff properly.

2   It helps keep high standards.

3   It makes a licensee retain proper control over his business even when he is not there.

4   Without the principle of vicarious liability, it would be difficult to convict those responsible for the business.

7.4.4 Criticisms of vicarious liability

1   It is unjust to penalise someone for the actions of another. This is especially so where the principal has taken steps to ensure that no offence is committed (*Coppen v Moore (No 2)* (1898), *Duke of Leinster* (1924)).

2   Where an offence requires *mens rea* it is unjust to convict someone who had no knowledge of the offence.

3   The rules of vicarious liability have not been created by Parliament; they are judge-made. In some cases, e.g. where Parliament has used the word 'knowingly' in an offence, the concept of vicarious liability appears to be contrary to the intentions of Parliament.

4   There is no evidence that it helps to promote high standards.

Key Cases Checklist

Children

JTB (2009)
S 34 Crime and Disorder Act 1998 has abolished the common law presumption of *doli incapax*

Corporations

Bolton (Engineering) v TJ Graham (1956)
There are people who represent the mind and will of the company

Tesco Supermarket v Natrass (1972)
Only those at a sufficiently high managerial level can make the company liable

Capacity

Mentally ill

Unfitness to plead
Antoine (2000)
Following a finding of unfitness to plead a jury should be empanelled to decide if D did the act alleged

Insanity: see 9.1

Diminished responsibility: see 10.3.1

Vicarious liability

Coppen v Moore (1898)
An act done within the scope of employment can make the employer liable

Adams v Camfoni (1929)
An act outside of the scope of employment does not make the employer liable

Allen v Whitehead (1930)
Where there is full delegation, the knowledge of the delegate will be imputed to the delegator

Vane v Yiannopoullos (1964)
Where there is only partial delegation, the knowledge of the delegate will NOT be imputed to the delegator

7.1.2   *JTB* [2009] UKHL 20   HL

Key Facts

D, aged 12, was charged with several offences of causing or inciting a child under 13 to engage in sexual activity. He admitted the activity, but said that he did not know it was wrong and that he should be allowed to put this as his defence. The trial judge ruled that the defence of *doli incapax* (under which a child aged 10–13 had a defence if they did not know that what they were doing was seriously wrong) was not available to him. It had been abolished. The House of Lords upheld the judge's ruling.

Key Law

Section 34 of the Crime and Disorder Act 1998 has abolished the common law presumption of *doli incapax* completely. It is no longer open to those aged 10–13 to put as a defence that they did not know that what they were doing was wrong.

Key Comment

At 10, the age of criminal responsibility in England and Wales is among the lowest in Europe. The abolition of the presumption of *doli incapax* makes a child of 10 'as responsible for his actions as if he were 40'. Should the same rules on intention apply to a child of 10 as they do to adults?

7.2.1   *Antoine* [2000] 2 All ER 208, [2000] 2 Cr App R 94   HL

Key Facts

D was charged with murder but was found by a jury to be unfit to plead. A new jury then tried D to decide if he had committed the act of murder. He wanted that jury to consider whether he was suffering from diminished responsibility.

Key Law

Section 4A of the Criminal Procedure (Insanity and Unfitness to Plead) Act 1991 means that the jury in the second hearing are only concerned with the *actus reus* and not the mental element of the offence.

Key Judgment: Lord Hutton

'The purpose of s 4A is to strike a fair balance between the need to protect a defendant who has, in fact, done nothing wrong and is unfit to plead at his trial and the need to protect the public from a defendant who has committed an injurious act which would constitute a crime if done with the requisite mens rea.'

Key Link

See the defence of insanity at **9.1** and the defence of diminished responsibility at **10.3**.

7.3.1   *HL Bolton (Engineering) Co Ltd v TJ Graham & Sons Ltd* [1956] 3 All ER 624   CCA

Key Facts

The case involved civil proceedings about a tenancy. The landlord was a limited company and the question arose whether the directors' intentions could be imputed to the company.

Key Law

Where senior officials of a company have intention, that intention can be imputed to the company.

Key Judgment: Lord Denning

'A company may in many ways be likened to a human body. It has a brain and a nerve centre which controls what it does. It also has hands which hold the tools and act in accordance with directions from the centre. Some of the people in the company are mere servants and agents who are nothing more than hands to do the work and cannot be said to represent the mind or will. Others are directors and managers who represent the directing mind and will of the company and control what it does. The state of mind of these managers is the state of mind of the company and is treated by the law as such.'

7.3.1

Tesco Supermarkets Ltd v Natrass [1972] AC 153   HL

Key Facts

A Tesco store advertised packets of washing machine powder at a reduced price. An employee did not tell the store manager when all the reduced price packets were sold and the adverts continued. The company was charged under s 11 of the Trade Descriptions Act 1968 with giving a false indication as to price.

Key Law

A store manager was at too low a level of management to be the 'mind and the will' of a company for the purpose of making the company criminally liable.

NOTE that corporations and other organisations can be liable for manslaughter under the Corporate Manslaughter and Corporate Homicide Act 2007.

7.4.1

Coppen v Moore (No 2) [1898] 2 QB 306   DC

Key Facts

The appellant owned six shops. He had issued instructions that any hams sold in them must not be given a specific place of origin. Despite this, an assistant in one of the shops sold a ham (which was American) as 'a Scotch ham'. The appellant was convicted of selling goods to which a false trade description had been applied.

Key Law

Where an offence is committed by an act such as 'selling', 'using' or 'driving' then a corporation can be liable for acts of its employees, provided that such act is done by an employee acting within the scope of employment.

Key Judgment: Lord Russell CJ

'[I]t was clearly the intention of the legislature to make the master criminally liable for acts [which were done within the scope or in the course of employment].'

| 7.4.1 | *Adams v Camfoni* [1929] 1 KB 95 | DC |

Key Facts

D, a licensee, was charged with selling alcohol outside the hours permitted by his licence. In fact, the sale had been made by a messenger boy who had no authority to sell anything. D's conviction was quashed.

Key Law

An employer is not liable for the acts of his employees where the act done was outside the scope of the employment.

| 7.4.2 | *Allen v Whitehead* [1930] 1 KB 211 | DC |

Key Facts

D was the owner and licensee of a café. He employed a manager to run the café. He instructed the manager not to allow prostitutes to enter the café. The manager allowed women, whom he knew to be prostitutes, to use the premises.

Key Law

An employer is liable for the acts of his employees where the act done was outside the scope of the employment.

The knowledge or intention of the person to whom responsibility has been delegated is treated as being the knowledge or intention of the principal.

| 7.4.2 | *Vane v Yiannopoullos* [1964] 3 All ER 820 | HL |

Key Facts

D was the licensee of a restaurant. He had given instruction to a waitress not to serve alcohol to people unless they ordered a meal. The restaurant was on two floors and, while the licensee was on another floor, the waitress served alcohol to two people who did not order a meal. D was charged with 'knowingly selling intoxicating liquor to persons to whom he was not entitled to sell'. His conviction was quashed.

Key Law

There must be complete delegation to make the principal liable through the knowledge or intention of his servant.

General defences

DURESS
- D's will is overborne by threats (*DPP for Northern Ireland v Lynch* (1975))
- The threats must be of death or serious injury (*Valderrama-Vega* (1985))
- There must be no avenue of escape (*R v Gill* (1963))
- There is a two-stage test:
  - Was D compelled to act as he did?
  - Would a sober person of reasonable firmness and same characteristics have responded in the same way? (*Graham* (1982))
- Characteristics include age, pregnancy, disability, mental illness, but not a low IQ (*Bowen* (1996))

SELF-INDUCED DURESS
- Where D joins a violent gang (*Sharp* (1987)) or associates with a violent criminal (*Hasan* (2005)), duress is not available as a defence

DURESS OF CIRCUMSTANCES
- D may be forced to act by surrounding circumstances (*Willer* (1986))
- There must be imminent peril of death or serious injury and this must operate on D's mind at the time (*Abdul-Hussain and others* (1999))

DURESS, NECESSITY AND MARITAL COERCION

NECESSITY
- This is a full defence
- It applies where D acted to avoid 'inevitable and irreparable evil' (*Re A (Conjoined Twins)* (2000))
- It can also form the basis of other defences

MARITAL COERCION
- A defence under s 47 of the Criminal Justice Act 1925
- It operates where offence was committed 'in the presence of, and under the coercion of, the husband'

▶ 8.1 Duress

1 Duress is a defence because the defendant has been effectively forced to commit the crime. It is an excuse based on concession to human frailty. The defendant has to choose between being killed or seriously injured or committing a crime. In such a situation there is no real choice. D's will has been overborne by threats of death or serious injury (*DPP for Northern Ireland v Lynch* (1975)).

2 Duress can be either through a direct threat by another (duress by threats) or through external circumstances (duress of circumstances). Duress of circumstances overlaps with the defence of necessity.

3 Duress can be used as defence to all crimes, except murder (*Howe* (1987)), attempted murder (*Gotts* (1991)) and, possibly, treason (*Steane* (1947)).

4 In *Wilson* (2007) it was held that duress is not available as a defence to murder even where the defendant was aged only 13.

8.1.1 Duress by threats

1 The threat must be of death or serious injury; lesser threats do not provide a defence (*Singh* (1971), *Valderrama-Vega* (1985)).

2 The threat must be to the defendant himself, or to a close member of his family (*Ortiz* (1986)). There is no authority to say that a threat to kill an unrelated third person will provide a defence. (NB The Law Commission's Draft Criminal Code would have allowed for this.)

3 Duress can only be used as a defence if the defendant is placed in a situation where he has no safe avenue of escape (*R v Gill* (1963)).

4 If the threat is not such that the defendant expects it to be carried out almost immediately, then D should take evasive action (such as going to the police) rather than commit the offence (*Hasan* (2005)).

5 The defence is only available if the threats to the defendant are aimed at making him commit a specific offence. Threats of violence to make the defendant repay debts did not provide a defence of duress when the defendant decided to commit a robbery in order to obtain the money (*Cole* (1994)).

6 The threat must be effective at the moment the crime is committed (*Hudson and Taylor* (1971)). But this does not mean that the threats need to be able to be carried out immediately (*Abdul-Hussain and others* (1999)).

7   There are both subjective and objective tests in deciding if the defence should succeed. This involves a two-stage test:

- was the defendant compelled to act as he did because he feared serious injury or death? (the subjective test); and

- if so, would a sober person of reasonable firmness, sharing the characteristics of the accused, have responded in the same way (the objective test) (*Graham* (1982), *Howe* (1987))?

8   The defendant's belief as to the elements of the threat must be reasonable and not merely genuine (*Hasan* (2005)).

9   Only characteristics which are relevant to the ability to resist pressure and threats can be taken into consideration. In *Bowen* (1996) it was accepted that the following could be relevant:

- age – as very young people and the very old could be more susceptible to threats;

- pregnancy – there is the additional fear for the safety of the unborn child;

- serious physical disability – which could make it more difficult for the defendant to protect himself;

- recognised mental illness or psychiatric disorder – this could include post-traumatic stress disorder or any other disorder which meant that a person might be more susceptible to threats: this did not include a low IQ (*Bowen* (1991));

- sex – although the Court of Appeal thought that many women might have as much moral courage as men.

Case on duress	Facts	Law
Valderrama-Vega (1985)	Smuggled cocaine because of death threats and threats to disclose homosexuality	Must be a threat of death or serious injury but can consider cumulative effect of threats
Graham (1982)	Helped kill his wife because he was threatened by his homosexual lover	Two-stage test: • was D compelled to act as he did because he reasonably believed he had good cause to fear serious injury or death? • if so, would a sober person of reasonable firmness, sharing the characteristics of the accused have responded in some way?

Case on duress	Facts	Law
Hasan (2005)	D associated with a violent drug dealer. He claimed he committed a burglary because of threats	D's belief in the threat must be genuine and reasonable
Bowen (1996)	Had a low IQ (68); obtained goods by deception for two men because of petrol-bomb threat	Cannot take low IQ into account Can consider: • age • pregnancy • recognised mental illness • sex
Gill (1963)	Threatened so that he stole a lorry but had time to escape and raise the alarm	Cannot use duress if has a 'safe avenue of escape'
Hudson and Taylor (1971)	Two girls lied on oath because of threats to cut them up	The threat need not be capable of being carried out immediately Take into account age and sex
Abdul-Hussain (1999)	Hijacked plane to escape from persecution in Iraq	Threat must be 'imminent' and operating on D's mind when he commits the offence

8.1.2 Self-induced duress

1   This may occur, for example, where a defendant has voluntarily joined a criminal gang and then been forced to commit further crimes under duress.

2   If the original crimes did not involve any violence then the defendant may use the defence of duress for the later crimes (*Shepherd* (1987)).

3   If, however, the defendant knew when he joined the gang that they were likely to use violence, duress will not be available as a defence (*Sharp* (1987)).

4   The defence of duress is not available if the defendant foresaw, or ought reasonably to have foreseen, the risk of being subjected to any compulsion by threats of violence (*Hasan* (2005)).

8.1.3 Duress of circumstances

1   Since the 1980s the courts have recognised that a defendant may be forced to act by the surrounding circumstances.

2   This was shown by *Willer* (1986), when the defendant, fearing for his safety, drove onto the pavement to get away from a gang of youths. He was charged with reckless driving but the Court of Appeal said that the jury should have been allowed to consider whether the defendant drove 'under that form of compulsion, that is, under duress'.

3   In *Martin* (1989), it was decided that duress of circumstances could be available as a defence if, from an objective viewpoint, the accused acted reasonably and proportionately to avoid a threat of death or serious injury and that the same two-stage test put forward in *Graham* (1982) applied.

4   In *Pommell* (1995), the Court of Appeal said that the defence of duress of circumstances was available for all crimes except murder, attempted murder and some forms of treason.

5   In *Abdul-Hussain* and others (1999) it was stated that:

   ● there must be imminent peril of death or serious injury to D, or to those for whom he has responsibility;

   ● the peril must operate on D's mind at the time of committing the otherwise criminal act, so as to overbear his will; this is a matter for the jury; and

   ● execution of the threat need not be immediately in prospect.

6   The jury must judge the defendant on what he reasonably believes to be the situation. So, a reasonable belief that a threat existed is sufficient to provide a defence, even if there was not a threat in fact (*Safi and others* (2003)).

7   In duress of circumstances the defence may be used for any offence which is an appropriate response to the danger posed by the circumstances (*Abdul-Hussain and others* (1999)).

▶ 8.2 Necessity

1   The courts have been reluctant to recognise a defence under this heading (*Dudley and Stephens* (1884)).

2   However, the defence has been implicitly recognised in some cases, especially *Bourne* (1938) and *Gillick v West Norfolk and Wisbech AHA* (1986).

3   In *Re A (Conjoined Twins)* (2000) the Court of Appeal approved the following four principles of the defence of necessity, as set out in Stephen's *Digest of Criminal Law* (1883):

   a) The act was done only in order to avoid consequences that could not otherwise be avoided.

   b) Those consequences, if they had happened, would have inflicted inevitable and irreparable evil.

   c) That no more was done than was reasonably necessary for that purpose.

   d) That the evil inflicted by it was not disproportionate to the evil avoided.

4   In *Shayler* (2001), the Court of Appeal did not distinguish between duress of circumstances and necessity, but treated them as the same defence. They used similar tests to those in point 3 above:

   ● the act must be done only to prevent an act of greater evil;

   ● the evil must be directed towards the defendant or a person or persons for whom he was responsible; and

   ● the act must be reasonable and proportionate to the evil avoided.

5   This blurring of the defences of duress of circumstances and necessity can be criticised on the following points:

   a) duress of circumstances is an excusatory defence but necessity is a defence of justification;

   b) necessity was accepted as a defence to murder in *Re A* (2000), but duress cannot be a defence to murder.

6   Cases such as *Quayle* (2005) and *Altham* (2006) show that courts are still reluctant to allow the defence of necessity.

8.2.1 The role of necessity in other defences

Necessity effectively forms the basis of other defences such as:

a) Statutory provisions – some Acts of Parliament set out defences based on necessity for certain crimes; these include allowing emergency vehicles a defence to breaking the speed limit 'if the observation of the limit would be likely to hinder the purpose for which the vehicle is being used'.

b) Self-defence – the essence of this defence is that the defendant is claiming that he acted as he did because it was necessary for his protection.

c) Duress of circumstances – as set out above, this defence, which might be considered necessity under a different title, is available for almost all crimes.

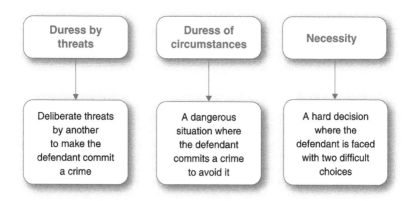

▶ 8.3 Marital coercion

1   Section 47 Criminal Justice Act 1925 provides that for a wife 'it shall be a good defence to prove that the offence was committed in the presence of, and under the coercion of, the husband'.

2   The defence is not available for murder or treason.

3   The burden of proving coercion lies on the defence.

4   It is a rarely used defence, though it was used in the case of *Fitton* (2000) on a charge of drink-driving.

5   It can be argued that the position of wives in the twenty-first century is very different from that in 1925 and the defence should no longer be available.

MISTAKE
- A mistake must be of fact
- It operates where *either* there was no *mens rea* for the offence, or D could rely on another defence
- D is judged on his genuine mistaken view (*Williams (Gladstone)* (1987))

INTOXICATED MISTAKE
- If the mistake negatives the *mens rea*, then D can rely on that mistake, even though the mistake was caused through intoxication
- If the intoxication causes D to make a mistake about another matter, D cannot rely on the mistake (*O'Grady* (1987))

MISTAKE, SELF-DEFENCE AND CONSENT

SELF-DEFENCE
- This is a full defence to any offence
- It includes defence of another and/or prevention of crime
- The force used must be reasonable in the circustances (*Palmer* (1971))
- D is judged on the facts as he believed them to be (Williams *(Gladstone)* (1987))
- S 76 Criminal Justice and Immigration Act 2008 has given statutory effect to the decisions in *Palmer* and *Williams*

CONSENT
- Consent is a full defence
- In some sexual offences consent is not a defence (e.g. where V is under 16)
- There must be true consent to the nature and the quality of the act (*Tabassum* (2000))
- Where injury is caused, consent is not usually a defence to an assault charge
- Consent to fighting in the street is not a defence (*A-G's Ref (No 6 of 1980)* (1981))
- Consent is not a defence to sado-masochistic acts (*Brown* (1993))
- Genuine belief V is consenting can be a defence (*Jones* (1986))

▶ 8.4 Mistake

1   To be a defence a mistake must be a mistake about a fact, so that if the facts had been as the defendant believed them to be, it would mean:

- either there was no *mens rea* for the offence; or

- that the defendant would have been able to rely on another defence.

2   Simple situations will illustrate these concepts:

●   if A picks up an umbrella from a stand as he is leaving a restaurant in the mistaken belief that it is his own umbrella, he does not have the *mens rea* required for theft as he is not dishonest;

●   if B, in the mistaken belief that V is pointing a gun at him, throws a stone at V and knocks him out, B can plead he should be judged on the basis that his action was in self-defence.

3   Provided the defendant genuinely makes a mistake, there will be a defence even if the mistake is unreasonable (*DPP v Morgan* (1976), *Williams (Gladstone)* (1987), *B v DPP* (2000)).

4   The defendant is judged according to his genuine mistaken view of the facts, regardless of whether his mistake was reasonable or unreasonable (*Williams* (1987)).

8.4.1 Drunken mistakes

1   If the mistake negatives the *mens rea* required for the offence then the defendant will have a defence.

2   If the mistake is about another aspect, for example the amount of force needed in self-defence, the defendant will not have a defence (*Lipman* (1970), *O'Grady* (1987)). *O'Grady* involved a charge of manslaughter but the case of *Hatton* (2005) confirmed that the same rule applies on a charge of murder.

3   The law is trying to balance the needs of the defendant and the protection of victims.

4   However, in *Richardson and Irwin* (1999) the Court of Appeal held that a mistaken belief by the defendant that the victim was consenting to run the risk of personal injury would enable the defendant to avoid liability even if that mistake was induced by intoxication.

5   Section 5 Criminal Damage Act 1971 allows an honest belief that the person to whom the property belonged would have consented to the damage or destruction as a lawful excuse to a charge of criminal damage, whether or not the belief is justified. This has been interpreted as giving a defendant a defence even where the mistake was made through intoxication (*Jaggard v Dickinson* (1981)).

8.4.2 Mistake and crimes of strict liability

For these crimes, a mistake, even if reasonable, will not be a defence (*Pharmaceutical Society of Great Britain v Storkwain* (1986)).

▶ 8.5 Self-defence

1 This covers not only actions needed to defend oneself from an attack, but also actions taken to defend another or prevent crime (s 3 Criminal Law Act 1967).

2 The defence can be a defence to any crime, including murder, as the defendant is justifying the use of force.

3 The force used to defend oneself or another must be reasonable in the circumstances (*Palmer v R* (1971)).

4 If excessive force is used the defence will fail (*Clegg* (1995)).

5 The defendant must be judged on the facts as he believed them to be (*Williams (Gladstone)* (1987)).

6 If the force is used after all danger from the assailant is over, the defence of self-defence is not available.

7 The decisions in *Palmer* and *Williams* were given statutory force by s 76 of the Criminal Justice and Immigration Act 2008.

8 Section 76 states that if D acts under a mistaken belief, then the reasonableness of that belief is relevant to the question of whether D genuinely held it, but if it is determined that D did genuinely hold it, D is entitled to rely on it whether or not it was a reasonable mistake to make (s 76(4)).

9 If D makes a mistake due to intoxication, he cannot rely on that mistaken belief as a defence (s 76(5)).

10 The degree of force must be reasonable in the circumstances as D believed them to be (s 76(3)).

11 Section 76(7) states that, in deciding whether the degree of force used was reasonable:

'(a) that a person acting for a legitimate purpose may not be able to weigh to a nicety the exact measure of any necessary action; and

(b) that evidence of a person's having only done what the person honestly and instinctively thought was necessary for a legitimate purpose constitutes strong evidence that only reasonable action was taken by that person for that purpose.'

12   Section 148 of the Legal Aid, Sentencing and Punishment of Offenders Act 2012 amends s 76 in order to clarify the law. In particular it states that the degree of force will not be reasonable if it is disproportionate in the circumstances as D believed them to be.

▶ 8.6 Consent

1   Whether the victim has consented or not is an essential factor in many offences.

2   Consent is not strictly speaking a defence, because where the other person consents there is no offence. This is particularly true of sexual offences.

3   For some statutory offences, Parliament has set down an age below which a person cannot consent.

8.6.1 Consent and theft

1   Consent to appropriation of property does not prevent the defendant from being liable for theft (*Gomez* (1991)).

2   This is so even where the consent has not been obtained by fraud (*Hinks* (2000)).

8.6.2 Consent and sexual offences

1   For offences such as rape and indecent assault, consent will normally mean that the act is not unlawful and so there is no offence.

2   Consent is never a defence to offences under the Sexual Offences Act 2003 where a child is under 13.

3   For an indecent assault (now sexual touching) where a victim only consents because they believe the defendant is medically qualified, there is no true consent. The consent is only to the nature of the act but not to its quality (*Tabassum* (2000)).

8.6.3 Consent and non-fatal assaults

1   Generally, the consent of the victim to an assault where there is no injury is a good defence as it prevents the act from being unlawful.

2   However, in some cases the courts have held that an unlawful act 'cannot be rendered lawful because the person to whose detriment it is done consents to it. No person can license another to commit a crime' (*Donovan* (1934)).

3   In *Attorney-General's Reference (No 6 of 1980)* (1981) where two young men agreed to fight in the street following a quarrel, the Court of Appeal held that consent could not be a defence to such an action as it was not in the public interest that people should cause each other injuries for no good reason.

4   In this case the Court of Appeal also said that consent was available as a defence to an assault in 'properly conducted games and sports, lawful chastisement or correction, reasonable surgical interference, dangerous exhibitions etc.'.

5   Although consent is not normally available as a defence where there is bodily harm, the defence may be available in contact sports (*Barnes* (2005)), particularly where the incident causing the injury is within the rules and practice of a sport.

6   The defence is not available if the conduct goes beyond what a player can reasonably be regarded as having consented to.

7   In *Brown* (1993), the House of Lords held that consent was not a defence to sado-masochistic acts, even though all the participants were adult and the injuries inflicted were transitory and trifling.

8   But in *Wilson* (1996), the Court of Appeal held that where a defendant branded his initials on his wife's buttocks with a hot knife at her request, this was not an unlawful act. It was not in the public interest that such consensual behaviour should be criminalised.

9   Consent must be willing and informed (*Dica* (2004), *Konzani* (2005)) where the defendants were guilty of causing GBH by infecting others with HIV during consensual sex but when they had not informed the others of their HIV positive status.

8.6.4 Mistaken belief in consent

Where the defendant genuinely believes that the victim is consenting then there is a defence to an assault (*Jones* (1986), *Aitken* (1992), *Richardson* (1999)).

Key Cases Checklist

Duress

***DPP for NI v Lynch* (1975)**
Duress is where D's will is overborne by threats of death or serious injury

***Howe (1987) / Wilson* (2007)**
The defence is not available for murder

***Valderrama-Vega* (1985)**
There must be threats of death or serious injury but a combination of these and other threats can be considered

***Hudson and Taylor* (1971)**
The threat has to be present and immediate

***Abdul-Hussain* (1999)**
(1) The threat must be imminent but it need not be immediate.
(2) The response to a threat need not be spontaneous.

***Graham* (1982)**
(1) D must have acted as he did because of threats of death or serious injury (subjective)
(2) A sober person of reasonable firmness, sharing the characteristics of D, would have responded in the same way (objective)

***Hasan (formerly Z)* (2005)**
The defence is not available where D has voluntarily associated with criminals whom he foresaw or ought reasonably to have foreseen might compel him to act through threats

Duress and Necessity

Duress of Circumstances

***Willer* (1986)**
Threats from circumstances can form the basis of the defence of duress

***Martin* (1989)**
The same principles for duress by threats set out in *Graham* (1982) apply to duress of circumstances

***Pommell* (1995)**
The defence of duress of circumstances is available to the same range of offences as the defence of duress by threats

Necessity

***Dudley and Stephens* (1884)**
Necessity is not a defence to murder

***Re A* (2000)**
Necessity is choosing the lesser of two evils to avoid greater harm.

DPP for Northern Ireland v Lynch [1975] 1 All ER 913, (1975) 61 Cr App R 6

Key Facts

D was ordered by M, a terrorist gunman, to drive M and others to a place where they shot and killed a policeman. M was well known as a ruthless killer. D said he feared that if he did not obey M, he, D, would be shot.

Key Law

Duress is where D's will is overborne by threats of death or serious injury, so that D commits an act which he would not otherwise do.

Howe [1987] 1 All ER 771, (1987) 85 Cr App R 32

Key Facts

D took part in two killings. D claimed that he did this because of threats. The trial judge ruled duress was available for the first killing where D was only a secondary party to the killing, but it was not available for the second killing where D was a principal offender. The House of Lords held that duress was not available as a defence for either murder.

Key Law

Duress is not available as a defence on a charge of murder. This is so whether D is a principal or a secondary party.

Key Judgment: Lord Hailsham LC

'I do not at all accept in relation to the defence of murder it is either good morals, good policy or good law to suggest . . . that the ordinary man of reasonable fortitude is not to be supposed to be capable of heroism if he is asked to take an innocent life rather than sacrifice his own.'

Key Problem

1) This ruling ignores situations such as a woman motorist being hijacked and forced to act as getaway driver.

Lord Griffiths simply dismissed such examples on the basis that it was inconceivable that such person would be prosecuted.

2) There is an anomaly that duress is not available for murder but is available for a charge under s 18 Offences against the Person Act 1861 where the *mens rea* of intention to cause grievous bodily harm can be the same as for murder.

8.1 *Wilson* [2007] 2 Cr App R 31

Key Facts

D, who was aged 13, and his father were charged with the murder of D's mother. D stated that he had helped his father with the murder because he was too frightened to disobey his father. The Court of Appeal held that D did not have a defence as the rule that duress provided no defence to murder applied, however susceptible D might be to the duress.

Key Law

Duress is not a defence to murder, even when D is only 13. The rule also applies whether D was a principal in the first or second degree.

Key Link

Gotts [1992] 1 All ER 832, (1992) 94 Cr App R 312.

8.1.1 *Valderrama-Vega* [1985] Crim LR 220

Key Facts

D was threatened with disclosure of his homosexuality and put under financial pressure. He was also threatened with death or serious injury. He took part in a scheme to bring cocaine into the UK. The trial judge directed the jury that duress was available only if D acted solely as a result of the threats of death or serious injury. His conviction was upheld, but the Court of Appeal held that the use of the word 'solely' was wrong.

Key Law

For the defence of duress to be available there must be threats of death or serious injury. However, if there are other threats together with those of death or serious injury, then the jury can take into account the combination of threats.

8.1.1

Hudson and Taylor [1971] 2 All ER 244, (1971) 56 Cr App R 1

Key Facts

Ds were girls aged 17 and 19 who committed perjury. They claimed they had been threatened by F with being 'cut up'. When they were giving evidence, F was in the public gallery. The trial judge ruled that the defence of duress was not available to them as there was no present, immediate threat. The threats could not have been carried out there and then. The Court of Appeal quashed their convictions.

Key Law

1) Although the threat had to be 'present and immediate', it was enough that it neutralised the will of D at the time D committed the offence.

2) In deciding whether D should have sought police protection, or otherwise made the threat ineffective, the jury should have regard to the age and circumstances of D.

Key Comment

This decision was criticised by the House of Lords in *Hasan (formerly Z)* (2005) (see below).

8.1.1

Abdul-Hussain and others [1999] Crim LR 570

Key Facts

Ds were Shiite Muslims from Iraq who had fled to Sudan. They feared they were going to be returned to Iraq where it was likely they would be tortured and killed. They hijacked a plane which eventually landed in England. The judge refused to allow the defence of duress to go to the jury and Ds were convicted. The Court of Appeal quashed the convictions.

Key Law

1) The threat must be imminent but it need not be immediate.

2) The response to a threat need not be spontaneous.

Key Judgment: Simon Brown LJ

'If Anne Frank had stolen a car to escape from Amsterdam and been charged with theft, the tenets of English law would not, in our judgment, have denied her a defence of duress of circumstances on the ground that she should have waited for the Gestapo's knock on the door.'

8.1.1

Graham [1982] 1 All ER 801, (1982) 74 Cr App R 235   CA

Key Facts

D was a homosexual who lived with his wife and another homosexual man, K. K was violent and bullied D. After both D and K had been drinking heavily, K put a flex around the wife's neck and told D to pull the other end of the flex. D did this for about a minute. The wife died. D claimed he had only held the flex because of his fear of K.

Key Law

For the defence of duress to be available, there are two tests:

1) D must have acted as he did because of threats of death or serious injury (subjective).

2) A sober person of reasonable firmness, sharing the characteristics of D, would have responded in the same way to such threats (objective).

Key Comment

The House of Lords in *Hasan (formerly Z)* (2005) (see below) confirmed the decision in *Graham* that D's belief in the threats must be reasonable and genuine.

8.1.1

Bowen [1996] 4 All ER 83, [1996] 2 Cr App R 157

 CA

Key Facts

D was of low IQ and abnormally suggestible. He was charged with obtaining services by deception and claimed he had been forced to do so by two men on the street who had threatened to petrol-bomb him and his family.

Key Law

Only certain characteristics can be considered for the objective test. These include categories of persons who are less able to resist pressure: examples are age, possibly sex, pregnancy, serious physical disability, recognised mental illness or psychiatric condition.

Key Judgment: Stuart-Smith LJ

'The mere fact that the accused is more pliable, vulnerable, timid or susceptible to threats than a normal person are not characteristics with which it is legitimate to invest the reasonable/ordinary person for the purpose of considering the objective test.'

 8.1.2

Sharp [1987] 3 All ER 103, (1987) 85 Cr App R 207

 CA

Key Facts

D voluntarily joined two others to commit a robbery. D knew that the others were violent and carried firearms. When he wished to withdraw from the robberies, one of the others threatened to kill him. D then took part in another robbery during which a sub-postmaster was shot dead.

Key Law

The defence of duress is not available where D voluntarily joins a gang whose members he knows are violent.

Key Comment

The courts have allowed duress to be available as a defence where D has voluntarily joined a non-violent gang; see *Shepherd* (1987) 86 Cr App R 47.

Key Link

Ali [1995] Crim LR 303; *Baker and Ward* [1999] EWCA Crim 913, [1999] 2 Cr App R 335. The leading case is now *Hasan (formerly Z)* (2005) (see below).

8.1.2   *Hasan (formerly Z)* [2005] UKHL 22   (HL)

Key Facts

D associated with a violent drug dealer, who threatened D and his family unless D burgled a house and stole money from a safe. D, carrying a knife, broke into the house but was unable to open the safe. He was convicted of aggravated burglary. The Court of Appeal allowed his appeal but the House of Lords reinstated his conviction.

Key Law

The defence of duress is excluded where D voluntarily associates with others who are engaged in criminal activity and he foresaw or ought reasonably to have foreseen the risk of being subjected to any compulsion by threats of violence.

Key Link

Israr Ali [2008] EWCA Crim 716.

8.1.3   *Willer* (1986) 83 Cr App R 225   (CA)

Key Facts

D was forced to drive his car on the pavement to escape from a gang of youths who were threatening him. He was convicted of reckless driving, but the Court of Appeal quashed the conviction on the basis of duress of circumstances.

Key Law

Threats from circumstances can form the basis of the defence of duress.

Key Comment

This is the first case in which the Court of Appeal accepted that there could be duress of circumstances. Prior to this a defendant could only put forward the defence of necessity. The judgment in *Willer* stated that D was 'wholly driven by force of circumstance into doing what he did and did not drive the car otherwise than under that form of compulsion, i.e. under duress'.

8.1.3   *Martin* [1989] 1 All ER 652, (1989) 88 Cr App R 343   CA

Key Facts

D, who was disqualified from driving, drove his stepson to work. He only did this because his wife became hysterical and threatened to commit suicide if he did not drive the boy to work and so prevent him from losing his job.

Key Law

Duress can arise from objective dangers threatening D or others. The same principles for duress by threats set out in *Graham* (1982) apply to duress of circumstances.

1) D must have acted as he did because he had good cause to fear that otherwise death or serious injury would result (subjective).

2) A sober person of reasonable firmness, sharing the characteristics of D, would have responded in the same way to that situation (objective).

8.1.3   *Pommell* [1995] 2 Cr App R 607   CA

Key Facts

D was found by police in bed at 8 am with a loaded sub-machine gun. He told police that at about 1 am he had taken it off another man who was going to use it 'to do some people some damage'. D said he had intended getting his brother to hand the gun in to the police that morning. The trial judge ruled that the defence of duress was not available and D was convicted. He appealed to the Court of Appeal who quashed the conviction and sent the case for retrial.

Key Law

The defence of duress of circumstances is available to the same range of offences as the defence of duress by threats.

8.2   *Dudley and Stephens* (1884) 14 QBD 273   CCR

Key Facts

Ds were shipwrecked with another man and V, a 17-year-old cabin boy, in a small boat about 1,600 miles from land. After drifting for 20 days, Ds killed and ate the cabin boy. Four days later, they were picked up by a passing ship and on their return to England were convicted of murder. Their claim of necessity to save themselves from dying was rejected.

Key Law

Necessity did not justify the killing of an innocent victim.

8.2   *Re A (Conjoined Twins)* [2000] 4 All ER 961, [2001] Crim LR 400   CA

Key Facts

Conjoined twins were born with one of them having no proper heart or lungs. She was being kept alive by the other twin, whose heart circulated blood for both of them. Their parents refused to consent to an operation to separate them. Doctors applied for a declaration that it was lawful to operate to separate the twins, even though the weaker twin would certainly die. The Court of Appeal gave the declaration. In the judgment, one of the points considered was the doctrine of necessity.

Key Law

Necessity can be distinguished from duress as the actor's mind is not 'irresistibly overborne by external pressures'.

Mistake

DPP v Morgan (1975)
A mistaken belief must be genuinely held, but the mistake need not be reasonable

Williams (Gladstone) (1987)
D must be judged on the facts as he genuinely believed them to be

B v DPP (2000)
Affirmed that D must be judged on the facts as he genuinely believed them to be

O'Grady (1987)
D is not entitled to rely on a mistake of fact which has been induced by voluntary intoxication

Self-Defence

Palmer v R (1971)
D may use what force is reasonably necessary in self-defence. The force must not be wholly out of proportion to the threat

Clegg (1995)
The defence is not available if excessive force is used

A-G's Ref (No 2 of 1983) (1984)
Where self-defence is necessary then acts preparatory to it are also lawful

Mistake, Consent, Self-Defence

Consent

Tabassum (2000)
There must be true consent to the nature and the quality of the act for D to establish a defence of consent

Dica (2004)
Where V is ignorant of D's infection, V is not consenting to the risk of infection

Donovan (1934)
Consent is not available as a defence where actual bodily harm is intended or likely to be caused

A-G's Ref (No 6 of 1980) (1981)
Consent is NOT available as a defence in private fights, but it is available as a defence in properly conducted games and sports

Brown (1993)
Consent is not available as a defence to charges of assault where injury was caused

Jones and others (1986)
It is a defence where D genuinely believes that V has consented to 'rough and undisciplined horseplay'

Necessity is choosing the lesser of two evils to avoid greater harm.

The requirements set out by Stephens in his Digest were held to be still the law. These state:

a) the act is needed to avoid inevitable and irreparable evil;

b) no more should be done than is reasonably necessary for the purpose to be achieved; and

c) the evil inflicted must not be disproportionate to the evil avoided.

8.4

DPP v Morgan [1975] 2 All ER 347, (1975) 61 Cr App R 136

HL

Key Facts

D invited friends to have sex with his wife, telling them that she was willing but might simulate reluctance for her own pleasure. In fact, the wife did not consent and struggled and shouted. The men were convicted of rape and D of incitement to rape. The trial judge directed the jury that the men would be guilty of rape if their belief in her consent was not based on reasonable grounds. They appealed.

Key Law

A mistaken belief must be genuinely held, but the mistake need not be reasonable.

Key Judgment: Lord Hailsham

'Since honest belief clearly negatives intent, the reasonableness or otherwise of that belief can only be evidence for or against the view that the belief and, therefore, the intent was actually held.'

8.4

Williams (Gladstone) [1987] 3 All ER 411, (1987) 78 Cr App R 276

CA

Key Facts

D saw V dragging a youth along the street and hitting him. The youth was calling for help. D punched V, believing that V was assaulting the youth. In fact, V was a police officer who had arrested the youth for mugging an old lady. The jury were directed that a mistake would only be relevant if it were a reasonable mistake. D's appeal was upheld and his conviction quashed.

Key Law

D must be judged on the facts as he genuinely believed them to be. The belief does not have to be reasonable.

Key Judgment: Lord Lane

'The reasonableness or unreasonableness of D's belief is material to the question of whether the belief was held by D at all. If the belief was in fact held, its unreasonableness, so far as guilt or innocence is concerned, is neither here nor there.'

Key Link

Beckford v R [1987] 3 All ER 425 Privy Council.

8.4   ***B v DPP* [2000] 1 All ER 823, [2000] 2 Cr App R 65**   (HL)

Key Facts

D, a boy of 15, sat next to a 13-year-old girl on a bus and repeatedly asked her to perform oral sex. He believed that the girl was 14 or over. D was charged with inciting a child under 14 to commit an act of gross indecency, under s 1(1) Indecency with Children Act 1960. The magistrates ruled that the offence was one of strict liability. D's conviction was quashed on appeal.

Key Law

The House of Lords affirmed the decision in *Williams (Gladstone)* (see above). D is to be judged on the facts as he genuinely believed them to be.

8.4.1

O'Grady [1987] 3 All ER 420, (1987) 85 Cr App R 315

CA

Key Facts

D and V drank a large amount of alcohol and then fell asleep at V's home. D woke up to find V attacking him. D hit back and then went to sleep again. In the morning he discovered that V was dead. He was convicted of manslaughter.

Key Law

Where D relies on the defence of self-defence, he is not entitled to rely on a mistake of fact which has been induced by voluntary intoxication.

8.5

Palmer v R [1971] 1 All ER 1077, (1971) 55 Cr App R 223

PC

Key Facts

D had gone with other men to buy drugs. A dispute arose and D and the others left without paying. They were chased and D shot and killed one of the chasers. He claimed that he was acting in self-defence, but he was convicted of murder.

Key Law

D may use what force is reasonably necessary in self-defence. The force must not be wholly out of proportion to the threat.

Key Judgment: Lord Morris

'It is both good law and good sense that a man who is attacked may defend himself, but [he] may only do what is reasonably necessary. But everything will depend on the particular facts and the circumstances . . . If there has been an attack so that defence is reasonably necessary, it will be recognised that a person defending himself cannot weigh to a nicety the exact measure of his necessary defensive action. If a jury thought that in a moment of unexpected anguish a person attacked had only done what he honestly and instinctively thought was

necessary, that would be most potent evidence that only reasonable defensive action had been taken.'

8.5   *Clegg* [1995] 1 All ER 334

Key Facts

D was a soldier on duty at a checkpoint in Northern Ireland. A car failed to stop at the checkpoint and D shouted at the driver to stop. D fired four shots at the car. One of the shots killed a passenger in the car. The evidence was that the car was some 50 yards past the checkpoint by the time the fatal shot was fired. D was convicted of murder.

Key Law

Where excessive force is used, then the defence of self-defence is not available.

Key Comment

The Criminal Justice and Immigration Act 2008 has now enacted that the question of whether the degree of force used by D was reasonable in the circumstances is to be decided by reference to the circumstances as D believed them to be. However, the degree of force is not to be regarded as reasonable in the circumstances as D believed them to be, if it was disproportionate in those circumstances.

8.6.2   *Tabassum* [2000] Crim LR 686, [2000] 2 Cr App R 328

Key Facts

Three women allowed D to touch their breasts for the purpose of preparing a database in relation to breast cancer. They thought D was medically qualified or trained and, because of this, they consented to the touching. D was not medically trained. He was convicted of indecent assault.

Key Law

There must be true consent to the nature and the quality of the act for D to establish a defence of consent.

8.6.3

Donovan [1934] All ER 207, (1934) 25 Cr App R 1

 CCA

Key Facts

D caned a 17-year-old girl for sexual gratification. This caused bruising and he was convicted of indecent assault and a common assault. D appealed on the basis that V had consented to the act. His conviction was quashed.

Key Law

In general, consent is not available as a defence where actual bodily harm is intended or likely to be caused. There are public policy exceptions which include 'mutual manly contests' and 'rough and undisciplined sport or play where there is no anger and no intention to cause bodily harm'.

8.6.3

Attorney-General's Reference (No 6 of 1980) [1981] 2 All ER 1057, (1981) 73 Cr App R 63

 CA

Key Facts

Two men who had quarrelled agreed to settle their differences by a fight in the street. One of them suffered a bloody nose and bruises.

Key Law

Consent is not available as a defence in private fights. Consent is available as a defence to properly conducted games and sports.

Key Judgment: Lord Lane CJ

'It is not in the public interest that people should try to cause, or should cause, each other bodily harm for no good reason. Minor struggles are another matter. So ... it is immaterial whether the act occurs in private or public: it is an assault if actual bodily harm is intended and/or caused. This means that most fights will be unlawful regardless of consent. Nothing which we have said is intended to cast doubt upon the accepted legality of properly conducted games and sports ... reasonable surgical interference, dangerous exhibitions, etc.'

8.6.3

Brown [1993] 2 All ER 75, (1993) 97 Cr App R 44

(HL)

Key Facts

Five men in a group of consenting adult sado-masochists were convicted of offences of assault causing actual bodily harm (s 47 Offences Against the Person Act 1861) and malicious wounding (s 20 Offences Against the Person Act 1861). They had carried out acts which included applying stinging nettles to the genital area and inserting map pins or fish hooks into the penises of each other. All the victims had consented and none had needed medical attention.

Key Law

Consent was not available as a defence to charges of assault where injury was caused, even though the acts were between adults in private and did not result in serious bodily injury.

8.6.3

Wilson [1996] 3 WLR 125, [1996] 2 Cr App R 241

(CA)

Key Facts

A husband used a heated butter knife to brand his initials on his wife's buttocks, at her request. The wife's burns became infected and she needed medical treatment. He was convicted of assault causing actual bodily harm (s 47 Offences Against the Person Act 1861) but the Court of Appeal quashed the conviction on appeal.

Key Law

Consensual activity between husband and wife should not normally be criminalised.

Dica [2004] EWCA Crim 1103

Key Facts

D, who knew he was HIV positive, had relationships with two women. They had unprotected sex with him and both became infected. They claimed that they did not know he was HIV positive and that if they had they would not have agreed to unprotected sex. The judge did not allow the issue of consent to go to the jury, so the Court of Appeal quashed the conviction but ordered a retrial.

Key Law

The consent must be informed and willing to provide a defence.

Key Link

Konzani [2005] 2 Cr App Rep 14.

 8.6.4

Jones and others (1986) 83 Cr App R 375   CA

Key Facts

The victims, two boys aged 14 and 15, were tossed in the air by the defendants who were older boys. One V suffered a broken arm and the other a ruptured spleen. Ds' convictions were quashed as the judge did not allow the issue of mistaken belief (that Vs had consented to the tossing) to go to the jury.

Key Law

There is no assault where D genuinely believes that V has consented to 'rough and undisciplined horseplay'. It is irrelevant whether that belief is reasonable or not.

9 Mental capacity defences

Some defences are a complete defence to all crimes. This is because the defence negates either the *mens rea* or the *actus reus* required for the offence. Other defences, which are based on excusing conduct in certain circumstances, are only a defence to crimes of specific intent or may not be available for certain crimes.

Availability of different defences		
Available for all offences	Only available for some offences	
		Limitation
Automatism	Intoxication	Not available for crimes of basic intent
Mistake	Duress	Not available for murder, attempted murder or, possibly, treason
Self-defence	Necessity	Very rarely successful as a defence
	Consent	Not available for murder or some assaults
	Insanity	Not available for strict liability offences

▶ 9.1 Insanity

1   The rules on insanity are based on the *M'Naghten* Rules 1843.

2   M'Naghten had been found not guilty of murder when he tried to kill Sir Robert Peel and actually killed his secretary. The judges in the House of Lords were asked a series of questions as to what the law was in respect of insanity.

3   The first rule is that 'in all cases every man is presumed to be sane and to possess a sufficient degree of reason to be responsible for his crimes'.

4   To establish the defence of insanity the defendant must prove that at the time of committing the act, 'he was labouring under such a defect of

reason, from disease of the mind, as not to know the nature and quality of the act he was doing, or if he did know it, that he did not know he was doing what was wrong'.

5   This defence has to be established on the balance of probabilities.

6   Where a defendant is found to be insane the verdict is 'Not guilty by reason of insanity'.

7   Insanity is a defence to all crimes, except for crimes of strict liability where no mental element is required (*DPP v H* (1997)).

9.1.1 Defect of reason

1   The defect of reason must be more than absent-mindedness or confusion (*Clarke* (1972)).

2   It must be due to a disease which affects the mind.

9.1.2 Disease of the mind

1   Disease of the mind is a legal term not a medical one. The disease can be a mental disease or a physical disease which affects the mind (*Sullivan* (1984)).

2   Any mental illness which has manifested itself in violence and is prone to recur is a disease of the mind (*Bratty v AG for Northern Ireland* (1963), *Burgess* (1991)).

3   The disease can be of any part of the body if it has an effect on the mind; for example, arteriosclerosis affecting the flow of blood to the brain (*Kemp* (1957)); or high blood sugar levels because of diabetes (*Hennessy* (1989)).

4   The disease can be one which causes a transient or intermittent impairment of reason, memory or understanding. The condition need not be permanent (*Sullivan* (1984)).

5   Where the cause is external and not a disease, then this is not insanity; for example, the effect of a drug (*Quick* (1973)).

9.1.3 Not knowing the nature and quality of the act or not knowing that it is wrong

1   Nature and quality refers to the physical character of the act (*Codere* (1916)).

2 a) The defendant may not know the nature and quality of the act because he is in a state of unconsciousness or impaired consciousness; or

   b) The defendant may be conscious but not know the nature and quality of the act as due to his mental condition he does not understand or know what he is doing.

3 Where the defendant knows the nature and quality of the act he can still use the defence of insanity if he does not know that he is doing wrong. Wrong in this sense means legally wrong, not morally wrong (*Windle* (1952)).

4 Where the defendant knows the nature and quality of the act and that it is legally wrong, he cannot use the defence of insanity. This is so even where the defendant is suffering from a mental illness (*Windle* (1952)).

5 In *Johnson* (2007), the Court of Appeal confirmed that *Windle* was still law and they were obliged to follow the decision, even though they were critical of it.

9.1.4 Reform of the law

1 Critics point out that the original statements by the judges in M'Naghten were made in 1843 when there was a very limited understanding of mental illness. The rules should be updated to reflect modern understanding.

2 Physical illnesses should not be covered by the label of 'insanity'.

3 The Butler Committee 1975 suggested that the verdict of not guilty by reason of insanity should be replaced by a verdict of not guilty on evidence of mental disorder.

4 The Draft Criminal Code suggests that a defendant should be not guilty on evidence of severe mental disorder or severe mental handicap.

▶ 9.2 Automatism

1 In *Bratty* (1963) automatism was defined as 'an act done by the muscles without any control by the mind, such as a spasm, a reflex action or a convulsion; or an act done by a person who is not conscious of what he is doing, such as an act done whilst suffering from concussion or whilst sleep-walking'.

2   This covers two types of automatism:

   a) insane automatism, where the cause of the automatism is a disease of the mind within the M'Naghten Rules. In such a case the defence is insanity and the verdict is not guilty by reason of insanity; and

   b) non-insane automatism, where the cause is an external one. Where such a defence succeeds, it is a complete defence and the defendant is not guilty.

9.2.1 Non-insane automatism

1   This is a defence because the *actus reus* done by the defendant is not voluntary.

2   The cause of the automatism must be external, such as a blow from a stone or an attack by a swarm of bees (*Hill v Baxter* (1958)) or sneezing (*Whoolley* (1997)).

3   Automatism caused by external pressures such as stress does not constitute non-insane automatism, but may be insane automatism (*Burgess* (1991)).

4   However, automatism caused by an exceptional event can constitute non-insane automatism as in *R v T* (1990) where the defendant suffered post-traumatic stress disorder after being raped.

5   Reduced or partial control of one's actions is not sufficient to constitute non-insane automatism. There must be 'total destruction of voluntary control' (*A-G's Reference (No 2 of 1992)* (1993)).

9.2.2 Self-induced automatism

1   This is where the defendant knows that his conduct is likely to bring on an automatic state, for example, a diabetic failing to eat after taking insulin.

2   If the offence charged is one of specific intent, then self-induced automatism can be a defence. This is because the defendant lacks the required *mens rea* (*Bailey* (1983)).

3   If the offence charged is one of basic intent then:

   a) If the defendant has been reckless in getting into a state of automatism, self-induced automatism cannot be a defence. Subjective recklessness is sufficient for the *mens rea* of crimes of basic intent (*Bailey* (1983)).

b) Similarly, where the self-induced automatic state is caused through drink or illegal drugs or other intoxicating substances, the defendant cannot use the defence of automatism. Becoming voluntarily intoxicated is a reckless course of conduct (*Majewski* (1977)).

c) Where the defendant does not know that his actions are likely to lead to a self-induced automatic state in which he may commit an offence, he has not been reckless and can use the defence of automatism (*Hardie* (1984)). If he knows he has been reckless and automation is not a defence (*Clarke* (2009)).

▶ 9.3 Intoxication

1   This covers intoxication by alcohol, drugs or other substances, such as glue-sniffing.

2   Intoxication does not provide a defence as such, but is relevant to whether or not the defendant has the required *mens rea* for the offence. If he does not have the required *mens rea* because of his intoxicated state he may be not guilty.

3   Whether the defendant is guilty or not depends on whether the offence charged is one of specific or basic intent and whether the intoxication was voluntary or involuntary.

9.3.1 Voluntary intoxication

1   Voluntary intoxication can negate the *mens rea* for a specific intent offence (*Beard* (1920), *Sheehan and Moore* (1975)).

2   However, if the defendant, despite his intoxicated state, still has the necessary *mens rea*, then he is guilty of the offence. The intoxication does not provide a defence (*A-G for Northern Ireland v Gallagher* (1963)).

3   Where the offence charged is one of basic intent, intoxication is not a defence. 'It is a reckless course of conduct and recklessness is enough to constitute the necessary *mens rea*' (*Majewski* (1977), *Metropolitan Police Comr v Caldwell* (1982)).

4   However, the prosecution must prove that the defendant would have foreseen the risk had he not been intoxicated (*Richardson and Irwin* (1999)).

5   *Heard* (2007) decided that voluntary intoxication was not a defence to s 3 Sexual Offences Act 2003 (sexual assault by touching) if the touching was deliberate. Section 3 was a basic intent offence.

9.3.2 Involuntary intoxication

1   This covers situations where the defendant did not know he was taking an intoxicating substance; for example, where a soft drink has been 'laced' with alcohol or the unexpected effect of prescribed drugs.

2   The test is: Did the defendant have the necessary *mens rea* when he committed the offence? If so, he will be guilty. The involuntary intoxication will not provide a defence (*Kingston* (1994)).

3   Even though the defendant would not have formed the *mens rea* if sober, he cannot use involuntary intoxication as a defence (*Davies* (1983)).

4   Where, however, the defendant did not have the necessary intent he will be not guilty, even if the crime is one of basic intent. This is so because in such circumstances the defendant has not been reckless (*Hardie* (1985)).

See also **8.4.1** for the effect of a drunken mistake.

9.3.3 Proposals for reform

1   In their report, *Intoxication and Criminal Liability*, the Law Commission recommended that the rule in *Majewski* (1977) should be enacted in statutory form.

2   They proposed a general rule that where:

- D was voluntarily intoxicated; and

- the fault element of the offence charged was not an integral fault, e.g. because it merely requires recklessness, then

- D should be treated as having been aware at the material time of anything which D would then have been aware of, but for the intoxication.

3   The following subjective fault elements should be excluded from the application of the general rule and should, therefore, always be proved:

- intention as to a consequence;

- knowledge as to something;

- belief as to something (where the belief is equivalent to knowledge as to something);

- fraud; and

- dishonesty.

4   D should not be able to rely on a mistake of fact arising from self-induced intoxication in support of a defence to which D's state of mind is relevant, regardless of the nature of the fault alleged. D's mistaken belief should be taken into account only if D would have held the same belief if D had not been intoxicated.

5   D's state of involuntary intoxication should be taken into consideration:

- in determining whether D acted with the subjective fault required for liability, regardless of the nature of the fault element; and

- in any case where D relies on a mistake of fact in support of a defence to which his or her state of mind is relevant.

	Specific intent crimes	**Basic intent crimes**
Voluntary intoxication	If defendant has *mens rea* he is guilty (*Gallagher*) If defendant has no *mens rea* he is not guilty	Becoming intoxicated is a reckless course of conduct. The defendant is guilty of the offence (*Majewski*)
Involuntary intoxication	If defendant has *mens rea* he is guilty (*Kingston*) If defendant has no *mens rea* he is not guilty (*Hardie*)	The defendant has not been reckless in becoming intoxicated, so not guilty (*Hardie*)
Drunken mistake	If the mistake negates *mens rea* the defendant is not guilty If the mistake is about the need to defend oneself it is not a defence. The defendant will be guilty.	This is a reckless course of conduct, so the defendant is guilty Exception: S 5 Criminal Damage Act 1971 (*Jaggard v Dickinson*)

Key Cases Checklist

Insanity

M'Naghten's case (1843)
Presumed sane until the contrary is proved. Must have a defect of reason caused by disease of the mind so as not to know the nature and quality of act or that what he was doing was wrong

Sullivan (1984)
Impairment can be organic or functional and need not be permanent

Burgess (1991)
A mental disorder which manifests itself in violence and is prone to recur is a disease of the mind

Hennessy (1989)
An internal cause is a disease of the mind, even where the disease is a physical one such as diabetes

Windle (1952)/Johnson (2007)
If D knows he is doing wrong, the defence of insanity is not available to him

Insanity, Automatism, Intoxication

Automatism

Bratty v A-G for NI (1961)
Automatism is an act done by the muscles without any control by the mind

Hill v Baxter (1958)
For the defence of automatism the cause must be an external one

A-G's Ref (No 2 of 1992) (1993)
Reduced or partial awareness is insuffcient for the defence

Bailey (1983)
(1) Self-induced automatism is a defence to a specifc intent offence
(2) Reckless self-induced automatism is NOT a defence to a basic intent offence

Hardie (1984)
If D is not reckless in getting into an automatic state then automatism is a defence to a basic intent offence

Clarke (2009)
If D knows that he may get into an automatic state automatism is not a defence

Intoxication

A-G for NI v Gallagher (1963)
A drunken intent is sufficient for *mens rea*

DPP v Majewski (1976)
Voluntary intoxication is not available as a defence for a basic intent offence

Kingston (1994)
The defence of involuntary intoxication is not available if D has the *mens rea* for the offence

| 9.1 | *M'Naghten's Case* (1843) 10 Cl & F 200 | HL |

Key Facts

D was charged with the murder of the Prime Minister's secretary. He was found not guilty by reason of insanity. Following this case, the issue of insanity was debated in the House of Lords and the judges were asked to explain the law.

Key Law

1) Every man is presumed to be sane and to possess a sufficient degree of reason to be responsible for his crimes.

2) To prove the defence of insanity, a defendant must show that he was labouring under such a defect of reason, from disease of the mind, as not to know the nature and quality of the act he was doing, or if he did know it, that he did not know he was doing what was wrong.

| 9.1.2 | *Sullivan* [1984] AC 156, (1983) 77 Cr App R 176 | HL |

Key Facts

While D was at the home of a friend, he had an epileptic fit. In the course of that fit he attacked and injured the friend. D argued that he should be allowed the defence of automatism. The trial judge ruled that his defence was insanity.

Key Law

Where D is suffering from a disease of the mind, then this can be within the definition of insanity.

The disease can be one which causes a transient or intermittent impairment of reason, memory or understanding. The condition need not be permanent.

9.1.2

Bratty v Attorney-General for Northern Ireland [1961] 3 All ER 523, (1961) 46 Cr App R 1   HL

Key Facts

D strangled a girl. He gave evidence that 'a blackness' came over him and he did not realise what he had done. There was evidence that he might have been suffering from epilepsy. His defence of insanity was rejected and he was convicted of murder.

Key Law

If an involuntary act was due to a disease of the mind then the defence is insanity. If the involuntariness of the act was caused by an external factor, then, provided there is evidence to raise the issue, the jury must consider the defence of automatism.

Key Judgment: Lord Denning

'Automatism is an act done by the muscles without any control by the mind, such as a spasm, a reflex action or a convulsion; or an act done by a person who is not conscious of what he is doing such as an act done whilst suffering from concussion or whilst sleep-walking.'

9.1.2

Burgess [1991] 2 All ER 769, (1991) 93 Cr App R 41   CA

Key Facts

D attacked a girl, with whom he had been watching a video, with a bottle and the video recorder and then put his hands round her neck. He claimed he was sleepwalking and that this should give him the defence of automatism. It was ruled that the evidence was of an internal cause and so the correct defence was insanity.

Key Law

Any mental disorder which has manifested itself in violence and which is prone to recur is a disease of the mind. Thus the correct defence is insanity.

9.1.2

Hennessy [1989] 2 All ER 9, (1989) 89 Cr App R 10

Key Facts

D was a diabetic who needed insulin to control the condition. He was charged with taking a car and driving whilst disqualified. His defence was that because he had failed to take his insulin, this had caused him to suffer hyperglycaemia. The trial judge ruled that this was an internal factor and therefore the defence of insanity.

Key Law

Where the cause of the involuntary behaviour is an internal cause, then it is a disease of the mind and the correct defence is insanity.

Key Problem

The decisions in this case and *Burgess* (1991) (above) have extended the meaning of insanity in the criminal law far beyond any medical definition. It is invidious that those with a physical disease such as diabetes should come within the definition of insanity.

Key Link

Kemp [1956] 3 All ER 249, (1956) 40 Cr App R 121.

9.1.2

Quick [1973] 3 All ER 347, (1973) 57 Cr App R 722

Key Facts

D, a nurse, was convicted of causing actual bodily harm to a patient. He said he had failed to eat after taking insulin for his diabetes. This had caused hypoglycaemia. The trial judge ruled this was the defence of insanity. The conviction was quashed because it was an external cause (the drug insulin) which had led to the involuntary act.

Key Law

Where there is an external cause, then it is not a disease of the mind and the correct defence is automatism.

The decisions in *Hennessy* and *Quick* have created an anomaly. If the cause is the failure to take insulin, this is an internal factor and considered a disease of the mind within the rules of insanity. However, if the cause is the taking of insulin, then this is an external cause and not within the rules of insanity.

9.1.3   *Windle* [1952] 2 QB 826, (1952) 36 Cr App R 85   `CCA`

Key Facts

D killed his wife by giving her about 100 tablets of aspirin. There was evidence that he was suffering from a mental illness. However, because he told the police 'I suppose they will hang me for this,' he was aware that what he had done was wrong.

Key Law

Where D knows that what he is doing is wrong, he cannot bring himself within the *M'Naghten* Rules. The defence of insanity is not available to him.

Key Comment

This case emphasises that those with mental illness may be denied the defence of insanity, even though they are not fully responsible for their actions. To meet this criticism, the defence of diminished responsibility was created in 1957 to provide a partial defence to murder.

9.1.3   *Johnson* [2007] EWCA Crim 1978   `CA`

Key Facts

D was convicted of wounding with intent to cause grievous bodily harm after he forced his way into a neighbour's flat and stabbed him. Evidence from two psychiatrists was that D was suffering from paranoid schizophrenia and had hallucinations. Despite this, the psychiatrists were of the view that D knew the nature and quality of his acts and knew that they were legally wrong. One psychiatrist thought D did not consider what he had done was morally wrong.

Key Law

The Court of Appeal upheld the judge's ruling that insanity was not available as D knew the nature and quality of his acts and that they were legally wrong. They followed the decision in *Windle*.

Key Comment

An Australian case, *R v Stapleton* (1952) 86 CLR 358, decided that if D believed his act to be right according to the ordinary standard of reasonable men, then he was entitled to be acquitted even if he knew that it was legally wrong. In *Johnson* the Court of Appeal thought that the reasoning in *Stapleton* was 'highly persuasive' but that they were bound by *Windle*.

9.2.1   *Hill v Baxter* [1958] 1 All ER 193, (1958) 42 Cr App R 51   DC

Key Facts

D was acquitted of dangerous driving by magistrates who accepted that he remembered nothing for some distance before going through a halt sign. The Divisional Court allowed the prosecution's appeal and remitted the case back to the magistrates with a direction to convict as there was no evidence to support a defence of automatism.

Key Law

Where an external cause makes D's actions involuntary, the defence of automatism is available.

Key Judgment

The court approved the judgment of Humphrey J in *Kay v Butterworth* (where he said):

'*A person should not be made liable at the criminal law who, through no fault of his own, becomes unconscious when driving, as, for example, a person who has been struck by a stone or overcome by a sudden illness, or when the car has been put temporarily out of his control owing to his being attacked by a swarm of bees.'*

9.2.1

T [1990] Crim LR 256

Key Facts

D was raped. Three days later she took part in a robbery and an assault. She claimed that at the time she was suffering from post-traumatic stress disorder as a result of the rape and that she had acted in a dream-like state. The trial judge allowed the defence of automatism to go to the jury, but D was convicted.

Key Law

An external cause of an automatic state is the defence of non-insane automatism rather than insanity.

Key Comment

This decision is only at Crown Court level. The recent trend of the appeal courts has been to regard behaviour that occurs after an external shock as having its source in the internal psychological or emotional state of D so that it provides a defence of insanity rather than non-insane automatism.

Key Link

Rabey (1980) SCR 513 Canada.

9.2.1

Attorney-General's Reference (No 2 of 1992) [1993] 4 All ER 683, (1993) 99 Cr App R 429

Key Facts

D was a lorry driver who, after driving for several hours, drove along the hard shoulder of a motorway for about half a mile and hit a broken-down car.

Key Law

Reduced or partial awareness is not enough to found a defence of automatism.

Bailey [1983] 2 All ER 503, (1983) 77 Cr App R 76   CA

Key Facts

D was a diabetic who failed to eat properly after taking insulin. This caused a hypoglycaemic state during which he hit V on the head with an iron bar. The trial judge ruled that the defence of automatism was not available. It was held that this ruling was wrong although D's conviction stood as there was insufficient evidence to raise the defence of automatism.

Key Law

1) Automatism, even if self-induced, is a defence to an offence which requires the prosecution to prove specific intent.

2) Self-induced automatism is also a defence to a basic intent offence if D was not reckless in getting into that state.

3) Where D is reckless in getting into a self-induced state of automatism, then he cannot rely on the defence for a basic intent offence.

Hardie [1984] 3 All ER 848, (1984) 80 Cr App R 157   CA

Key Facts

D, who was upset by the breakdown of a relationship, took some Valium belonging to his ex-girlfriend. She encouraged him to do this, stating that it would calm him down. He later started a fire in the bedroom of their flat. He was charged under s 1(2) Criminal Damage Act 1971. D argued that the effect of the drug prevented him having the *mens rea* for the offence. The trial judge ruled against this. The Court of Appeal quashed the conviction.

Key Law

To be guilty of a basic intent offence, D must have acted recklessly in taking the drug that caused the automatic state. Where the intoxicating effect of a drug is not generally known, then the prosecution need to prove that D knew there was a risk that it could make him intoxicated.

9.2.2

Clarke [2009] EWCA Crim 921

Key Facts

D was a diabetic who suffered a hypoglycaemic episode while driving. He lost control of his car and hit and killed a pedestrian. He was convicted of causing death by dangerous driving. The conviction was upheld.

Key Judgment: Moses LJ

'Automatism due to a hypoglycaemic attack will not be a defence if the attack might reasonably have been avoided. If the driver ought to have tested his blood glucose level before embarking on his journey, or appreciated the onset of symptoms during the journey, then the fact that he did suffer a hypoglycaemic attack . . . would be no defence.'

9.3.1

Attorney-General for Northern Ireland v Gallagher [1963] AC 349, (1961) 45 Cr App Rep 316

Key Facts

D decided to kill his wife. He then bought a knife and a bottle of whisky. After drinking a large amount of the whisky he killed his wife. He claimed that at the time of the killing he was drunk. He was convicted of murder but the conviction was quashed by the Court of Appeal. The House of Lords restored his conviction.

Key Law

Where D forms the required *mens rea* for an offence then drunkenness is not a defence. This is the law both for specific intent offences and basic intent offences.

Key Judgment: Lord Denning

'If a man, whilst sane and sober, forms an intention to kill and makes preparation for it, knowing it is a wrong thing to do, and then gets himself drunk so as to give himself Dutch courage to do the killing, and while drunk carries out his intention, he cannot rely on this self-induced drunkenness as a defence to a charge of murder.'

9.3.1

DPP v Majewski [1976] 2 All ER 142, (1976) 62 Cr App R 262

Key Facts

As a result of taking drugs and alcohol, D became aggressive and assaulted a barman and police officers who were called to the scene. He claimed he had 'completely blanked out' and did not know what he was doing. He was convicted of offences of assault occasioning actual bodily harm and of assaulting a police officer in the execution of his duty.

Key Law

Where an offence is one of basic intent then voluntary intoxication is not available as a defence.

Key Judgment: Lord Elwyn-Jones LC

'If a man, of his own volition, takes a substance which causes him to cast off the restraints of reason and conscience, no wrong is done to him by holding him answerable criminally for any injury he may do while in that condition. His course of conduct in reducing himself by drugs and drink to that condition, in my view, supplies the evidence of mens rea, of guilty mind certainly sufficient for crimes of basic intent.'

Key Problem

In such situations the recklessness is at the point when D consumes enough alcohol to make him drunk. The *actus reus* may be several hours later when D actually commits an assault. Is there coincidence of *mens rea* and *actus reus* in such situations? The courts appear to disregard this point in order to justify what may be seen as a public policy decision.

9.3.2

Kingston [1994] 3 All ER 353, [1994] Crim LR 846

HL

Key Facts

D claimed his coffee had been spiked by someone who knew that D had paedophilic tendencies and wished to put

D into a compromising position for the purposes of black-mail. D was then shown a 15-year-old boy who had been drugged. D indecently assaulted the boy.

Key Law

1) Where D has the required *mens rea* for an offence then he cannot use the defence of involuntary intoxication even though the involuntary intoxication caused him to lose control or become less inhibited.

2) Where involuntary intoxication causes lack of *mens rea* then it is a defence.

Key Link

See *O'Grady* [1987] 3 All ER 420 on intoxication and mistake at **8.4.1**.

Key Link

Richardson and Irwin [1999] Crim LR 494.

10 Homicide

Homicide is the unlawful killing of a human being. There are different offences depending on the *mens rea* of the defendant and whether there is a special defence available to the defendant.

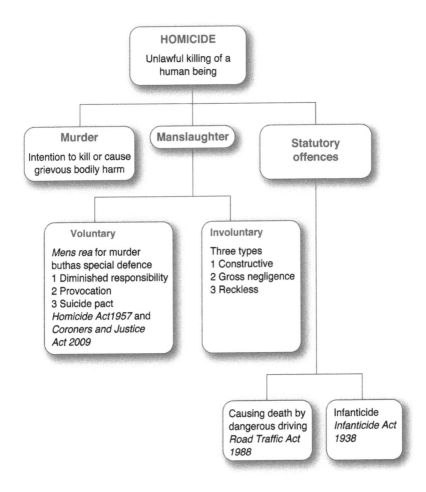

▶ 10.1 *Actus reus* of homicide

1   This is the killing of a human being (reasonable creature in being).

• A homicide offence cannot be charged in respect of the killing of a foetus. However, if the foetus is injured and the child is born alive but dies afterwards as a result of the injuries this can be the *actus reus* for murder or manslaughter (*Attorney-General's Reference (No 3 of 1994) (1997)*).

• A person who is 'brain dead' is not considered a 'reasonable creature in being'. This is important as it allows doctors to switch off life-support machines without being liable for homicide (*Malcherek and Steel (1981)*).

• In *Airedale NHS Trust v Bland* (1993) there were *obiter dicta* statements that brain-stem death was the test. Doctors were allowed to withdraw all artificial means (including feeding by tubes) of keeping the victim alive.

2   The death must be caused by the defendant's act or omission (see 2.4 for the rules on causation).

3   There used to be a rule that death must have occurred within a year and a day, but this was abolished by the Law Reform (Year and a Day Rule) Act 1996.

4   There is now no time limit on when the death may occur after the unlawful act, but, where it is more than three years later, the consent of the Attorney-General is needed for the prosecution.

▶ 10.2 Murder

1   There is no statutory definition of murder.

2   The accepted definition is based on that in Lord Coke's Institutes. This is that murder is 'unlawfully killing a reasonable person who is in being and under the King's Peace with malice aforethought, express or implied'.

3   Jurisdiction over murder extends to any murder in any country by a British citizen. This means that even though the alleged offence was committed in another country, the defendant may be tried for murder in an English court.

10.2.1 The *actus reus* of murder

1   See 10.1 for general rules.

2   In addition, the death can be caused by an act or by an omission (*Gibbins and Proctor* (1918)).

3   Under the King's (or Queen's) Peace means that the killing of an enemy in the course of war is not murder. However, the killing of a prisoner of war would be sufficient for the *actus reus* of murder.

10.2.2 The *mens rea* of murder

1   This is malice aforethought, express or implied. Express malice aforethought is the intention to kill. Implied malice aforethought is the intention to cause grievous bodily harm.

2   Either of these two intentions will suffice. This means that a person can be guilty of murder even though they did not intend to kill (*Vickers* (1957), *Cunningham* (1982)).

3   However, in *Attorney-General's Reference (No 3 of 1994)* (1997) the House of Lords described implied malice as a 'conspicuous anomaly'.

4   Grievous bodily harm has the natural meaning of 'really serious harm' (*DPP v Smith* (1961)). However, a direction to the jury which left out the word 'really' was not considered a misdirection (*Saunders* (1985)).

5   Intention has been described as 'a decision to bring about, in so far as it lies within the accused's power, (the prohibited consequence), no matter whether the accused desired that consequence of his act or not' (*Mohan* (1976)) (see 3.2 for fuller discussion).

6   Foresight of consequences is evidence from which intention may be inferred (*Moloney* (1985)).

7   In *Woollin* (1998) it was said that the jury should be directed that they are not entitled to find the necessary intention unless they feel sure that (the consequence) was a virtual certainty as a result of the defendant's actions and that the defendant appreciated that such was the case.

10.2.3 Proposals for reform

1   At the end of 2006, the Law Commission published a Report (Law Com 304) on the law of murder.

2   The key proposal is that murder should be split into two degrees.

3   First-degree murder would apply only where the defendant had an intention to kill or intended to do serious injury and was aware that there was a serious risk of causing death.

4   Second-degree murder would include a variety of situations where D has killed V and it is more serious than involuntary manslaughter.

These situations are:

- where D had intended to do serious harm;
- where D intended to cause some injury or fear or risk of injury and was aware of a serious risk of causing death; and
- where D had a partial defence through diminished responsibility, provocation or duress to what would otherwise be first-degree murder.

▶ 10.3 Voluntary manslaughter

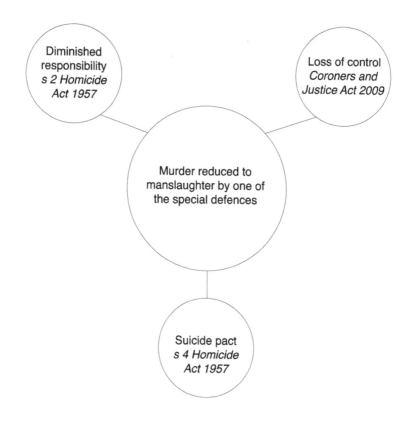

10.3.1 Diminished responsibility

1   Section 2(1) Homicide Act 1957 as amended by s 52 Coroners and Justice Act 2009 now defines diminished responsibility as follows:

> A person (D) who kills or is a party to the killing of another is not to be convicted of murder if D was suffering from an abnormality of mental functioning which:
>
> ● arose from a recognised medical condition
>
> ● substantially impaired D's ability to do one or more of the things mentioned in ss 2(1A)
>
> ● provides an explanation for D's acts and omissions in doing or being a party to the killing.'

2   The things listed in ss 2(1A) are:

● to understand the nature of his conduct;

● to form a rational judgment; and

● to exercise self-control.

This list in ss 2(1A) is similar to that under the old law in the case of *Byrne* (1960).

3   The abnormality of mental functioning must arise from a recognised medical condition.

4   The abnormality of mental functioning must substantially impair D's ability to do one or more of the things listed in 2 above. 'Substantially' means more than trivial (*Lloyd* (1966), *Brown* (2011))

5   The abnormality of mental functioning must provide an explanation for D doing or being a party to the killing.

10.3.2 Diminished responsibility and intoxication

1   There have been problems where a defendant who pleads diminished responsibility was also intoxicated at the time of the killing.

2   Voluntary intoxication alone is NOT capable of being a foundation for diminished responsibility (*Dowds* (2012)).

3   In *Dietschmann* (2003) the House of Lords stated that:

● the abnormality of mind (under the old law – now mental functioning) and the drink might each play a part in impairing the defendant's mental responsibility for the killing;

- the jury's task is to decide whether, despite the disinhibiting effect of the drink on the defendant's mind, the abnormality of mind nevertheless substantially impaired his mental responsibility for his fatal acts;

- it is not correct for the judge to direct the jury that, unless they were satisfied that if the defendant had not taken drink he would have killed, the defence must fail.

5   If the brain has been injured through alcoholism then that injury or disease can support a finding of diminished responsibility.

6   Alcohol dependency syndrome can be a source of the abnormality of mental functioning.

7   In *Wood* (2008) the House of Lords stated that a jury could take into consideration the effect of any drinking that they decided was involuntary when determining whether D's mental responsibility for the actions at the time of the killing was substantially impaired.

10.3.3 Scope of the defence

1   The defence is available only where the defendant is charged with murder and it is only a partial defence reducing the charge of murder to manslaughter.

2   The burden of proving the defence is on the defendant (s 2(2) Homicide Act 1957). But the defendant need only prove it on the balance of probabilities.

3   The defence of diminished responsibility is usually raised by the defence, although the court may decide that there is evidence to raise it even though the defence has not specifically done so.

Comparison of diminished responsibility and insanity	
Diminished responsibility	Insanity
Only available as a defence to murder	Available as a defence for all crimes (except, possibly, strict liability offences)
Verdict is not guilty of murder but guilty of manslaughter	Verdict is not guilty by reason of insanity
Must be an abnormality of mental functioning	Must be a defect of reason
This must arise from a recognised medical condition	This must be due to disease of the mind This may be a physical or mental disease The cause must be internal
The abnormality must substantially impair D's ability to: • understand the nature of his conduct • form a rational judgment • exercise self-control	The defendant must either: • not know the nature and quality of his acts; or • not know he was doing wrong
The defence must prove diminished responsibility on the balance of probabilities	The defence must prove insanity on the balance of probabilities

10.3.4 Loss of control

1   This a defence under s 54 Coroners and Justice Act 2009.

2   It replaces the old defence of provocation.

3   Loss of control is only available as a defence if it was due to a 'qualifying trigger' which must be:

   ● fear of serious violence from V or another; or

   ● things said and/or done; or

   ● a combination of both of these (s 55 Coroners and Justice Act 2009).

4   Where the qualifying trigger is things said or done, then these must have:

   ● constituted circumstances of an extremely grave character; and

   ● caused D to have a justifiable sense of being seriously wronged.

5   These are higher levels of test than under the previous law of provocation (*Zebedee* (2012)).

6   D cannot rely on V's sexual infidelity as a qualifying trigger if it is the only qualifying trigger. But it can be taken into account if it is 'integral to and forms an essential part of the context' (*Clinton* (2012)).

7   D cannot rely on a qualifying trigger if D incited the fear of violence or the things said or done.

8   Loss of control will only be a defence if a person of D's sex and age with a normal degree of tolerance and self-restraint, and in the circumstances of D, might have reacted in the same or in a similar way to D.

9   'The circumstances of D' above is a reference to all of D's circumstances other than those whose only relevance to D's conduct is that they bear on D's general capacity for tolerance or self-restraint.

10   The loss of control does not have to be sudden. This is a change from the old law of provocation where D had to show that the provocation caused a sudden loss of control.

10.3.5 Suicide pact

1   'It shall be manslaughter and shall not be murder, for a person acting in pursuance of a suicide pact between him and another to kill the other or be a party to the other being killed by a third party' (s 4(1) Homicide Act 1957).

2   A suicide pact is 'a common agreement between two or more persons having for its object the death of all of them' (s 4(3) Homicide Act 1957).

3   The defendant's acts will only be counted as being in pursuance of a suicide pact if 'it is done while he has the settled intention of dying in pursuance of the pact' (s 4(3) Homicide Act 1957).

4   The burden of proving the defence is on the defendant (s 4(2) Homicide Act 1957). But the defendant need only prove it on the balance of probabilities.

▶ 10.4 Involuntary manslaughter

Involuntary manslaughter		
Three different ways of committing the offence		
Constructive manslaughter	Gross negligence manslaughter	Reckless manslaughter
Unlawful act Objectively dangerous as to the risk of harm to the victim – **Church (1966)** Act can be aimed at property – **Goodfellow (1986)** Defendant must have *mens rea* for the unlawful act BUT need not realise it is dangerous – **Newbury and Jones (1977)**	Lawful act or omission Defendant must owe victim a duty of care – **Adomako (1994)** Act or omission must be so negligent that it 'goes beyond a matter of mere compensation' – **Bateman (1925)**	Act or omission Subjectively reckless as to an obvious risk of injury to health – **Stone and Dobinson (1977)**, **Lidar (2000)** Possibly only exists for 'motor' manslaughter cases – **Adomako (1994)**

10.4.1 Constructive manslaughter

1   The death must be caused by an unlawful act. A civil wrong is not enough (*Franklin* (1883)).

2   There have been difficulties in deciding whether there is an unlawful act where the defendant prepares an injection of a drug but the victim then injects himself. This creates difficulty also on the issue of whether the defendant has caused the death. The current law appears to be that:

- where the defendant supplies the drug but does nothing towards the administration of it, he has not caused the death (*Dalby* (1982), *Kennedy No 2* (2007));

- where the defendant assists in the injection in some way, for example by applying a tourniquet to raise the vein, he has participated in the unlawful act of administering a noxious substance, and where this act causes the death he is guilty of manslaughter (*Rogers* (2003)).

3   There must be an act: an omission cannot not create liability for constructive manslaughter (*Lowe* (1973)).

4   The unlawful act must be dangerous on an objective test; i.e. it must be 'such as all sober and reasonable people would inevitably recognise must subject the other person to, at least, the risk of some harm resulting therefrom, albeit not serious harm' (*Church* (1966)).

5   The act need not be aimed at a person; it can be aimed at property, provided it is 'such that all sober and reasonable people would inevitably recognise must subject another person to, at least, the risk of some harm' (*Goodfellow* (1986)).

6   The risk of harm refers to physical harm; fear and apprehension are not sufficient, even if they cause the victim to have a heart attack (*Dawson* (1985)).

7   However, where a reasonable person would be aware of the victim's frailty and the risk of physical harm to him, then the defendant will be liable (*Watson* (1989)).

8   It must be proved that the defendant had the *mens rea* for the unlawful act, but it is not necessary for the defendant to realise that the act is unlawful or dangerous (*DPP v Newbury and Jones* (1977), *Attorney-General's Reference (No 2 of 1999)* (2000)).

10.4.2 Gross negligence manslaughter

1   This is where a defendant who owes the victim a duty of care does a lawful act or omission in a very negligent way.

2   A duty of care has been held to exist for the purposes of the criminal law in various situations, including:

● the duty of a doctor to his patient (*Adomako* (1994));

● the duty of managing and maintaining property where there was a faulty gas fire (*Singh* (1999));

● the duty of the owner and master of a sailing ship to the crew (*Litchfield* (1998));

● the duty of care a lorry driver held to illegal immigrants he knew were in the back of his lorry and dependent on him to open the air vent (*Wacker* (2002)).

3   In *Khan* (1998) the Court of Appeal held that duty situations could be extended to include a duty to summon medical assistance in certain circumstances.

4   The fact that D and V were engaged on a criminal enterprise does not prevent a duty of care from arising (*Wacker* (2002), *Willoughby* (2004)).

10.4.3 What is gross negligence?

1   The negligence is 'gross' when it goes 'beyond a matter of mere compensation between subjects and showed such disregard for the life and safety of others as to amount to a crime against the State and conduct deserving of punishment' (*Bateman* (1925)).

2   The disregard must be as to the risk of death. Risk of injury is not enough (*Singh (Gurpal)* (1999), *Misra* (2004), *Yaqoob* (2005)).

3   In *Adomako* (1994) the House of Lords reinforced the test from *Bateman*. Lord MacKay said the ordinary principles of negligence apply:

- Is the defendant in breach of a duty of care?

- Did the breach cause the death?

- If so, the jury must consider whether the breach is gross negligence and therefore a crime. This depends on the seriousness of the breach of duty in all the circumstances in which the defendant was placed.

4   Lord MacKay stated that: 'the essence of the matter, which is supremely a jury question, is whether having regard to the risk of death involved, the conduct of the defendant is so bad as to amount in their judgment to a criminal act or omission'.

5   The Law Commission criticised this test as being 'circular'. The jury must be directed to convict the defendant of a crime if they think his or her conduct was 'criminal'.

6   There is also the criticism that the use of the civil terminology of duty of care and negligence is unclear in the criminal law context.

7   In *Misra: Srivastava* (2004) the Court of Appeal held that the elements of gross negligence manslaughter were set out sufficiently clearly in *Adomako* (1994) so that there was no breach of Article 7 of the European Convention on Human Rights.

10.4.4 Reckless manslaughter

1   Prior to *Adomako* (1994) it was held that manslaughter could be committed by recklessness, based on an objective standard.

2   In *Adomako* it was stated that this was the wrong test for manslaughter, though the word 'reckless' might be appropriate. Reckless should have the meaning that the defendant had been indifferent to an obvious risk of injury to health, or actually to have foreseen the risk but determined to run it (*Stone and Dobinson* (1977)).

3   In *Lidar* (2000) the Court of Appeal approved of a direction on manslaughter by recklessness, where the risk of injury was appreciated by the defendant.

4   It is probable that reckless manslaughter only exists in 'motor' manslaughter cases (*Adomako* (1994)).

▶ 10.5 Causing death by dangerous driving

1   'A person who causes the death of another by driving a mechanically propelled vehicle dangerously on a road or other public place is guilty of an offence' (s 1 Road Traffic Act 1988).

2   The test for what is dangerous is an objective one. 'A person is to be regarded as driving dangerously if:

● the way he drives falls far below what would be expected of a competent and careful driver, and

● it would be obvious to a competent and careful driver that driving in that way would be dangerous' (s 2A Road Traffic Act 1988).

3   The maximum sentence is 10 years' imprisonment and/or a fine.

▶ 10.6 Infanticide

1   The offence of infanticide is set out in s 1 Infanticide Act 1938, as amended by the Coroners and Justice Act 2009.

2   The offence is committed when a woman 'by any wilful act or omission causes the death of her child' and:

● the child is under the age of 12 months; and

● D's balance of mind was disturbed by reason of her not having fully recovered from the effect of giving birth to the child or by reason of the effect of lactation consequent upon the birth of the child.

3   Infanticide can be charged as an offence in its own right or used as a partial defence to a charge of murder or manslaughter.

4   The law used to be that it was not necessary to prove the *mens rea* for murder (*R v Gore* (2008)). However, the law was changed by the Coroners and Justice Act so that now it has to be proved that D had the intention to murder.

> # 10.7 Causing or allowing the death of a child or vulnerable adult

1   Section 5 of the Domestic Violence, Crime and Victims Act 2004 created a new offence of causing or allowing the death of a child or vulnerable adult.

2   The elements of the offence are that:

- D was aware or ought to have been aware that V was at significant risk of serious physical harm from a member of the household;

- D failed to take reasonable steps to prevent that person coming to harm; and

- the person subsequently died from the unlawful act of a member of the household in circumstances the defendant foresaw or ought to have foreseen.

3   One of the situations that s 5 was created to cover is where it is impossible to prove which of two people killed V (*Ikram and Parveen* (2008)).

4   Leaving a child with a person who has been violent to it in the past can come under this section (*Mujuru* (2007)).

5   Where V is an adult, the fact that they are utterly dependent on others may bring them within the category of 'vulnerable adult' even though they are young and fit (*Kahn and others* (2009)).

6   The state of vulnerability does not need to be long-standing. It can be short or temporary.

> # 10.8 Offences against a foetus

Killing a foetus is not murder or manslaughter, but there are other offences which may be charged.

10.8.1 Child destruction

1   'Any person who, with intent to destroy the life of a child capable of being born alive, by any wilful act causes a child to die before it has an existence independent of its mother, shall be guilty of an offence' (s 1(1) Infant Life (Preservation) Act 1929).

2   Where a woman is 28 weeks or more pregnant, this is *prima facie* proof that the child was capable of being born alive (s 1(2) Infant Life (Preservation) Act 1929).

3   However, the prosecution can try to prove that the child was capable of being born alive even though the foetus was less than 28 weeks.

4   It is not an offence if the act is done with the 'purpose of preserving the life of the mother' (*Bourne* (1939)).

5   There is no offence if the pregnancy is terminated by a registered medical practitioner in accordance with the terms of the Abortion Act 1967.

10.8.2 Abortion

1   Under s 58 Offences Against the Person Act 1861 it is an offence to try to procure a miscarriage.

2   The offence can be committed by the woman herself or by another by unlawfully administering any poison or other noxious thing or unlawfully using an instrument or any other means.

3   It is not necessary to show that a miscarriage has actually been caused.

4   Where another person is charged with the offence it is not even necessary to prove that the woman was pregnant, provided the other acted with the intent of procuring a miscarriage.

5   By s 1(1) Abortion Act 1967, there is no offence if the pregnancy is terminated by a registered medical practitioner where two doctors are of the opinion that:

● the pregnancy has not exceeded the 24th week and that the continuance of the pregnancy involves greater risk of injury to health of the woman or any existing children of her family than if the pregnancy was terminated; or

● at any time during the pregnancy if the termination is necessary to prevent grave permanent injury to the physical or mental health of the pregnant woman; or

● at any time during the pregnancy if the continuance of the pregnancy would involve greater risk to the life of the pregnant woman than if the pregnancy was terminated; or

● there is a substantial risk that if the child were born it would suffer from a serious physical or mental handicap.

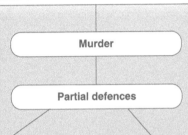

Key Cases Checklist

Mens rea for murder

Vickers (1957)
Intention to cause grievous bodily harm is sufficient for the *mens rea* of murder

Moloney (1985)
Foresight of consequences is only evidence from which the intention for murder may be found

Woollin (1998)
The jury are not entitled to find the necessary intention unless they feel sure that death or serious bodily harm was a virtual certainty as a result of D's act and that D realised this

Murder

Partial defences

Diminished responsibility
S 2 Homicide Act 1957 as amended by s 52 Coroners and Justice Act 2009

Byrne (1960)
Old definition: 'Abnormality of mind' is wide enough to cover perception, ability to form rational judgment and to exercise willpower

Dietschmann (2003)
The abnormality does not have to be the sole cause of D's acts in doing the killing

Wood (2008)
Alcohol dependency syndrome can amount to an abnormality [of mind]

Dowds (2012)
Voluntary intoxication on its own cannot give rise to the defence

Loss of Control

Zebedee (2012)
There must be circumstances of an extremely grave character

Clinton (2012)
Sexual infidelity on its own cannot be a qualifying trigger, but may be considered if integral to whole context

10.1

Attorney-General's Reference (No 3 of 1994) [1997] 3 All ER 936, [1998] 1 Cr App R 91

HL

Key Facts

See 3.6.

Key Law

A foetus is not a person and there is no liability for murder or manslaughter for killing a foetus. However, where the foetus suffers an attack while in the womb, is afterwards born as a living child, but then dies as a result of the attack on it when it was a foetus, D can be liable for murder or manslaughter depending on his intention.

10.2.2

Vickers [1957] 2 All ER 741, (1957) 41 Cr App R 189

CCA

Key Facts

D broke into the cellar of a local sweet shop. He was interrupted by the old lady who ran the shop. D hit her several blows with his fists and kicked her once in the head. She died as a result of her injuries. The Court of Appeal upheld his conviction for murder.

Key Law

An intention to cause grievous bodily harm is sufficient for the *mens rea* of murder. It does not have to be proved that D had the intention to kill.

Key Comment

The old common law definition of murder states that the *mens rea* of murder is 'malice aforethought express or implied'. Express malice is the intention to kill: implied malice is the intention to cause grievous bodily harm.

Key Problem

In 2005 the Law Commission published a consultation paper on murder which proposed that only an intention to kill would be sufficient for first-tier murder.

10.2.2

Moloney [1985] 1 All ER 1025, (1985) 81 Cr App R 93

HL

Key Facts

See 3.2.1.

Key Law

Foresight by D that death or grievous bodily harm is virtually certain to result from D's acts or omissions is evidence from which the required intention for murder can be found.

10.2.2

Woollin [1998] 4 All ER 103, [1999] 1 Cr App R 8

HL

Key Facts

See 3.2.1.

Key Law

The model direction to a jury considering foresight of consequences should be:

'the jury should be directed that they are not entitled to *find* the necessary intention unless they feel sure that death or serious bodily harm was a virtual certainty (barring some unforeseen intervention) as a result of D's actions and that D appreciated that such was the case'.

Key Links

Hancock and Shankland [1986] 1 All ER 641 and *Nedrick* [1986] 3 All ER 1. See 3.2.1.

10.3.1

Byrne [1960] 3 All ER 1, (1960) 44 Cr App R 246

CCA

Key Facts

D was a sexual psychopath who strangled a young woman and then mutilated her body. The medical evidence was that, because of his condition, he was unable to control his perverted desires. He was convicted of murder, but the Court of Appeal quashed the conviction and substituted a conviction for manslaughter.

Key Law

The phrase 'abnormality of mind' in the Homicide Act 1957 was wide enough to cover:

- the perception of physical acts and matters;
- the ability to form a rational judgment as to whether an act is right or wrong; and
- an ability to exercise willpower to control physical acts in accordance with that rational judgment.

Note: The old definition of diminished responsibility used the phrase 'abnormality of mind'. The new definition uses the phrase 'abnormality of mental functioning'.

10.3.2 | ## *Dowds* [2012] EWCA Crim 281

Key Facts

D and his girlfriend, V, were heavy binge drinkers. D, in a drunken state, stabbed V 60 times, killing her. D was convicted of murder. He appealed on the basis that his state of 'acute intoxication' should have been left to the jury as providing a possible defence of diminished responsibility. His appeal was rejected and his conviction for murder upheld.

Key Law

Voluntary acute intoxication is not capable of founding diminished responsibility.

10.3.2 | ## *Dietschmann* [2003] UKHL 10

Key Facts

D, who was suffering from an adjustment disorder in the form of depressed grief reaction to the death of his aunt, was upset by V's disrespectful behaviour. D killed V by repeatedly kicking him and stamping on him. D had also drunk a large amount of alcohol before the killing. He was convicted. The House of Lords allowed his appeal.

Key Law

The abnormality does not have to be the sole cause of D's acts in doing the killing. Even if D would not have killed if he had not taken the drink, the causative effect of the drink does not necessarily prevent an abnormality of mind from substantially impairing his mental responsibility.

Key Link

Gittens [1984] 3 WLR 327.

10.3.2   *Wood* [2008] EWCA Crim 1305   CA

Key Facts

After drinking heavily, D killed V in a frenzied attack with a meat cleaver. He suffered from alcohol dependency syndrome. At the trial the judge directed the jury that the defence of diminished responsibility was only available if D's drinking was truly involuntary. The Court of Appeal quashed his conviction for murder and substituted a verdict of manslaughter.

Key Law

There was no need to prove brain damage as a result of drinking. Alcohol dependency syndrome could amount to an abnormality of mind (now abnormality of mental functioning).

10.3.4   *Zebedee* [2012] EWCA Crim 1428   CA

Key Facts

D lost control when his 94-year-old father, who suffered from Alzheimer's, repeatedly soiled himself. D killed his father. D put forward the defence of loss of control, but was convicted of murder and his conviction upheld.

Key Law

In order for things done or things said to be a qualifying trigger under s 55 Coroners and Justice Act 2009, they must constitute circumstances of an extremely grave character.

10.3.4

Clinton [2012] EWCA Crim 2, [2012] All ER 947

Key Facts

D killed his wife. The day before, she had told him she was having an affair. She also taunted him about looking up suicide websites, saying he had not got the courage to commit suicide. They also argued. D then killed V. He was convicted of murder but appealed on the basis that the defence of loss of control should have been left to the jury. The Court of Appeal agreed and quashed the conviction.

Key Law

Sexual infidelity alone could not amount to a qualifying trigger for the defence of loss of control. However, it did not have to be disregarded. It could be considered if it was integral to and formed an essential part of the context.

Unlawful Manslaughter

Lowe (1973)
An omission is not sufficient for the *actus reus* of unlawful act manslaughter

Church (1965)
The unlawful act must be one which a sober and reasonable person would recognise put V at risk of some harm

Goodfellow (1986)
The unlawful act can be aimed at property, provided it puts a person at risk of harm

Dawson (1985)
Causing fear is not a dangerous act unless D knows V is at risk of injury from the fear

DPP v Newbury and Jones (1976)
D need only have the *mens rea* for the unlawful act: there is no need to prove that D foresaw harm

---

Involuntary Manslaughter

Gross Negligence Manslaughter

Bateman (1925)
Gross negligence is conduct which goes beyond the civil tort of negligence so as to be considered criminal

Adomako (1994)
There must be a duty of care, breach of that duty which causes V's death, and the negligence must be so bad as to amount in all the circumstances to a criminal act or omission

Khan and Khan (1998)
The categories of duty of care can be extended on a case-by-case basis

Wacker (2003)
Even though V is involved with D in a criminal act, D can still owe a duty of care to V

10.4.1   *Kennedy (No 2)* [2007] UKHL 38   HL

Key Facts

D had prepared an injection of heroin and water for V to inject himself. He handed the syringe to V who injected himself and then handed the syringe back to D. V died. Initially D was convicted and the Court of Appeal upheld his conviction. The Criminal Case Review Commission referred the case back to the Court of Appeal. Again the Court of Appeal upheld the conviction on the basis that filling the syringe and handing it to V was administering a noxious substance and an unlawful act. The case was then appealed to the House of Lords who quashed the conviction.

Key Law

The Law Lords pointed out that the criminal law generally assumes the existence of free will. V had freely and voluntarily administered the injection to himself. The defendant could only be guilty if he was involved in administering the injection. In this case he had not been and so had not done an unlawful act which caused the death.

Key Comment

The case overrules *Rogers* [2003] 2 Cr App R 160.

10.4.1   *Lowe* [1973] 1 All ER 805, (1973) 57
Cr App R 365   CA

Key Facts

D was convicted of wilfully neglecting his baby son and of his manslaughter. The Court of Appeal quashed the conviction for manslaughter because the finding of wilful neglect involved a failure to act and this could not support a conviction for unlawful act manslaughter.

Key Law

An omission is not sufficient for the *actus reus* of unlawful act manslaughter.

10.4.1

Church [1965] 2 All ER 72, (1965) 49 Cr App R 206

Key Facts

D had a fight with a woman and knocked her out. He tried for half an hour, unsuccessfully, to bring her round. He thought she was dead and pushed her into a river. In fact, she was alive when she entered the river but died through drowning.

Key Law

The unlawful act must be one which a sober and reasonable person would recognise put V at risk of some harm.

Key Judgment: Edmund Davies J

'The unlawful act must be such as all sober and reasonable people would inevitably recognise must subject the other person to, at least, the risk of some harm resulting therefrom, albeit not serious harm.'

10.4.1

Goodfellow (1986) 83 Cr App R 23

Key Facts

D decided to set fire to his council flat so that the council would have to re-house him. The fire got out of control and his wife, son and another woman died in the fire. He was convicted of manslaughter and appealed. The Court of Appeal upheld the conviction because all the elements of unlawful act manslaughter were present.

Key Law

Even though the unlawful act was aimed at property, the elements of unlawful act manslaughter were present:

- the act was committed intentionally;
- it was unlawful;
- reasonable people would recognise that it might cause some harm to another person;
- the act caused the death.

10.4.1 · *Dawson* (1985) 81 Cr App R 150

 CA

Key Facts

Three defendants attempted to rob a petrol station. They were masked and armed with pickaxe handles. The petrol station attendant pressed the alarm and the robbers fled. The attendant, who had a serious heart condition, then died from a heart attack. Ds' convictions were quashed.

Key Law

The act must be one likely to cause some harm in the eyes of reasonable people. Frightening a man of 60 would not normally be expected to cause harm and so was not a dangerous act for unlawful act manslaughter.

10.4.1 · *Watson* [1989] 2 All ER 865, (1989) 89 Cr App R 211

 CA

Key Facts

Two defendants threw a brick through the window of a house and got into it, intending to steal property. The occupier was a frail 87-year-old man who heard the noise and came to investigate what had happened. The two defendants physically abused him and then left. The man died of a heart attack 90 minutes later.

Key Law

Where a reasonable person would be aware of V's frailty and the risk of harm to him, then the unlawful act is dangerous within the *Church* test.

10.4.1 · *DPP v Newbury and Jones* [1976] 2 All ER 365, (1976) 62 Cr App R 291

 HL

Key Facts

The defendants were two teenage boys who pushed a piece of paving stone from a bridge onto a railway line as a train was approaching. The stone hit the train and killed the guard. They were convicted of manslaughter.

Key Law

It was not necessary to prove that the defendant foresaw any harm from his act. The defendant could be convicted provided the unlawful act was dangerous and the defendant had the necessary *mens rea* for that act.

Key Link

Attorney-General's Reference (No 2 of 1999) [2000] 3 All ER 187.

10.4.2   *Adomako* **[1994] 3 All ER 79**   (HL)

Key Facts

D was an anaesthetist. He failed to notice that during an operation one of the tubes supplying oxygen to a patient became disconnected. The lack of oxygen caused the patient to suffer a heart attack and brain damage. As a result, the patient died six months later.

Key Law

1) The elements of gross negligence manslaughter are:
   - the existence of a duty of care towards the victim;
   - a breach of that duty of care which causes death;
   - gross negligence which the jury considers to be criminal.

2) To be considered gross negligence, the conduct of the defendant must be so bad in all the circumstances and having regard to the risk of death involved, as to amount, in the judgment of the jury, to a criminal act or omission.

Key Judgment: Lord Mackay

'The ordinary principles of the law of negligence apply to ascertain whether or not the defendant has been in breach of a duty of care towards the victim . . . The jury will have to consider whether the extent to which the defendant's conduct departed from the proper standard of care incumbent upon him involving as it must have done a risk of death . . ., was such that it should be judged criminal.'

10.4.2   *Wacker* [2003] 1 Cr App R 22   CA

Key Facts

D agreed to bring 60 illegal immigrants into England. They were put in the back of his lorry for a cross-channel ferry crossing. The only air into the lorry was through a small vent and it was agreed that this vent should be closed at certain times to prevent the immigrants being discovered. D closed the vent before boarding the ferry. The crossing took an hour longer than usual and at Dover the Customs officers found 58 of the immigrants were dead.

Key Law

Although no action could arise in a civil case because the victims were involved in criminal behaviour, it was still possible for there to be a breach of a duty of care in a criminal case.

10.4.2   *Khan and Khan* [1998] Crim LR 830   CA

Key Facts

The two defendants had supplied heroin to a new user who took it in their presence and then collapsed. They left her alone and by the time they returned to the flat she had died. Their conviction for unlawful act manslaughter was quashed but the Court of Appeal thought there could be a duty to summon medical assistance in certain circumstances.

Key Law

The categories of duty of care can be extended on a case-by-case basis.

10.4.3   *Bateman* [1925] All ER Rep 45, (1925) 19 Cr App R 8   CCA

Key Facts

D, a doctor, attended V for the birth of her child at her home, during which part of V's uterus came away. D did not send V to hospital for five days, and she later died. D's

conviction was quashed on the basis that he had acted as any competent doctor would have done. He had not been grossly negligent.

Key Law

Gross negligence is conduct which goes so far beyond the civil tort of negligence as to be considered criminal.

Key Judgment: Lord Hewart

'The facts must be such that, in the opinion of the jury, the negligence of the accused went beyond a mere matter of compensation between subjects and showed such disregard for the life and safety of others as to amount to a crime against the State and conduct deserving of punishment.'

10.4.3   *Misra and another* [2004] EWCA Crim 2375, [2005] 1 Cr App R 21

CA

Key Facts

The two defendants were senior house doctors responsible for the post-operative care of V. They failed to identify and treat V for an infection which occurred after the operation. V died from the infection.

Key Law

The test in gross negligence manslaughter involves consideration of the risk of death. It is not sufficient to show a risk of bodily injury or injury to health.

Key Comment

The defendants had appealed on the basis that the elements of gross negligence manslaughter were uncertain and so breached Article 7 European Convention on Human Rights. The Court of Appeal held that *Adomako* had clearly laid down the elements, so there was no breach of Article 7.

Key Link

Evans [2009] EWCA Crim 650. See 2.3.1

Causing or Allowing the Death of a Child or Vulnerable Adult

s 5 Domestic Violence and Victims Act 2004

***Ikram and Parveen* (2008)**
s 5 was created for instances where it was impossible to prove which of two people killed the child

***Mujuru* (2007)**
s 5 covers leaving a child with a person who had been violent towards it

***Khan and others* (2009)**
An adult may be vulnerable if they are utterly dependent on others
The state of vulnerability can be short or temporary

Other Offences of Homicide

Infanticide

s 1 Infanticide Act as amended by Coroners and Justice Act 2009 D must be proved to have the intent for murder

Causing Death by Dangerous Driving

s 2A Road Traffic Act 1988

***Marchant and Muntz* (2003)**
There is no an offence where the dangerousness comes from an inherent design of the vehicle

---

10.7   *Ikram and Parveen* [2008] EWCA Crim 586

Key Facts

V was the 16-month-old son of D. D lived with E. V died as a result of a fractured leg and other injuries. D and E were the only adults in the house in the hours before V's death. It was impossible to prove murder as it was not known which of them caused the injuries. Both were convicted of causing or allowing the death of a child under s 5 Domestic Violence, Crime and Victims Act 2004.

Key Comment

This was the type of situation for which s 5 was created.

10.7

Mujuru [2007] EWCA Crim 2810   CA

Key Facts

D went to work leaving her four-month-old daughter with her partner, whom she knew was violent and who had previously broken the child's arm. V was killed by the partner. He was convicted of murder. D was convicted under s 5 Domestic Violence, Crime and Victims Act 2004.

Key Law

By leaving the child with a man who had previously broken the child's arm, D had 'failed to take such steps as she could reasonably have been expected to take to protect' V from the 'significant risk of serious physical harm'.

Khan and others [2009] EWCA Crim 2   CA

Key Facts

V, aged 19, was murdered by her husband. Medical evidence showed that V had suffered numerous injuries in three distinct attacks over an extended period of time. His two sisters and brother-in-law lived in the same house. They were all convicted under s 5 Domestic Violence, Crime and Victims Act 2004.

Key Law

An adult who is utterly dependent on others may fall within the protection of s 5, even though physically young and apparently fit. The state of vulnerability does not need to be long-standing. It may be short or temporary.

11 Non-fatal offences against the person

Offence	Actus reus plus consequence		Mens rea
Common assault S 39 Criminal Justice Act 1988	**Assault** – causing V to fear immediate unlawful violence **Battery** – application of unlawful violence, even the slightest touching (**Wilson v Pringle (1986)**)	No injury is required	**Assault** – intention or subjective recklessness as to causing V to fear immediate unlawful violence **Battery** – intention of, or subjective recklessness as to applying unlawful force (**Venna (1976)**)
Assault occasioning actual bodily harm S 47 Offences Against the Person Act 1861 (OAPA 1861)	Assault (i.e. an assault or battery)	Actual bodily harm (e.g. bruising) This includes: • nervous shock (**Miller (1954)**) • psychiatric harm (**Chan Fook (1994)**)	Intention or subjective recklessness as to causing fear of unlawful violence or of applying unlawful force (as above)
Maliciously wounding or inflicting grievous bodily harm s 20 OAPA 1861	A direct or indirect act or omission (**Martin (1881)**) No need to prove an assault (**Mandair (1994), Burstow (1998))**	Either a wound (a cutting of the whole skin) (**JJC v Eisenhower (1984)**) or grievous bodily harm (really serious harm) which includes psychiatric harm (**Burstow (1998)**)	Intention or subjective recklessness as to causing some injury (though not serious) (**Savage: DPP v Parmenter (1991)**)
Wounding or causing grievous bodily harm with intent S 18 OAPA 1861	A direct or indirect act or omission which causes V's injury	A wound or grievous bodily harm (as above)	Specific intention to cause grievous bodily harm or to resist or prevent arrest

The main offences are set out in the Offences Against the Person Act (OAPA) 1861. This did not create a coherent set of offences and there have been many problems in the law. The Law Commission has proposed a complete reform of the law but, as yet, Parliament has not reformed the law.

The chart at the start of the chapter shows key points of four important offences against the person.

▶ 11.1 Common assault

1   There are two ways of committing this:

●   assault; and

●   battery.

2   Both of these offences are charged under s 39 Criminal Justice Act 1988 and are summary offences.

11.1.1 Assault

1   This is also known as a technical assault or a psychic assault.

2   The defendant intentionally or subjectively recklessly causes another person to fear immediate unlawful personal violence.

Actus reus of an assault

1   An assault requires some act or words; an omission is not enough (*Fagan v Metropolitan Police Commissioner* (1969)).

2   Words are sufficient for an assault; even silent telephone calls can be an assault (*Ireland* (1998)).

3   Words indicating there will be no violence may prevent an act from being an assault (*Tuberville v Savage* (1669)), but not in all circumstances (*Light* (1843)).

4   Fear of immediate force is necessary; this does not mean instantaneous, but 'imminent', so an assault can be through a closed window (*Smith v Chief Superintendent of Woking* (1983)) or via a telephone call (*Ireland* (1998)).

5   Fear of any unwanted touching is sufficient: the force or unlawful personal violence that is feared need not be serious.

Mens rea of an assault

1   The *mens rea* must be either an intention to cause another to fear immediate unlawful personal violence or recklessness as to whether such fear is caused.

2   The test for recklessness is subjective; the defendant must realise the risk that his acts/words could cause another to fear unlawful personal violence.

11.1.2 Battery

The defendant intentionally or subjectively recklessly applies unlawful force to another.

Actus reus of battery

1   Force can include the slightest touching; but not the ordinary 'jostlings' of everyday life (*Wilson v Pringle* (1986)).

2   It may be through a continuing act (*Fagan v Metropolitan Police Commissioner* (1969)).

3   It may be through an indirect act such as a booby trap (*Martin* (1881), *DPP v K* (1990)); or causing a child to fall to the floor by punching the person holding the child (*Haystead* (2000)).

4   It has been held that a defendant's failure to tell a policewoman searching his pockets that there was a hypodermic needle in one of them can amount to the *actus reus* (*DPP v Santana-Bermudez* (2003)).

5   Where police officers held D by the arm when they did not intend to arrest D, this was held to be unlawful force (*Collins v Wilcock* (1984), *Wood (Fraser) v DPP* (2008)).

6   The unlawfulness of the force may be negated by the victim's consent (see 8.6) or if it is used in self-defence (see 8.5).

Mens rea of battery

1   The *mens rea* must be either an intention to apply unlawful physical force or recklessness.

2   Where recklessness is relied on, it is a subjective test, i.e. the defendant must realise the risk of physical contact and take that risk (*Venna* (1976)).

▶ 11.2 Assault occasioning actual bodily harm

1   This is an offence under s 47 Offences against the Person Act 1861.

2   This states 'whosoever shall be convicted of any assault occasioning actual bodily harm shall be liable . . . to imprisonment for five years'.

3   The offence is triable either way.

11.2.1 *Actus reus* of an assault occasioning actual bodily harm

1   It requires a technical assault or a battery.

2   This must 'occasion' (cause) actual bodily harm.

3   Actual bodily harm is 'any hurt or injury calculated to interfere with the health or comfort' of the victim (*Miller* (1954)).

4   Momentary unconsciousness can be actual bodily harm (*T v DPP* (2003)).

5   Cutting V's hair can be actual bodily harm (*Smith (Michael)* (2006)).

6   Psychiatric injury is sufficient, but not 'mere emotions such as fear, distress or panic' (*Chan Fook* (1994)).

11.2.2 *Mens rea* of an assault occasioning actual bodily harm

1   The defendant must intend or be subjectively reckless as to whether the victim fears or is subjected to unlawful force (i.e. the *mens rea* for an assault or a battery).

2   There is no need for the defendant to intend or be reckless as to whether actual bodily harm is caused (*Roberts* (1971), *Savage* (1991)).

▶ 11.3 Malicious wounding/inflicting grievous bodily harm

1   This is an offence under s 20 Offences against the Person Act 1861.

2   The Act states: 'Whosoever shall unlawfully and maliciously wound or inflict any grievous bodily harm upon any other person, either with or without a weapon or instrument, shall be guilty of an offence.'

3   The offence is known as 'malicious wounding'.

4   The offence is triable either way and the maximum sentence is five years. This is the same as for a s 47 offence, despite the fact that s 20 is a more serious offence.

11.3.1 *Actus reus* of malicious wounding

1   The word 'inflict' does not require a technical assault or a battery (*Burstow* (1998)). It can be by an indirect act (*Martin* (1881)).

2   Grievous bodily harm means 'really serious harm' (*Smith* (1961)); but this does not have to be life-threatening.

3   Severe bruising may be grievous bodily harm when the victim is a very young child or frail person (*Bollom* (2004)).

4   Serious psychiatric injury can be grievous bodily harm (*Burstow* (1997)).

5   Wound means a cut or a break in the continuity of the whole skin. A cut of internal skin, such as in the cheek, is sufficient, but internal bleeding where there is no cut of the skin is not sufficient (*JCC v Eisenhower* (1984)).

11.3.2 *Mens rea* of malicious wounding

1   The defendant must intend to cause another person some harm or be subjectively reckless as to whether he suffers some harm (*Mowatt* (1967)).

2   There is no need for the defendant to foresee serious injury (*Savage* (1991), *Parmenter* (1991)).

▶ 11.4 Wounding or causing grievous bodily harm with intent

1   This is an offence under s 18 Offences Against the Person Act 1861.

2   The Act states: 'Whosoever shall unlawfully and maliciously by any means whatsoever wound or cause any grievous bodily harm to any person, with intent to do some grievous bodily harm to any person, or with intent to resist or prevent the lawful apprehension or detainer of any person, shall be guilty of an offence.'

3   This is an indictable offence and the maximum sentence is life imprisonment.

11.4.1 *Actus reus* of wounding or causing grievous bodily harm with intent

1 The word 'cause' is very wide so that it is only necessary to prove that the defendant's act was a substantial cause of the wound or grievous bodily harm.

2 The meanings of 'wound' and 'grievous bodily harm' are the same as for s 20 (see 11.3.1 above).

11.4.2 *Mens rea* of wounding or causing grievous bodily harm with intent

1 This is a specific intent offence. The defendant must be proved to have intended to:

● do some grievous bodily harm; or

● resist or prevent the lawful apprehension or detainer of any person.

2 See 3.2 for explanation of intention as a concept.

3 Where the charge is intending to cause grievous bodily harm then, although the word 'maliciously' appears in s 18, it has been held that this adds nothing to the *mens rea*.

4 An intent to wound is not sufficient for the *mens rea* of s 18. There must be intent to cause grievous bodily harm (*Taylor* (2009)).

5 Where the charge is causing grievous bodily harm or wounding when intending to resist or prevent arrest or detention, then the word 'maliciously' is important. The prosecution must prove that the defendant had specific intention to resist or prevent arrest but they need only prove that he was reckless as to whether his actions would cause a wound or injury (*Morrison* (1989)).

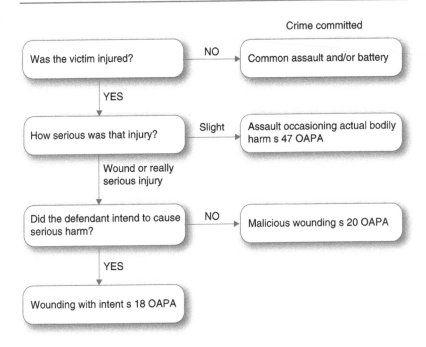

▶ 11.5 Racially aggravated assaults

1   Under s 29 Crime and Disorder Act 1998, a common assault or an offence under s 47 or s 20 Offences Against the Person Act 1861 becomes a racially aggravated assault if either:

● at the time of committing the offence, or immediately before or after doing so, the offender demonstrates towards the victim of the offence hostility based on the victim's membership (or presumed membership) of a racial group; or

● the offence is motivated (wholly or partly) by hostility towards members of a racial group based on their membership of that group.

2   Where an offence is racially aggravated in this way, the maximum penalty is increased from six months to two years for common assault and from five years to seven years for both s 47 and s 20.

▶ 11.6 Administering poison

1   The Offences Against the Person Act 1861 creates two offences:

- s 23 'Whosoever shall unlawfully and maliciously administer to or cause to be administered to or taken by any other person any poison or other destructive or noxious thing, so as to endanger the life of such person, or so as thereby to inflict upon such person any grievous bodily harm, shall be guilty of (an offence) . . .'.

- s 24 'Whosoever shall unlawfully and maliciously administer to or cause to be administered to or taken by any other person any poison or other destructive or noxious thing, with intent to injure, aggrieve, or annoy such person shall be guilty of an (offence) . . .'.

2   'Administer' has been held to include spraying with CS gas (*Gillard* (1998)).

3   For s 24, a harmless substance, such as a sedative or a laxative, may become 'noxious' if administered in large quantities (*Marcus* (1981)).

4   The word 'maliciously' in both sections has the meaning given to it in *Cunningham* (1957) that the defendant must intend or be subjectively reckless about the administration of the substance.

5   Section 24 has an additional requirement for *mens rea* of intent to injure, aggrieve or annoy.

Key Cases Checklist

Assault and Battery

Ireland (1998); Smith v Chief Superintendent of Woking (1983)
Putting V in fear of the possibility of immediate force is sufficient

Collins v Wilcock (1984)
The slightest physical restraint can be battery

DPP v Santana-Bermudez (2003)
An omission is sufficient for the *actus reus*

Mens rea

Venna (1976)
Subjective recklessness is sufficient

Assault Occasioning ABH (s 47)

Actual bodily harm

T v DPP (2003)
Momentary loss of consciousness can be ABH

Chan Fook (1994)
Psychiatric injury can be ABH

Mens rea

Savage (1991)
There is no need to prove any intention to injury

Assaults

Actus Reus of s 20 and s 18 OAPA 1861

Burstow (1997)
It is not necessary to prove an assault for either 'inflict' or 'cause'

Martin (1881)
An indirect act is sufficient for s 20

JCC v Eisenhower (1983)
There must be a cut of the external skin to constitute a wound

DPP v Smith (1961)
GBH means really serious harm

Bollom (2004)
The age and health of the victim must be considered in deciding the seriousness

Mens Rea of s 20 and s 18

Mowatt (1967)
'Maliciously' for s 20 means an intention to injure or taking the risk of some injury

Parmenter (1991)
Affirmed *Mowatt* – there is no need for D to realise that serious injury could be caused

Morrison (1989)
In s 18 where the ulterior intent is to resist arrest, maliciously means taking the risk of injuring V

11.1.1

Ireland [1997] 4 All ER 225, [1998] 1 Cr App R 177

 HL

Key Facts

D made a large number of silent telephone calls to three women. This caused them psychiatric injury. He was convicted of an assault occasioning actual bodily harm under s 47 of the Offences Against the Person Act 1861.

Key Law

It was held that *making* telephone calls, even silent ones, can amount to an assault.

Key Judgment: Lord Steyn

'Take now the case of the silent caller. He intends by his silence to cause fear and he is so understood. The victim is assailed by uncertainty about his intentions. Fear may dominate her emotions, and it may be the fear that the caller's arrival at her door may be imminent. She may fear the possibility of immediate personal violence.'

Key Link

Constanza [1997] Crim LR 576 CA.

Key Comment

Such cases could now also be charged under the Protection from Harassment Act 1997. Section 4 of this Act defines harassment as 'causing another to fear, on at least two occasions, that violence will be used against him'.

11.1.1

Tuberville v Savage (1669) 1 Mod Rep 3

Key Facts

D placed his hand on the hilt of his sword and said to V: 'If it were not assize-time, I would not take such language from you.' D was held not guilty of assault.

Key Law

The accompanying words made it clear that no violence was going to be used. There was no reason for V to fear immediate force, so there was no assault.

11.1.1   *Light* **[1843–60] All ER 934**   (CCR)

Key Facts

D raised a sword above his wife's head, telling her: 'Were it not for the bloody policeman outside, I would split your head open.' D was held guilty of assault.

Key Law

There was an assault as, despite the words, V had cause to fear immediate force in these circumstances.

Key Comment

These two cases can be distinguished on the basis that the assizes were an ongoing event, whereas in *Light* the police officer could have walked away. In addition, it can be argued that in *Tuberville v Savage*, D had not drawn his sword, whereas, in *Light*, D had raised the sword above V's head.

11.1.1   *Smith v Chief Superintendent of Woking Police Station* **[1983] Crim LR 323**   (DC)

Key Facts

D got into a garden and looked through a woman's ground-floor bedroom window at about 11 pm. She was in her nightclothes and was terrified. D was convicted of being on enclosed premises for an unlawful purpose (i.e. an assault).

Key Law

Although D was outside the house and no attack could be made at that immediate moment, the court held that his conduct was an assault. The woman feared some imme-diate and unlawful force and this was sufficient for the purposes of an assault.

11.1.2

DPP v Santana-Bermudez [2003] EWHC 2908 (Admin)

Key Facts

A policewoman, before searching the defendant's pockets, asked him if he had any needles or other sharp objects on him. The defendant said 'no', but when the police officer put her hand in his pocket she was injured by a needle, which caused bleeding. He was convicted of assault occasioning actual bodily harm under s 47 Offences Against the Person Act 1861.

Key Law

Failure to tell the police officer about the needle could amount to the *actus reus* for the purposes of an assault causing actual bodily harm.

11.1.2

Collins v Wilcock [1984] 3 All ER 374 (1984) 79 Cr App Rep 229

Key Facts

Two police officers saw two women apparently soliciting for the purposes of prostitution. They asked D to get into the police car for questioning but she refused and walked away. One of the officers walked after her to try to find out her identity. She refused to speak to the officer and again walked away. The officer then took hold of her by the arm to prevent her leaving. D became abusive and scratched the officer's arm. Her conviction of assaulting a police officer in the execution of his duty was quashed on the basis that the officer was not acting in the execution of his duty, but was acting unlawfully by holding the defendant's arm. The court held that the officer had committed a battery and the defendant was entitled to free herself.

Key Law

Touching a person to get his attention is acceptable provided that only necessary physical contact is used; physical restraint is not acceptable and will be a battery unless there is consent to the touching.

Key Judgment: Goff LJ

'The fundamental principle . . . is that every person's body is inviolate. It has long been established that any touching of another person, however slight, may amount to battery.'

Key Link

Wood (Fraser) v DPP [2008] EWHC 1056 (Admin).

11.1.2   ***Venna* [1976] QB 421, (1976) 61 Cr App R 310**

Key Facts

D and others were causing a disturbance in the street. The police were sent for. When the police tried to arrest D, he kicked out, causing a fracture to a small bone in the officer's hand. D was convicted of assault occasioning actual bodily harm.

Key Law

Subjective recklessness was sufficient for the *mens rea* of battery.

Key Judgment: James LJ

'We see no reason in logic or in law why a person who recklessly applies physical force to the person of another should be outside the criminal law of assault.'

11.2.1   ***T v DPP* [2003] Crim LR 622**

Key Facts

D and a group of other youths chased V. V fell to the ground and saw D coming towards him. V covered his head with his arms and was kicked. He momentarily lost consciousness and remembered nothing until being woken by a police officer. D was convicted of assault occasioning actual bodily harm.

Key Law

Momentary loss of consciousness could be actual bodily harm. 'Harm' was a synonym for injury. 'Actual' indicated that the injury should not be so trivial as to be wholly insignificant. Loss of consciousness fell within the meaning of actual bodily harm.

11.2.1   *Chan Fook* [1994] 2 All ER 552, (1994) 99 Cr App R 147   CA

Key Facts

D thought that V had stolen his fiancée's ring. D dragged V upstairs and locked him in a second-floor room. V tried to escape but was injured when he fell to the ground. At D's trial on a s 47 charge it was claimed that V had suffered trauma before the escape bid and that this amounted to ABH. The judge directed the jury that a hysterical or nervous condition was capable of being ABH. D was convicted, but the Court of Appeal quashed the conviction.

Key Law

Psychiatric injury is capable of amounting to actual bodily harm but 'mere emotions such as fear, distress or panic' do not amount to ABH.

Key Judgment: Hobhouse LJ

'The body of the victim includes all parts of his body, including his organs, his nervous system and his brain. Bodily injury therefore may include injury to any of those parts of his body responsible for his mental and other faculties.'

Key Links

Ireland [1997] 4 All ER 225: see 11.1.
Burstow [1997] 4 All ER 225: see 11.3.

11.2.2 *Savage* [1991] 4 All ER 698, (1991) 94 Cr App R 193 HL

Key Facts

D threw beer over another woman in a pub. In doing this the glass slipped from D's hand and V's hand was cut by the glass. D said that she had only intended to throw beer over the woman. D had not intended her to be injured, nor had she realised that there was a risk of injury. She was convicted of a s 20 offence but the Court of Appeal quashed that and substituted a conviction under s 47 (assault occasioning actual bodily harm). She appealed against this to the House of Lords. The Law Lords dismissed her appeal.

Key Law

Intention to apply unlawful force is sufficient for the *mens rea* of a s 47 offence. The prosecution need not prove that D intended or was reckless as to any injury.

Key Judgment: Lord Ackner

'The verdict of assault occasioning actual bodily harm may be returned upon proof of an assault together with proof of the fact that actual bodily harm was occasioned by the assault. The prosecution is not obliged to prove that the defendant intended to cause some actual bodily harm or was reckless as to whether such harm would be caused.'

11.3.1 *Burstow* [1997] 4 All ER 225, [1998] 1 Cr App R 177 HL

Key Facts

D carried out an eight-month campaign of harassment against a woman with whom he had had a brief relationship some three years earlier. The harassment consisted of both silent and abusive telephone calls, hate mail and stalking. This caused V to suffer from severe depression.

Key Law

It was decided that 'inflict' does not require a technical assault or a battery. This decision means that there now appears to be little, if any, difference in the *actus reus* of the offences under s 20 ('causing') and s 18 ('inflicting').

Key Judgment: Lord Hope

'I would add that there is this difference, the word "inflict" implies that the consequence of the act is something which the victim is likely to find unpleasant or harmful. The relationship between cause and effect, when the word "cause" is used, is neutral. It may embrace pleasure as well as pain. The relationship when the word "inflict" is used is more precise, because it invariably implies detriment to the victim of some kind.'

Key Problem

The wording of the 1861 Act is unclear and the offences do not form a coherent range. The Law Commission set out a draft Bill proposing reform of the law, but this has never been enacted.

Key Link

Serious psychiatric injury can amount to grievous bodily harm. This case was heard together with *Ireland* (see 11.1).

11.3.1   *Martin* **(1881) 8 QBD 54** (CCR)

Key Facts

D placed an iron bar across the doorway of a theatre. He then switched off the lights and yelled 'fire'. In the panic which followed several of the audience were injured when they were trapped and unable to open the door. Martin was convicted of an offence under s 20 OAPA 1861.

Key Law

Grievous bodily harm can be 'inflicted' for the purposes of s 20 through an indirect act such as a booby trap.

11.3.1

DPP v Smith [1961] AC 290, (1960) 44 Cr App R 261   HL

Key Facts

D was charged with murder when he drove erratically while a police officer was clinging to his car. The officer was eventually thrown off the car into the path of another vehicle which ran over him causing him fatal injuries. Since the *mens rea* for murder includes an intention to cause grievous bodily harm, one of the issues was the meaning of 'grievous bodily harm'.

Key Law

Grievous bodily harm should be given its ordinary and natural meaning of 'really serious harm'. GBH does not have to be life-threatening, nor does the harm have to have lasting consequences.

Key Judgment: Viscount Kilmuir LC

'The words "grievous bodily harm" are to be given their ordinary and natural meaning. "Bodily harm" needs no explanation, and "grievous" means . . . really serious . . . The prosecution does not have to prove that the harm was life-threatening, dangerous or permanent . . . There is no requirement that the victim should require treatment or that the harm should extend beyond soft tissue damage.'

11.3.1

Bollom [2004] 2 Cr App R 50   CA

Key Facts

A 17-month-old child had bruising to her abdomen, both arms and left leg. D was charged with causing grievous bodily harm.

Key Law

The severity of the injuries should be assessed according to V's age and health. Bruising could amount to grievous bodily harm. Bruising of this severity would be less serious on an adult in full health than on a very young child.

11.3.1

JCC v Eisenhower [1983] 3 All ER 230

Key Facts

V was hit in the eye by a shotgun pellet. This did not penetrate the eye but caused severe bleeding under the surface. As there was no cut, it was held that this was not a wound. The cut must be of the whole skin, so that a scratch is not considered a wound.

Key Law

To constitute a wound, all the external layers of the skin must be broken. Internal bleeding will not suffice for a wound.

11.3.2

Mowatt [1967] 3 All ER 47, (1967) 51 Cr App R 402

Key Facts

Either D or his friend had taken £5 from V's pocket. V realised this and seized D. D hit out at V, allegedly in self-defence, punching him repeatedly until V was nearly unconscious. D was convicted under s 20 OAPA 1861. The Court of Appeal upheld his conviction.

Key Law

For s 20 there is no need to prove that D had intention to cause serious injury or that he realised there was a risk of serious injury. It is sufficient to prove that D foresaw that some harm might result.

Key Judgment: Diplock LJ

'The word "maliciously" does import . . . an awareness that his act may have the consequence of causing some physical harm to some other person

. . . It is quite unnecessary that the accused should have foreseen that his unlawful act might cause physical harm of the gravity described in [s 20], i.e. a wound or serious phys-

ical injury. It is enough that he should have foreseen that some physical harm to some person, albeit of a minor character, might result.'

Key Comment

The judgment refers only to physical harm. However, since *Mowatt* was decided, it has been established that serious psychiatric injury also comes within the meaning of grievous bodily harm. So D has the required *mens rea* if he realises that his acts might cause serious psychiatric injury to V.

11.3.2   *Parmenter* [1991] 4 All ER 698, (1991) 94 Cr App R 193   HL

Key Facts

D injured his three-month-old baby when he threw the child in the air and caught him. D said that he had often done this with slightly older children and did not realise that there was risk of any injury. He was convicted of an offence under s 20. The House of Lords quashed this conviction but substituted a conviction for assault occasioning actual bodily harm under s 47.

Key Law

The word 'maliciously' in s 20 means only that D must be aware that some injury might be caused by his act.

11.4.2   *Morrison* (1989) 89 Cr App R 17   CA

Key Facts

A police officer seized hold of D and told him that she was arresting him. He dived through a window, dragging her with him as far as the window so that her face was badly cut by the glass. His conviction for wounding with intent to resist arrest (s 18) was quashed because the trial judge directed the jury that D would be guilty if either he foresaw the risk of injury or it would have been obvious to an ordinary prudent man. The Court of Appeal quashed the conviction, holding that the direction was wrong.

Key Law

Where the ulterior intent for s 18 was an intent to resist arrest, 'maliciously' has the same meaning as in *Cunningham*. This means that the prosecution must prove that D realised there was a risk of injury and took that risk.

Key Problem

One unresolved point is that, for the offence of wounding with intent, what degree of harm does the defendant need to foresee? Does he need to foresee that serious harm or a wound will be caused, or does he only need to foresee that some harm will be caused? Under s 20, the test is that the defendant should foresee that some physical harm will be caused. For consistency it seems reasonable that the same test should apply.

11.6   *Cunningham* **[1957] 2 All ER 412, (1957) 41 Cr App R 155**

Key Facts

See 3.3.

12 Sexual offences

Rape

- S 1 Sexual Offences Act 2003 penetration of vagina, anus or mouth
- Slight penetration is sufficient
- Lack of consent by V
- Intention to penetrate vagina, anus or mouth
- Lack of reasonable belief in V's consent

Marital rape is an offence (*R v R* (1991))

SEXUAL OFFENCES

Sexual assaults

- Assault by penetration (s 2)
- Sexual assault (s 3)

Sexual offences on children

- Rape of a child under 13 (s 5)
- Assault of a child under 13 by penetration (s 6)
- Sexual assault of a child under 13 (s 7)
- Sexual activity with a child under 16 (s 9)

Offences involving family members

- Sexual activity with a child family member (s 25)
- Sex with an adult relative; penetration (s 64)
- Sex with an adult relative consenting to penetration (s 65)

Forbidden relationships are parent, grandparent, brother, sister, aunt, uncle, foster parent

Bigamy

S 57 Offences Against the Person Act 1861

- Going through a ceremony of marriage while married to another
- Prosecution must prove first spouse is alive
- Reasonable belief that first spouse is dead is a defence

▶ 12.1 Rape

1   Rape is now defined by s 1(1) Sexual Offences Act 2003 (SOA 2003).

2   A person commits rape if:

  a) he intentionally penetrates the vagina, anus or mouth of another person with his penis;

  b) V does not consent to the penetration; and

  c) D does not reasonably believe that V consents.

3   Note that though the section uses the word 'person', it is clear that only a man can be the principal offender as the penetration has to be by 'his penis'. However, a woman can be guilty of rape as a secondary party.

12.1.1 *Actus reus* of rape

1   This consists of:

  ● penetration of vagina, anus or mouth; and

  ● lack of consent by V.

2   Penetration means any penetration, however slight, by D's penis.

3   Section 79 SOA 2003 states that 'penetration is a continuing act from entry to withdrawal'. This gives statutory effect to decisions in cases such as *Kaitamaki* (1985) and *Cooper and Schaub* (1994).

4   There must be absence of consent. Section 74 SOA 2003 states that a person 'consents if he agrees by choice, and has the freedom and capacity to make that choice'.

5   An intoxicated person is capable of consenting to intercourse. The jury must decide if the alleged V did consent and if they had the freedom and capacity to consent (*Bree* (2007)).

6   Section 75 makes evidential presumptions about consent. It provides that where D knows that certain circumstances exist, V is taken not to have consented. The circumstances are that at the time of the relevant act:

  ● any person was using violence at the time or immediately before, against V or another person, or causing V to fear that immediate violence would be used against V or another person, as was the situation in *Olugboja* (1981);

  ● V was unlawfully detained and D was not unlawfully detained, as in *McFall* (1994) where he had kidnapped his former girlfriend at gunpoint;

- V was asleep or otherwise unconscious;
- because of physical disability, V would not have been able to communicate whether V consented;
- without V's knowledge, a person had administered to or caused V to take a substance that caused V to be stupefied or overpowered.

7   The presumption can be rebutted by proof of consent.

8   Under s 76 SOA 2003 it is conclusively presumed that V did not consent in certain circumstances and that D did not believe that V had consented. The circumstances are:

- D intentionally deceived V as to the nature or purpose of the act; this covers situations such as those in *Flattery* (1877) and *Willliams* (1923);
- D intentionally induced V to consent to the act by impersonating a person known personally to V; this covers cases such as *Elbekkay* (1995).

9   If V is deceived in some other way, then there is no conclusive presumption under s 76 (*Jheeta* (2007)).

12.1.2 *Mens rea* of rape

1   There must be an intention to penetrate V's vagina, anus or mouth.

2   There must be lack of reasonable belief in V's consent.

3   Prior to SOA 2003, it had been a defence if D honestly believed that V consented, even if that belief was not reasonable (*DPP v Morgan* (1976)).

12.1.3 Marital rape

1   The original view at common law was that by marrying, a woman gave consent to sexual intercourse with her husband and she could not withdraw that consent while she remained married to him. (See Hale's *History of the Pleas of the Crown* (1736).)

2   The statutory definition of rape in the Sexual Offences Act 1956 used the phrase 'unlawful sexual intercourse'. It was initially held that 'unlawful' referred to sexual intercourse outside marriage (*Chapman* (1959)).

3   However, during the second half of the twentieth century, judicial opinion gradually changed. Marital rape was recognised initially in limited situations:

- where there was a magistrates' court order that the wife need no longer cohabit with her husband (*Clarke* (1949));

- where there was a *decree nisi* of divorce, even though the divorce had not been finalised (*O'Brien* (1974)); and

- where the parties had entered into a formal separation agreement (*Roberts* (1986)).

4   Finally, in R *v* R (1991) the House of Lords ruled that marital rape was an offence. They pointed out that:

- the status of women had changed;

- a modern marriage is regarded as a partnership of equals; and

- the use of the word 'unlawful' meant something contrary to law rather than outside marriage.

▶ 12.2 Assault by penetration

1   The Sexual Offences Act 2003 creates a new offence of assault by penetration (s 2(1)) which is committed if the defendant:

- intentionally penetrates the vagina or anus of another person with a part of his body or anything else, e.g. a finger as in *Coomber* (2005);

- the penetration is sexual;

- the other person does not consent to the penetration; and

- the defendant does not reasonably believe that V consents.

2   This would previously have been charged as an indecent assault.

3   Section 78 Sexual Offences Act 2003 states that 'penetration, touching or any other activity is sexual if a reasonable person would consider that:

a)   whatever its circumstances or any person's purpose in relation to it, it is because of its nature sexual, or

b)   because of its nature it may be sexual and because of its circumstances or the purpose of any person in relation to it (or both) it is sexual.'

▶ 12.3 Sexual assault

1   This is a new offence under s 3 Sexual Offences Act 2003 which effectively replaces the old offence of indecent assault.

2   It is committed if:

  ● the defendant intentionally touches another person;

  ● the touching is sexual;

  ● the victim does not consent to the touching; and

  ● the defendant does not reasonably believe that V consents.

3   Sexual has the meaning given in s 78 of the Act (see 12.2).

4   Touching is defined in s 79(8) as including touching:

  a) with any part of the body;

  b) with anything else; or

  c) through anything.

  There no longer needs to be an assault.

5   Touching V's clothing can be sufficient to amount to touching for the purposes of s 3 (*H* (2005)).

6   'Touching amounting to penetration' also included making a deliberate overlap between the offences in ss 2(1) and 3(1) Sexual Offences Act 2003.

7   Under the definition of 'sexual' in s 78, certain 'touchings' are automatically 'sexual'. Whether others are depends on the circumstances and/or D's purpose.

8   'Sexual' touching is a wide concept. The following have been accepted as 'sexual' touchings:

  ● touching V's breasts;

  ● kissing V's face;

  ● sniffing V's hair whilst stroking her arm.

9   Section 3 is a basic intent offence. D will be guilty if the touching was deliberate even though he was voluntarily intoxicated (*Heard* (2007)).

▶ 12.4 Victims with a mental disorder

1   Sections 30–34 Sexual Offences Act 2003 create offences where V has a mental disorder which impedes their ability to consent to engaging in sexual activity.

2   For each offence it must be shown that V was unable to refuse because of, or for a reason related to, mental disorder *and* D either knew, or could reasonably be expected to know, that V had a mental disorder and was likely to be unable to refuse.

3 V is deemed unable to refuse if he lacks the capacity to choose whether to agree to the touching or other activity. This may be because he lacks sufficient understanding of the nature or reasonably foreseeable consequences of what is being done (C (2010)).

▶ 12.5 Rape and other offences against children under 13

1 Section 5(1) Sexual Offences Act 2003 creates the offence of rape of a child under 13. This is committed if:

● the defendant penetrates the victim's vagina, anus or mouth with his penis; and

● the victim is under 13.

2 Note that lack of consent is not an element of the *actus reus*.

3 The only *mens rea* element is that the defendant intended to penetrate the victim's vagina, anus or mouth. Liability is strict with regard to the victim's age. The defendant has no defence even if he honestly thought that the child was 13 or over (G (2006)).

4 Section 6(1) of the Act creates the offence of assault of a child under 13 by penetration. The *actus reus* elements are that the defendant must penetrate the child's vagina or anus with a body part or anything else and the penetration must be 'sexual'. Again the only *mens rea* element stated is that the defendant intended to penetrate the child's vagina or anus. Liability is strict with regard to the child's age.

5 Section 7(1) of the Act creates the offence of sexual assault of a child under 13. The *actus reus* elements are that the defendant touches the child, the touching is 'sexual' and the child is under 13. Consent is irrelevant. The only *mens rea* requirement is that the defendant intended to touch the child. Liability is strict with regard to both:

a) the 'sexual' nature of the touching; and

b) the child's age.

6 A woman can be guilty of a s 7(1) offence, as in *Davies* (2005) where D kissed two young girls on the lips.

▶ 12.6 Sexual activity with a child

1 Section 9(1) of the 2003 Act creates a new offence of 'sexual activity with a child'. This replaces the offence of unlawful sexual intercourse with a girl under 16 (s 6 Sexual Offences Act 1956).

2   It is committed if the defendant is aged 18 or over and touches a child under 16. The touching must be 'sexual' (s 78 SOA 2003).

3   The touching need not necessarily involve D's penis nor is it necessary that V's vagina, anus or mouth be penetrated. However, if the touching involves any of the following:

   ● penetration of anus or vagina with a part of the defendant's body or anything else;

   ● penetration of the mouth with the defendant's penis;

   ● penetration of the defendant's anus or vagina with a part of the child's body; or

   ● penetration of the defendant's mouth with the child's penis;

   then the offence is indictable (s 9(2)).

   Other touchings (not involving penetration) are triable either way (s 9(3) SOA 2003).

4   If the defendant is under 18 the charge is brought under s 13(1) and the maximum sentence is lower.

▶ 12.7 Offences involving family members

1   The Sexual Offences Act 2003 replaces the previous offence of incest with new offences of:

   ● sexual activity with a child family member (s 25);

   ● sex with an adult relative: penetration (s 64);

   ● sex with an adult relative: consenting to penetration (s 65).

2   An adopted child and a foster child are included in the definition of 'child family member'.

3   The relationships that can make D liable under these offences are:

   ● parent;

   ● grandparent;

   ● brother or sister;

   ● half-brother or half-sister;

   ● aunt or uncle;

   ● foster parents – for these it is enough if they have been the foster parent even though the fostering arrangement no longer exists.

▶ 12.8 Other crimes under the Sexual Offences Act 2003

1   The Sexual Offences Act 2003 creates a number of other offences. The main ones are given below.

2   Grooming a child by intentionally arranging or facilitating an offence under ss 9–13 of the Act (s 14).

3   Meeting a child, where the defendant is 18 or over and intentionally meets a child under 16 intending to commit a relevant offence (s 15). This section is aimed at paedophiles who contact children on the internet.

4   Abuse of a position of trust which involves sexual touching of a victim under the age of 18 where the defendant is in a position of trust (s 16).

5   Trespass with intent to commit a sexual offence (s 63). This can be committed by trespassing on any premises (not only in a building as previously in burglary with intent to rape under s 9(1)(a) of the Theft Act 1968).

▶ 12.9 Bigamy

1   This is an offence under s 57 of the Offences against the Person Act 1861.

2   The *actus reus* of the offence is going through a ceremony of marriage while already being married to another person.

3   The prosecution must prove that the first spouse is still alive at the time of the ceremony.

4   If the first marriage has been annulled or dissolved through divorce, then no offence has been committed.

5   There is no offence where the defendant believed on reasonable grounds that the first spouse was dead (*Tolson* (1889)); or that the marriage had been dissolved (*Gould* (1968)).

Key Cases Checklist

Rape

Williams (1923)
Consent induced by fraud as to the nature of the act is not a defence

Jheeta (2007)
S 74 Sexual Offences Act 2003 – consent must be a free choice

R (1991)
A man may be prosecuted for raping his wife

Sexual offences

Other Offences

H (2005)
(1) Touching can include touching clothing
(2) There is a two-stage approach in deciding whether a touching is sexual under s 78(b)

Heard (2007)
A drunken intent is still intent for touching

C (2010)
S 30 Sexual Offences Act 2003
D is liable if V's inability to refuse sexual activity is because of, or for a reason relating to, a mental disorder

Bigamy

Tolson (1889)
Where D has honest and reasonable belief in mistaken facts, then the defence of mistake is available

---

12.1.1

Williams [1923] 1 KB 340, (1923) 17 Cr App R 56

 CCA

Key Facts

A choir master had sexual intercourse with a 16-year-old girl after telling her that he was going to perform a procedure that would help her singing. She did not realise it was sexual intercourse. His conviction for rape was upheld.

Key Law

There is no genuine consent to sexual intercourse when the consent is obtained by fraud.

Key Link

Elbekkay [1995] Crim LR 163.

R [1991] 4 All ER 481, (1991) 94 Cr App R 216

Key Facts

See 1.2.2.

Key Law

The common law rule that a man could not rape his wife was abolished. If a wife does not consent to sexual intercourse with her husband then he can be guilty of rape.

12.1.1   *Jheeta* [2007] EWCA Crim 1699

Key Facts

V told D she wished to end their relationship. D sent V threatening texts. V, not knowing that D had sent the texts, sought protection from him. D then had sexual intercourse with her on a number of occasions. D was convicted of rape and his conviction upheld by the House of Lords.

Key Law

V's apparent consent was not a free choice. Therefore it was not consent under the definition of consent in s 74 Sexual Offences Act 2003.

12.3   ### *H* [2005] EWCA Crim 732   CA

Key Facts

D approached V in the street and said, 'Do you fancy a shag?' V ignored him, but D then grabbed the side of her tracksuit bottoms and attempted to pull her towards him. She broke free and ran off. D's conviction for sexual assault under s 3 Sexual Offences Act 2003 was upheld.

Key Law

1) Touching can include touching clothing.
2) Section 78(b) creates a two-stage approach in deciding whether a touching is 'sexual'.

12.3   ### *Heard* [2007] 1 Cr App R 37   CA

Key Facts

D, who was drunk, undid his trousers, pulled his penis out and rubbed it against the thigh of a policeman. D was convicted of intentional sexual assault under s 3 Sexual Offences Act 2003.

Key Law

To be an offence under s 3, the sexual touching must be intentional, that is, deliberate. Voluntary intoxication cannot be relied on as negating the necessary intention.

Key Problem

This decision seems to stretch the meaning of intention. It also raises the problem of whether the courts will try to extend this principle to other areas of law.

12.4   ### *C* [2010] UKHL 42   HL

Key Facts

V was a woman with a schizo-affected disorder, an emotionally unstable personality disorder and an IQ of less than 75. She attended a community mental health centre. C also attended the centre. When he saw her in the car park of the centre, he asked her to give him a 'blow job'; V submitted to oral sex. Psychiatric evidence was given that she would not have had the ability to consent to sexual contact at the time. C's conviction under s 30 Sexual Offences Act 2003 was upheld by the House of Lords.

Key Law

Under the 2003 Act, a person would be unable to refuse sexual touching if he or she lacked the capacity to choose whether to agree to the touching or not. This would be so whether he or she lacked sufficient understanding of the nature or reasonably foreseeable consequences of what was being done or for any other reason.

Key Problem

When dealing with ss 30–34 of the Sexual Offences Act 2003 (offences against persons with a mental disorder which impeded their choice), the courts have to tread a difficult line. They must provide mentally disordered individuals with protection from abuse, but must not restrict their right to engage in consensual sexual activity.

12.9   *Tolson* (1889) 23 QBD 168   CCR

Key Facts

D believed her husband had drowned when his boat sank at sea. In fact, her husband had jumped ship and was not on board when it sank. Believing that he was dead, D remarried. She was convicted of bigamy.

Key Law

The defence of mistake is available where D honestly and reasonably held a mistaken belief in facts which would, if true, have afforded a defence.

Key Judgment: Cave J

'At common law an honest and reasonable belief in the existence of circumstances which, if true, would make the act for which the prisoner is indicted an innocent act has always been held to be a good defence.'

13 Theft

Theft	
Actus reus	*Mens rea*
Appropriation (s 3) Any assumption of the rights of an owner Can be appropriation even though the owner has consented to it (**Gomez (1991), Hinks (2000)**) If property is come by without stealing it, then any later assumption of a right to it is an appropriation (s 3(1))	**Dishonesty (s 2)** Two-stage test: (**Ghosh (1982)**) 1. Was it dishonest by standards of reasonable and honest people? 2. Did the defendant realise it was dishonest? Can be dishonest even though willing to pay Not dishonest if believes: • has right in law • would have the other's consent • owner of property cannot be found
Property (s 4) Includes money and all other property, real and personal Land can only be stolen by a trustee etc. Fixtures can be severed from land and stolen Wild creatures cannot be stolen (s 4(4)) Knowledge cannot be stolen (**Oxford v Moss (1979)**)	**Intention of permanently depriving (s 6)** Intends to treat the thing as his own regardless of the other's rights Borrowing an item until all the goodness has gone out of it is equivalent to an outright taking (**Lloyd (1985)**) Dealing with another's property in such a manner that he knows he is risking its loss (**Fernandez (1996)**)
Belonging to another (s 5) Any person owning or having possession or control of the property Can steal own property where another has control of it and a right over it (**Turner (No 2) (1971)**)	

▶ 13.1 Theft

1   This is an offence under s 1 Theft Act 1968.

2   The Act states 'A person is guilty of theft if he dishonestly appropriates property belonging to another with the intention of permanently depriving that other of it . . .'

3   The various parts of the definition are explained in ss 2 to 6 of the Act.

4   For the *actus reus* of theft, three points have to be proved:

● there was an appropriation

● of property

● which belonged to another.

5   For the *mens rea* of theft, two points must be proved:

● dishonesty; and

● intention to permanently deprive.

13.1.1 Appropriation

1   'Any assumption by a person of the rights of an owner amounts to an appropriation' (s 3(1) Theft Act 1968).

2   This includes where the person has come by the property (innocently or not) without stealing it, any later assumption of a right to it by keeping or dealing with it as an owner (s 3(1) Theft Act 1968).

3   From this it can be seen that the meaning of 'appropriation' is very wide. It obviously includes physically taking property, but exercising any of the rights of an owner has been held to be an appropriation. Such rights include:

● using;

● selling;

● changing price labels on goods (*Anderton v Burnside* (1983));

● damaging or destroying (this means that there can be an overlap with criminal damage).

4   The main problem has been whether there can be theft when the owner of the property has consented to the appropriation. In *Lawrence* (1971) taking more than was due for a taxi fare from a person who did not understand English money was held to be an appropriation, even though the person held out his wallet and allowed the taxi driver to take the money.

5   In *Morris* (1983) it was stated that there had to be an element of adverse interference with or usurpation of any of the rights of the owner. The use of the word 'adverse' suggested that where the owner consented to the defendant's act, then there was no appropriation.

6   In *Gomez* (1991) goods were supplied and 'paid for' by cheques which were stolen. The shop consented to the goods being taken. It was held that this could amount to an appropriation of the goods. It did not matter that the owner had consented. The use of the word 'adverse' in Morris was held to be wrong. The decision in *Gomez* creates an overlap between obtaining property by deception (s 15 Theft Act 1968) and theft.

7   This was further confirmed in *Hinks* (2001) where there was no fraud in the obtaining of the consent to the transfer of the property. The word 'appropriation' was taken to be a neutral word with the meaning 'any assumption by a person of the rights of an owner' given it in s 3(1) Theft Act 1968. Whether it amounted to theft would depend on whether it was done dishonestly.

Appropriation of credit balances

The law on where and when appropriation takes places in banking cases is a little uncertain, but the principles appear to be:

●   presenting a cheque – appropriation is at place and point of presentation (*Ngan* (1998));

●   telex instructions – appropriation is possibly at the place of receipt of instructions or more probably at place and point of sending telex (conflicting cases of *Tomsett* (1985) and *Governor of Pentonville Prison, ex p Osman* (1989));

●   computer instructions – appropriation is at place and point of receipt of instructions since operation of the keyboard produced a 'virtually instantaneous' result (*Governor of Brixton Prison, ex p Levin* (1997)).

13.1.2 Property

1   Property is defined as including 'money and all other property, real and personal, including things in action and other intangible property' (s 4(1) Theft Act 1968).

2   Money is coins and banknotes.

3   Real property is land, but there are limitations as to when land can be stolen under s 4(2) Theft Act 1968. Land can only be stolen:

- where a trustee or personal representative or other authorised person disposes of it in 'breach of the confidence reposed in him'; or

- when a person not in control of the land severs something from the land; or

- where a tenant misappropriates fixtures attached to the land.

4   A person who picks mushrooms, flowers, fruit or foliage growing wild does not steal what he picks unless he does it for reward or sale (s 4(3) Theft Act 1968).

5   Personal property is any physical item which is not attached to land, e.g. car, boat, jewellery, furniture, paintings, etc.

6   Things in action and other intangible property includes patents, copyright, and a credit balance in a bank account.

7   The following property has been held NOT to be capable of being stolen:

- wild creatures unless they have been tamed or kept in captivity or in another person's possession (s 4(4) Theft Act 1968) (*Cresswell and Currie v DPP* (2006));

- electricity (but there is a separate offence of dishonestly abstracting electricity (s 13 Theft Act (1968));

- information or knowledge, such as the contents of an examination paper (*Oxford v Moss* (1979)); but note that the piece of paper on which the examination is written can be stolen;

- a corpse or part of a corpse unless they have been preserved for scientific analysis (*Kelly and Lindsay* (1998)).

13.1.3 Belonging to another

1   Property shall be regarded as belonging to any person having possession or control of it, or having in it any proprietary right (s 5(1) Theft Act 1968).

2   This means that property can be stolen from people other than the owner.

3   It is even possible for a person to steal his own property if it is in control of another as in *Turner (No 2)* (1971) where the owner of a car was held guilty of theft of it from a garage that had done repair work on it, when he took it without informing the garage and without paying for the repairs.

4   Where property is subject to a trust, the persons to whom it belongs include any person having a right to enforce the trust (s 5(2) Theft Act

1968). This allows a charge of theft to be brought against a trustee who dishonestly appropriates trust property of which he is in possession and control.

5 a) Where a person receives property from another and is under an obligation to deal with that property in a particular way, the property shall be regarded (as against him) as belonging to the other (s 5(3) Theft Act 1968).

   b) For example, in *Davidge v Bennett* (1984) the defendant was guilty of theft when she spent money given to her by the other flat-sharers to pay the gas bill.

6 a) Where a person gets property by another's mistake, and is under an obligation to make restoration, the property shall be regarded (as against him) as belonging to the person entitled to the restoration (s 5(4) Theft Act 1968).

   b) This covers situations where money is paid into the 'wrong' bank account by mistake of the bank or where an employee is paid more than they are entitled to by their employers. The person will only be guilty of theft if they are aware of the mistake, are being dishonest and intend to permanently deprive the other of it (*A-G's Reference (No 1 of 1983)* (1985)).

13.1.4 Dishonestly

1 The Theft Act 1968 does not give a definition of dishonestly.

2 However, s 2(1) gives three situations in which appropriation of property is not to be regarded as dishonest. These are:

   a) where the person believes that he has in law the right to deprive the other of it;

   b) where the person believes he would have the other's consent if the other knew of the appropriation and the circumstances of it; or

   c) where the person believes that the owner of the property cannot be discovered by taking reasonable steps.

3 A person's appropriation of property belonging to another may be dishonest even though he is willing to pay for the property (s 2(2) Theft Act 1968).

4 The main case on the meaning of dishonestly is *Ghosh* (1982). This gave a two-stage test to be applied:

- Was what was done dishonest according to the standards of reasonable and honest people? If so,

- Did the defendant realise that what he was doing was dishonest by those standards?

5   The two tests must be applied separately and in the above order (*Gohill and Walsh v DPP* (2007)).

13.1.5 Intention to permanently deprive

1   This is appropriating property and not intending to give it back. For example, taking money from an employer's till to use, but intending to replace those coins or notes with some to the same value. There is an intention to permanently deprive of the original coins and notes (*Velumyl* (1989)).

2   An intention to permanently deprive includes where the defendant does not mean the other permanently to lose the thing, but the defendant intends 'to treat the thing as his own to dispose of regardless of the other's rights' (s 6(1) Theft Act 1968).

3   Taking V's car and demanding money to return it was treating the car as their own 'to dispose of regardless of the other's rights' (*Raphael* (2008)).

4   Disposal includes 'dealing with' property (*DPP v Lavender* (1994)).

5   A borrowing or lending of the item may amount to an intention to permanently deprive if it is 'for a period and in circumstances making it equivalent to an outright taking or disposal' (s 6(1) Theft Act 1968).

6   In *Lloyd* (1985) it was held that this meant borrowing the property and keeping it until 'the goodness, the virtue, the practical value . . . has gone out of the article'. In this case a film had been taken for a short time and copied, then the original film replaced undamaged. Held, there was no intention to permanently deprive.

7   In *Fernandez* (1996) it was said that s 6 'may apply to a person in control of another's property, who dishonestly and for his own purpose, deals with that property in such a manner that he knows he is risking its loss'.

Key Cases Checklist

Appropriation

Lawrence (1971)
There can be an appropriation where V does not genuinely consent to the taking

Gomez (1993)
Appropriation is the assumption of any of the rights of an owner

Hinks (2000)
Appropriation is a neutral word. There is no differentiation between cases of consent induced by fraud and consent given in any other circumstance

Property

Oxford v Moss (1979)
Information or knowledge is not property and cannot be stolen

Kelly and Lindsay (1998)
A corpse is not property and cannot be stolen unless it has acquired 'different attributes'

Belonging to another

Turner (No 2) (1971)
Property is regarded as belonging to any person having possession or control

Davidge v Bennett (1984)
Property handed over by another to be retained and dealt with in a particular way belongs to that other

A-G's Ref (No 1 of 1983) (1984)
Where property is obtained by a mistake and there is a legal obligation to make restoration to another, then that property is regarded as belonging to that other

Theft

Mens rea

Ghosh (1982)
Two-part test for dishonesty:
(1) Is it dishonest by ordinary standard?
(2) If so, did D know it was dishonest by those standards?

DPP v Lavender (1994)
Disposal can include 'dealing with' property

Lloyd (1985)
Borrowing can be equivalent to an outright taking where the property is kept until the goodness or the value has gone

13.1.1 | *Lawrence* (1971) 57 Cr App R 64

Key Facts

An Italian student, who had just arrived in England, took a taxi ride. It should have cost 50p, but D took £7 when the student offered his wallet to D to take the correct money for the fare.

Key Law

There can be an appropriation where V does not genuinely consent to the taking.

13.1.1 | *Gomez* [1993] 1 All ER 1

Key Facts

Gomez was the assistant manager of a shop. He persuaded the manager to sell electrical goods worth over £17,000 to an accomplice and to accept payment by two cheques, telling him they were as good as cash. The cheques were stolen and had no value. Gomez was convicted of theft of the goods.

Key Law

An assumption of any of the rights of an owner is sufficient for an appropriation. There is no need for adverse interference with or usurpation of some right of the owner.

13.1.1 | *Hinks* [2000] 4 All ER 833, [2001] 1 Cr App R 252

Key Facts

D was a 38-year-old woman who had befriended a man of low IQ who was very naïve. He was, however, mentally capable of understanding the concept of ownership and of making a valid gift. D gradually withdrew about £60,000 from his building society account and this money was deposited in D's account. The man also gave D a television set. She was convicted of theft of the money and the TV set.

Key Law

'Appropriation' is a neutral word. There is no differentiation between cases of consent induced by fraud and consent given in any other circumstance. All situations are appropriation, even where there is a gift.

Key Problem

Although there may be appropriation, there are problems with the other elements of theft in gift situations. Lord Hobhouse dissented because of these problems. He pointed out that, as a gift transfers the ownership in the goods to the donee at the moment the owner completes the transfer, the property ceased to be 'property belonging to another' unless it could be brought within the situations identified in s 5 of the Theft Act 1968. Also, under s 6, the donee would not be acting regardless of the donor's rights as the donor has already surrendered his rights.

13.1.2   *Oxford v Moss* (1978) 68 Cr App R 183   `DC`

Key Facts

D was a university student who acquired a proof of an examination paper he was due to sit. It was accepted that D did not intend to permanently deprive the university of the piece of paper on which the questions were printed. But he was charged with theft of confidential information (i.e. the knowledge of the questions). He was found not guilty.

Key Law

Knowledge of the questions was not intangible property within the definition of s 4 of the Theft Act 1968.

13.1.2   *Kelly and Lindsay* [1998] 3 All ER 741   `CA`

Key Facts

K was a sculptor who asked L, a laboratory assistant at the Royal College of Surgeons, to take body parts from there.

K then made casts of the parts. Both were convicted of theft of the body parts.

Key Law

Body parts, which had acquired 'different attributes' by the application of skill such as dissection or preservation, were capable of being property within the definition in s 4 of the Theft Act 1968. Normally, a dead body is not property under that definition.

13.1.3 ### *Turner (No 2)* [1971] 2 All ER 441, (1971) 55 Cr App R 336 (CA)

Key Facts

D left his car at a garage for repairs. It was agreed that he would pay for the repairs when he collected the car after the repairs had been completed. When the repairs were almost finished the garage left the car parked on the roadway outside their premises. D used a spare key to take the car during the night, without paying for the repairs. D was convicted of theft of the car.

Key Law

For the purposes of the definition of theft, property is regarded as belonging to any person who has possession or control over it as well as anyone having a proprietary right. This means that the owner of an item can be charged with theft if V has possession or control of it.

13.1.3 ### *Davidge v Bennett* [1984] Crim LR 297 (DC)

Key Facts

D was given money by her flatmates to pay the gas bill but instead used it to buy Christmas presents. She was convicted of theft of the money.

Key Law

Under s 5(3) of the Theft Act 1968 property belongs to the other where it is received from the other under an obligation to retain or deal with it in a particular way.

Key Link

Klineberg and Marsden [1999] Crim LR 417.

13.1.3 *Attorney-General's Reference (No 1 of 1983)* [1984] 3 All ER 369, (1984) 79 Cr App R 288 CA

Key Facts

D's salary was paid into her bank account by transfer. On one occasion, her employers mistakenly overpaid her by £74.74. She did not return the money. She was acquitted by the jury of theft but the prosecution sought a ruling on a point of law.

Key Law

When D receives property by mistake and there is a legal obligation to make restoration, then that property belongs to the other for the purposes of the Theft Act 1968.

Key Link

Gilks [1972] 3 All ER 280.

13.1.4 *Ghosh* [1982] 2 All ER 689, (1982) 75 Cr App R 154 CA

Key Facts

D was a doctor acting as a locum consultant in a hospital. He claimed fees for an operation he had not carried out. D said that he was not dishonest as he was owed the same amount for consultation fees. The trial judge directed the jury that they must apply their own standards to decide if what he did was dishonest. He was convicted and the Court of Appeal upheld the conviction.

Key Law

There is a two-part test for dishonesty:

1) The jury must first of all decide whether according to the ordinary standards of reasonable and honest people what was done was dishonest; if it is then:

2) The jury must consider whether the defendant himself must have realised that what he was doing was, by those standards, dishonest.

Key Judgment: Lord Lane CJ

'It is dishonest for a defendant to act in a way which he knows ordinary people consider to be dishonest, even if he asserts or genuinely believes that he was morally justified in acting as he did. For example, Robin Hood or those ardent anti-vivisectionists who remove animals from vivisection laboratories are acting dishonestly, even though they may consider themselves to be morally justified in doing what they do, because they know that ordinary people would consider these actions to be dishonest.'

Key Link

DPP v Gohill and another [2007] EWHC 239 (Admin).

13.1.5   ***DPP v Lavender* [1994] Crim LR 297**   DC

Key Facts

D took doors from a council property which was being repaired and used them to replace damaged doors in his girlfriend's council flat. The doors were still in the possession of the council but had been transferred without permission from one council property to another. D was convicted of theft.

Key Law

Disposal can include 'dealing with' property. So if D intended to treat the doors as his own, regardless of the rights of the council, then s 6 of the Theft Act 1968 is satisfied.

13.1.5

Lloyd [1985] 2 All ER 661, (1986) 81 Cr App R 182

Key Facts

The projectionist at a local cinema gave D a film that was showing at the cinema so that D could make an illegal copy. D returned the film in time for the next screening at the cinema. His conviction for theft was quashed because, by returning the film in its original state, it was not possible to prove an intention to permanently deprive.

Key Law

Borrowing is not theft unless it is for a period and in circumstances making it equivalent to an outright taking or disposal. This can occur where property is kept until the goodness or the value has gone.

Key Judgment: Lord Lane CJ

'[Section 6(1)] is intended to make clear that a mere borrowing is never enough to constitute the necessary guilty mind unless the intention is to return the "thing" in such a changed state that it can truly be said that all its goodness or virtue has gone.'

14 Other offences under the Theft Acts

ROBBERY

- An offence under s 8 of the Theft Act 1968.
- D must steal and use force or put V in fear of force *Robinson* (1977)
- The force must be immediately before or at the time of the theft *Hale* (1978)
- The force can be minimal *Clouden* (1987)
- D must have the intention for theft and the intention to use force or be subjectively reckless as to the use of force

ROBBERY AND BURGLARY

BURGLARY

- This is an offence under s 9 of the Theft Act 1968
- For a s 9(1)(a) offence, D must enter a building or part thereof as a trespasser with the intention to:
  - steal; or
  - inflict grievous bodily harm; or
  - do unlawful damage to the building or anything in it
- For a s 9(1)(b) offence, D, having entered a building or part thereof as a trespasser, must:
  - steal or attempt to do so; or
  - inflict or attempt to inflict grievous bodily harm
- Entry has to be effective *Brown* (1985)
- A building must be a structure with a degree of permanence: building also includes an inhabited vehicle or vessel (s 9(4))
- Where a person has permission to enter, they are not a trespasser *Collins* (1973)
- But if they go beyond their permission they can be a trespasser *Smith and Jones* (1976)

▶ 14.1 Robbery

1   This is an offence under s 8 Theft Act 1968.

2   The Act states: 'A person is guilty of robbery if he steals, and immediately before or at the time of doing so, and in order to do so, he uses force on any person or puts or seeks to put any person in fear of being then and there subjected to force.'

14.1.1 *Actus reus* of robbery

1   This is theft together with the use of force or putting someone in fear of force being used on them.

2   Where the force and the theft are quite separate from each other, this is not robbery (*Robinson* (1977)).

3   However, the act of appropriation can be a continuing one, so that any force used in order to steal while it is continuing would make this robbery (*Hale* (1978), where one accomplice tied up the householder while the other stole jewellery from rooms upstairs).

4   Only minimal force is needed (*Dawson* (1976), where the victim was 'nudged' or 'jostled' and his wallet taken as he stumbled, also *B and R v DPP* (2007)).

5   Wrenching property from the victim is sufficient force (*Clouden* (1987)).

14.1.2 *Mens rea* of robbery

1   There must be the *mens rea* for theft (dishonesty and an intention to permanently deprive (*Mitchell* (2008)).

2   There must also be intention to use force or subjective recklessness as to the use of force.

▶ 14.2 Burglary

Burglary	
Section 9(1)(a)	**Section 9(1)(b)**
Enters a building or part of a building as a trespasser	Having entered a building or part of a building as a trespasser
with intent to: • steal • inflict grievous bodily harm • do unlawful damage	• steals or attempts to steal; or • inflicts or attempts to inflict grievous bodily harm

1   Burglary is an offence under s 9 Theft Act 1968.

2   There are two different ways in which burglary can be committed. These are:

   a)   under s 9(1)(a) he enters any building or part of a building as a trespasser and with intent to:

- steal anything in the building;

- inflict grievous bodily harm to any person in the building;

- do unlawful damage to the building or anything in it;

   b)   under s 9(1)(b) having entered any building or part of a building as a trespasser he:

- steals or attempts to steal anything in the building; or

- inflicts or attempts to inflict grievous bodily harm on any person in the building.

3   These two separate offences of burglary have three elements in common:

- entry;

- of a building or part of a building; or

- as a trespasser.

4   The distinguishing features between the subsections are:

- the intention at the time of entry; for s 9(1)(a) the defendant must intend to do one of the three listed offences (known as ulterior offences) at the time of entering; and

- that for s 9(1)(b) the defendant must actually commit or attempt to commit one of the two listed offences; for s 9(1)(a) there is no need for the ulterior offence even to be attempted.

14.2.1 Entry

1   In *Collins* (1973) it was held that the entry had to be 'substantial and effective'.

2   However, in *Brown* (1985) it was held that all that was required was that the entry be effective. Brown was standing outside the building leaning in through a window, rummaging for goods.

3   Further, in *Ryan* (1996) it was held that the defendant had entered when he was part-way through a window, even though he was stuck in the window.

14.2.2 Building or part of a building

1   A building includes an inhabited vehicle or vessel, even when there is no-one present in the vehicle or vessel (s 9(4) Theft Act 1968).

2   No other definition is provided by the Theft Act 1968, but the courts have held that there must be a degree of permanence for a structure to be a building.

3   There are conflicting cases on whether a large storage container is a building:

   ● In *B and S v Leathley* (1979) a 25-foot-long freezer container that had been in a yard for two years and was connected to the electricity supply was held to be a building.

   ● But in *Norfolk Constabulary v Seekings and Gould* (1986) a lorry trailer with wheels was held not to be a building, even though it was connected to the electricity supply.

4   Part of a building refers to situations in which the defendant may have permission to be in one part of the building (and therefore is not a trespasser in that part) but does not have permission to be in another part. Examples are storerooms in shops where shoppers would not have permission to enter or behind the counter of a shop (*Walkington* (1979)).

14.2.3 Trespasser

1   Where a person has permission to enter they are not a trespasser (*Collins* (1973)).

2   However, where the defendant goes beyond the permission given, he may be considered a trespasser (*Smith and Jones* (1976)).

3   The defendant must know, or be subjectively reckless as to, whether he is trespassing.

14.2.4 *Mens rea* for burglary

1   As stated above, the defendant must know, or be subjectively reckless as to, whether he is trespassing.

2   In addition, for s 9(1)(a) the defendant must have the intention to commit one of the ulterior offences at the time of entering the building.

3   While for s 9(1)(b), the defendant must have the *mens rea* for theft or grievous bodily harm when committing the *actus reus* of these offences.

▶ 14.3 Aggravated burglary

1   This is an offence under s 10(1) Theft Act 1968.

2   The Act states that the offence is committed where the defendant commits any burglary and at the time has with him any firearm or imitation firearm, any weapon of offence, or any explosive.

● Firearm includes an air gun or air pistol (s 10(1)(a)).

● An imitation firearm means anything that has the appearance of being a firearm, whether capable of being fired or not (s 10(1)(a)).

● Weapon of offence means any article made or adapted for use for causing injury, or intended by the person having it with him for such use (s 10(1)(b)).

● Explosive means any article manufactured for the purpose of producing a practical effect by explosion, or intended by the person having it with him for that purpose (s 10(1)(c)).

3   By putting the four 'weapons' into a different order, it is easy to remember that aggravated burglary is when the burglar takes his WIFE with him!

● Weapon of offence

● Imitation firearm

● Firearm

● Explosive.

14.3.1 'At the time has with him'

1   The defendant must have one of the four items with him at the time of the burglary. Thus for a s 9(1)(a) burglary he must have it at the moment of entry, but for a s 9(1)(b) burglary he must have it at the point when he commits or attempts to commit the ulterior offence.

2   Where this is so, the defendant is guilty of aggravated burglary, even though he does not use the item.

3 The defendant must know he has the item 'with him'.

4 Where one of two defendants who commit burglary jointly has such an item, then if the other knows of it, he will also be guilty of aggravated burglary.

5 However, if an accomplice with such an item remains outside the building, the person entering will not have committed aggravated burglary (*Klass* (1998)).

TAKING A CONVEYANCE WITHOUT CONSENT
- This is an offence under s 12 of the Theft Act 1968
- 'Conveyance' covers 'any conveyance constructed or adapted for the carriage of a person or persons whether by land, water or air'
- The offence can be committed by:
  - taking;
  - driving; or
  - allowing oneself to be carried
- Taking is where a person assumes possession or control of the conveyance and intention causes it to move
- If D believes he has lawful authority then he is not guilty
- Where D drives or allows himself to be carried he is guilty if he knew or believed that the conveyance had been taken without lawful authority

HANDLING STOLEN GOODS
- This is an offence under s 22 of the Theft Act 1968
- It can be committed by receiving stolen goods or undertaking, assisting or arranging their:
  - retention
  - removal
  - disposal
- D must know or believe the goods are stolen
- The handling must be done dishonestly (*Ghosh test*)

TAKING A CONVEYANCE WITHOUT CONSENT, HANDLING STOLEN GOODS, GOING EQUIPPED FOR STEALING AND BLACKMAIL

GOING EQUIPPED FOR STEALING
- This is an offence under s 25 of the Theft Act 1968
- D must have with him 'any article for use in the course of or in connection with any burglary, theft or cheat'
- D must not be in his place of abode
- D must intend to use it in the course of or in connection with any burglary, theft or cheat
- The use must be for future offences

BLACKMAIL
- This is an offence under s 25 of the Theft Act 1968
- D must make a demand
- The demand must be made with menaces
- Menaces are threats that would influence an ordinary person or actually intimidated V
- The demand must be unwarranted
- The demand must be made with a view to gain for oneself or cause a loss to another

▶ ## 14.4 Taking a conveyance without consent

1   This is an offence under s 12(1) Theft Act 1968.

2   The Act states that 'a person shall be guilty of an offence if, without the consent of the owner or other lawful authority, he takes any conveyance for his own or another's use or, knowing that any conveyance has been taken without such authority, drives it or allows himself to be carried in or on it'.

3   The rationale for the offence is to cover temporary use of a conveyance, since it is often difficult to prove that there was the intention to permanently deprive, which is necessary for proving theft.

14.4.1 Meaning of conveyance

1   A conveyance is 'any conveyance constructed or adapted for the carriage of a person or persons whether by land, water or air' (s 12(7)(a) Theft Act 1968).

2   However, pedal cycles are not included under a s 12(1) offence. There is a separate offence under s 12(5) Theft Act 1968 of taking a pedal cycle without authority.

14.4.2 *Actus reus* of taking a conveyance without consent

1   There are three ways in which the offence can be committed:
   - taking;
   - driving;
   - allowing oneself to be carried.

2   Taking is when a person assumes possession or control of the conveyance and intentionally causes it to move or be moved (*Bogacki* (1973)).

3   There can also be a taking where the defendant fails to return a conveyance or goes beyond the authority given to him to take it. For example, using an employer's lorry to drive friends to a pub (*McKnight v Davies* (1974)).

4   The taking, driving or allowing oneself to be carried must be without the consent of the owner (or other lawful authority). Consent obtained by fraud or force is not valid consent.

14.4.3 *Mens rea* of taking a conveyance without consent

1   If the defendant believes that he has lawful authority or that he would have the owner's consent if the owner knew of his actions, then he is not guilty (s 12(6) Theft Act 1968).

2   Where the defendant is charged with driving or allowing himself to be carried, then he must know that the conveyance has been taken without consent or authority. 'Know' probably includes wilful blindness as to this fact.

14.5 Aggravated vehicle-taking

1   This is an offence under s 12A Theft Act 1968. This section was added to the Theft Act by the Aggravated Vehicle-taking Act 1992.

2   The 1992 Act makes the taking of a vehicle a more serious offence than s 12 in the following circumstances:

- where the vehicle is driven dangerously (s 12A(2)(a) Theft Act 1968); the test for dangerous is that 'it would be obvious to a competent and careful driver that driving in that way would be dangerous';

- that, owing to the driving of the vehicle, an accident occurred by which injury was caused to any person (s 12A(2)(b) Theft Act 1968);

- that, owing to the driving of the vehicle, an accident occurred by which damage was caused to any property, other than the vehicle (s 12A(2)(c) Theft Act 1968);

- that damage was caused to the vehicle (s 12A(2)(d) Theft Act 1968).

For these last three situations it is not necessary to prove any fault in the driving of the defendant (*Marsh* (1997)).

14.6 Handling stolen goods

1   This is an offence under s 22 Theft Act 1968.

2   A person handles stolen goods if (otherwise than in the course of stealing), knowing or believing them to be stolen goods, he dishonestly receives the goods, or dishonestly undertakes or assists in their retention, removal, disposal or realisation by or for the benefit of another person or he arranges to do so.

3   The goods must be stolen for the full offence of handling to be committed (*A-G's Ref (No 1 of 1974)* (1974), but where the defendant believes the goods are stolen, there can be an attempt to handle them (*Shivpuri* (1986)).

4   Note that the thief cannot be charged with handling for anything done in the course of the theft. The correct charge against him is theft.

14.6.1 *Actus reus* of handling

1   The section creates a number of ways in which the *actus reus* may be committed:

- receiving stolen goods (taking possession or control);
- undertaking or assisting or arranging their:
  - retention (keeping possession of, not losing, continuing to have *Pitchley* (1972), *Kanwar* (1982))
  - removal (transporting or carrying)
  - disposal (destroying, giving them away, melting down silver, etc.);
- undertaking their realisation (selling them).

Note the last four can be by another person or by the defendant for another's benefit.

2   These different ways appear to cover all possible ways of unlawfully dealing with stolen goods.

14.6.2 *Mens rea* of handling

1   The defendant must know or believe the goods to be stolen.

2   'Know' is where the handler has first-hand information about the fact the goods are stolen, e.g. he has been told by the thief that this is so.

3   'Believe' is the state of mind where the defendant says to himself 'I cannot say I know for certain that these goods are stolen, but there can be no other reasonable conclusion in the light of all the circumstances' (*Hall* (1985)).

4   Mere suspicion that the goods might be stolen is not enough (*Grainge* (1974)).

5   The handling must be done dishonestly. The test for dishonest is the same as for theft (see 13.1.4).

▶ 14.7 Going equipped for stealing

1   This is an offence under s 25 Theft Act 1968.

2   'A person shall be guilty of an offence if, when not at his place of abode, he has with him any article for use in the course of or in connection with any burglary, theft or cheat' (s 25(1) Theft Act 1968).

14.7.1 *Actus reus* of going equipped

1   It must be proved that:

- D has with him any article for use in the course of or in connection with any burglary, theft or cheat
- D must not be at his place of abode.

2   Proof that a person had with him any article made or adapted for use in committing a burglary, theft or cheat shall be evidence that he had it with him for such use (s 25(3) Theft Act 1968).

3   Where the item has an innocent use, then it is for the prosecution to prove that the defendant intended to use it for a burglary, theft or cheat.

4   In *Doukas* (1978) a wine waiter was found guilty of this offence when he sold his own wine instead of his employer's wine to customers.

14.7.2 *Mens rea* of going equipped

1   D must know he had the article with him.

2   D must intend to use it in the course of or in connection with any burglary, theft or cheat.

3   That intention must be to commit future crimes. Use for past crimes is not sufficient (*Ellames* (1974)).

▶ 14.8 Making off without payment

1   This is an offence under s 3 Theft Act 1978. (Note this is a different Act from the Theft Act 1968.)

2   This makes it an offence when a person who, knowing that payment on the spot for any goods supplied or service done is required or expected from him, dishonestly makes off without having paid as required or expected and with intent to avoid payment of the amount due (s 3(1) Theft Act 1978).

3   This offence was created as there were situations in which it was difficult to prove theft or obtaining by deception.

14.8.1 *Actus reus* of making off without payment

1   There must be either goods supplied or a service done which is lawful. If the supply of goods is unlawful (e.g. cigarettes to someone under 16) or the service is not legally enforceable (e.g. prostitution), then no offence has been committed (s 3(3) Theft Act 1978).

2   Payment on the spot must be required. If there is an agreement to defer payment, then the offence cannot be committed (*Vincent* (2001)).

3   D must make off. This is a question of fact (*McDavitt* (1981)).

14.8.2 *Mens rea* of making off without payment

1   The *mens rea* of the offence involves:
   - dishonesty (this is the same test as for theft; see 13.1.4);
   - knowledge that payment on the spot is required; and
   - an intention to avoid payment permanently (*Allen* (1985)).

▶ 14.9 Blackmail

1   This is an offence under s 21 Theft Act 1968.

2   A person is guilty of blackmail if, with a view to gain for himself or another or with intent to cause loss to another, he makes any unwarranted demand with menaces.

14.9.1 *Actus reus* of blackmail

1   There must be a demand. If a demand is sent through the post then the demand is made when the letter is posted (*Treacy* (1971)).

2   The demand must be made with menaces. Menaces have been held to be a serious threat. This threat can be of violence or any action detrimental or unpleasant to the victim (*Thorne v Motor Trade Association* (1937)).

3   The threat must either be:

- 'of such a nature and extent that the mind of an ordinary person of normal stability and courage might be influenced or made apprehensive by it' (*Clear* (1968)); in which case it is not necessary to prove that the victim was actually intimidated; or

- one which actually intimidated the victim; but if that threat was such as would not affect a normal person, the prosecution must prove that the defendant was aware of the likely effect on the victim (*Garwood* (1987)).

14.9.2 *Mens rea* of blackmail

1   The demand must be unwarranted. A demand with menaces is unwarranted unless the person making it does so in the belief:

- that he has reasonable grounds for making the demand; and

- that the use of menaces is a proper means of reinforcing the demand (s 21(1) Theft Act 1968).

2   The defendant must make the demand with a view to gain for himself. This need not be a monetary gain. In *Bevans* (1987) a demand for a morphine injection was held to be both a gain for the defendant and a loss to the doctor from whom it was demanded.

Key Cases Checklist

Robbery

Robinson (1977)
All the elements of theft must be present for the offence of robbery to be committed

Clouden (1987)
Only minimal force is needed

Hale (1978)
Theft is a continuing act for the purposes of robbery. Force used to escape is still at the time of the theft and in order to steal

Robbery and burglary

Burglary

Collins (1972)
(1) D must know he is a trespasser or be reckless as to that fact
(2) The entry must be 'effective and substantial'

Brown (1985)
The entry must be 'effective': there is no need for it to be substantial

Ryan (1996)
The entry need not be effective as to the ulterior offence

Walkington (1979)
Any clearly defined area of a building can be 'part of a building'

Smith and Jones (1976)
If D goes beyond the permission given for entry, he may become a trespasser

14.1.1   *Robinson* [1977] Crim LR 173

Key Facts

D was owed £7 by V's wife. D threatened V. During a struggle V dropped a £5 note and D took it. D's conviction for robbery was quashed because the trial judge had wrongly directed the jury that D had honestly to believe he was entitled to get the money in that way.

Key Law

1) There must be a completed theft for there to be robbery.

2) If D had a genuine belief that he had a right in law to the money, then his actions are not dishonest under s 2(1)(a) Theft Act 1968.

14.1.1   *Hale* (1978) 68 Cr App R 415

Key Facts

Two defendants forced their way into V's house. D1 put his hand over V's mouth to stop her screaming while D2 went upstairs and took a jewellery box. Before they left the house they tied up V and gagged her. Their convictions for burglary were upheld.

Key Law

For the purposes of robbery, theft is a continuous act. Appropriation does not cease when D picks up an item. It is open to the jury to decide if the theft is still ongoing at the point when force is used.

Key Problem

The tying up of V was considered as force 'at the time' of the theft. Although this does seem a sensible interpretation, it is not consistent with the court's decision in *Gomez* (1993) (see 14.1). In *Gomez*, it was held that the point of appropriation is when D first does an act assuming the right of an owner. At this point the theft is completed.

Key Link

Lockley [1995] Crim LR 656.

14.1.1   *Clouden* [1987] Crim LR 56

Key Facts

D wrenched a shopping basket from V's hand. He was convicted of robbery. The Court of Appeal upheld his conviction as the trial judge had been right to leave the question of whether D had used force on a person to the jury.

Key Law

'Force' is an ordinary word and it is for the jury to decide if force has been used.

Key Comment

The Criminal Law Revision Committee, who put forward the draft Bill for the Theft Act 1978, stated that they would 'not regard mere snatching of property, such as a handbag, from an unresisting owner as using force for the purpose of the definition [of robbery]'. The courts have ignored this in their decisions on force.

Key Link

Dawson and James (1976) 64 Cr App R 170.

14.2.1   *Collins* [1972] 2 All ER 1105, (1972) 56 Cr App R 554

Key Facts

D climbed a ladder to an open window. He saw a naked girl asleep in bed. He then went down the ladder, took off all his clothes except for his socks and climbed back. As he was on the windowsill outside the room, she woke up, thought he was her boyfriend and helped him into the room where they had sex. D's conviction for burglary was quashed as it could not be proved that he was a trespasser at the time of entry.

Key Law

1) There must be an effective and substantial entry as a trespasser for D to be liable for burglary.

2) To be a trespasser D must enter either knowing he is a trespasser, or being reckless as to whether or not he has consent to enter the premises.

14.2.1

Brown [1985] Crim LR 212

Key Facts

D was leaning in through a shop window, rummaging through goods. His feet and lower part of his body were outside the shop. He was convicted of burglary.

Key Law

The word 'substantial' used by the Court of Appeal in *Collins* (1973) does not materially assist the definition of entry. It is sufficient if the entry is effective.

14.2.1

Ryan [1996] Crim LR 320

Key Facts

D was trapped when trying to get through a window into a house. His head and right arm were inside the house but the rest of his body was outside. The fire brigade had to be called to release him. The Court of Appeal upheld his conviction for burglary.

Key Law

There need only be proof of entry. The entry does not have to be effective to commit the ulterior offence.

Key Problem

There is no definition of 'entry' in the Theft Act 1968. The wording of 'effective and substantial entry' was first used in *Collins*. However, *Brown* and *Ryan* have moved away from that test put forward in *Collins*.

Walkington [1979] 2 All ER 716, (1979) 63 Cr App R 427

CA

Key Facts

D went into a counter area in a shop and opened a till. D's conviction for burglary under s 9(1)(a) was upheld as he had entered part of a building as a trespasser.

Key Law

D can be a trespasser in part of a building, even though he has permission to be in the rest of the building.

Smith and Jones [1976] 3 All ER 54, (1976) 63 Cr App Rep 47

CA

Key Facts

Smith and his friend went to Smith's father's house and took two television sets without the father's knowledge or permission. The father said his son had a general permission to enter. Their convictions for burglary were upheld as they had gone beyond the permission given them to enter.

Key Law

Entering a building with intent to steal removes any permission that normally exists for D to enter that building. D becomes a trespasser if he knowingly enters in excess of the permission that has been given to him to enter, or when he is reckless whether he is entering in excess of the permission.

Taking a conveyance without consent

Bogacki (1973)
There must be some movement of the vehicle for a taking

McKnight v Davies (1974)
If D goes beyond the permission for use, he can be guilty of this offence

Marsh (1997)
For aggravated vehicle-taking there is no need for D to be at fault in respect of any injury or damage done

Taking a conveyance without consent and handling

Handling

A-G's Ref (No 1 of 1974) (1974)
The goods must be stolen goods: if they have been reduced into police possession they may no longer be stolen

Pitchley (1972)
Retention means 'keep possession of, not lose, continue to have'

Kanwar (1982)
Assisting in retention can include representations such as lying about the origin of goods

14.4.2   *Bogacki* [1973] 2 All ER 864, (1973) 57 Cr App R 593   CA

Key Facts

Three defendants had got onto a bus in a depot and tried, unsuccessfully, to start it. The Court of Appeal quashed their conviction for taking without consent as there was no 'taking'.

Key Law

There must be unauthorised taking possession or control of the vehicle by D, adverse to the rights of the true owner, coupled with some movement of the vehicle. The movement need only be very small.

14.4.2   *McKnight v Davies* [1974] RTR 4, [1974] Crim LR 62   DC

Key Facts

D was a lorry driver who had not returned a lorry at the end of his working day but had used it for his own purposes. He then returned it in the early hours of the following morning. His conviction for an offence under s 12 of the Theft Act 1968 was upheld.

Key Law

Where the owner has given consent for D to use the conveyance for a particular purpose, D can be guilty of taking without consent if he goes beyond the permission given.

14.5   *Marsh* [1997] 1 Cr App R 67   CA

Key Facts

D was driving when a pedestrian ran out in front of the car D had taken and was slightly injured. D was not to blame for the incident. D's conviction for aggravated vehicle-taking was upheld.

Key Law

For aggravated vehicle-taking, the prosecution needs to prove only that D committed the basic offence of taking and that one of the prohibited events then occurred. There is no need to prove fault in respect of the prohibited happenings, i.e. injury owing to the driving, damage to other property owing to the driving or damage to the vehicle.

14.6 *Attorney-General's Reference (No 1 of 1974)* [1974] 2 All ER 899   CA

Key Facts

A police officer suspected that goods in the back of a parked car were stolen, so he removed the rotor arm of the car to prevent it being driven away and kept watch. When D returned to the car the officer arrested him because he could not give a satisfactory explanation. D was acquitted of handling stolen goods. The point at issue was whether the goods were still stolen goods or whether they had been taken into police possession.

Key Law

The goods must be stolen goods at the time of the handling. If the goods have been restored to their original owner or taken into police possession, they are no longer stolen goods. This will depend on the specific facts of each case.

14.6.1 *Pitchley* (1972) 57 Cr App R 30   CA

Key Facts

D was given £150 in cash by his son who asked him to take care of it for him. D put the money into his Post Office savings account. At the time of receiving the money, D was not aware that it was stolen. Two days later, D found out that it was stolen. He left the money in the account. He was convicted of handling. By leaving the money in the account he had retained it on behalf of another person.

Key Law

'Retention' in s 24 of the Theft Act 1968 means 'keep possession of, not lose, continue to have'.

14.6.1   *Kanwar* [1982] 2 All ER 528, (1982) 75 Cr App R 87

CA

Key Facts

D's husband had used stolen goods to furnish their home. D was aware that the items were stolen. When the police called and made inquiries about them, she gave false answers about where the items had come from.

Key Law

Verbal representations, whether oral or in writing, for the purpose of concealing the identity of stolen goods may, if made dishonestly and for the benefit of another, amount to handling stolen goods by assisting in their retention.

Going equipped

Doukas (1978)
The items must be for use in an offence

Ellames (1974)
'For use' applies only to future offences: there is no offence if D has completed the offence

Making off without payment

Vincent (2001)
It has to be proved that payment 'on the spot' was required or expected

Allen (1985)
There must be an intention to evade payment altogether

McDavitt (1981)
D must have 'made off' from the spot

Going equipped, blackmail and making off without payment

Blackmail

Treacy (1971)
The offence is committed when the demand is made

Clear (1968)
It is not necessary to prove that V was actually intimidated by the threats

Garwood (1987)
A threat which would not affect a normal person can be menaces if D was aware of the likely effect it would have on the specific victim

Bevans (1988)
Any property can be the subject of the 'gain' or 'loss'

14.7.1

Doukas [1978] 1 All ER 1061, (1978) 66 Cr App R 228

 CA

Key Facts

D was a wine waiter in a hotel. He took bottles of wine into the hotel intending to sell them to people dining at the hotel so that he could pocket the money. The main point on appeal was whether they were for use in a s 15 offence of obtaining money by deception. His conviction was upheld.

Key Law

There was a potential offence of obtaining money by deception as diners in the hotel would refuse to have the wine if they knew that it was brought in by D for his own profit. They were being deceived.

14.7.2

Ellames [1974] 3 All ER 130

 CA

Key Facts

D was stopped by the police and found to have with him masks, guns and gloves which had been used in a robbery. D was trying to get rid of these. His conviction was quashed as he did not have the article 'for use' as the robbery was in the past.

Key Law

The 'for use' applies only to future offences. Where D has already committed the offence and does not intend to commit further offences with the items, there is no offence of going equipped.

14.8.1

Vincent [2001] EWCA Crim 295, [2001] Cr App R 150

 CA

Key Facts

D had stayed at two hotels and not paid his bills. He said that he had arranged with the proprietors of each to pay when he could, so payment on the spot was not required or expected. His conviction was quashed.

Key Law

It has to be proved that payment 'on the spot' was required or expected. If there is an agreement to defer payment then payment 'on the spot' is not required and there is no offence under s 3.

14.8.1   *McDavitt* [1981] 1 Crim LR 843   CA

Key Facts

D had an argument with the manager of a restaurant and refused to pay his bill for a meal. He got up and started to walk out but was advised not to leave as the police had been called. He then went into the toilet and stayed there until the police came. The judge directed the jury to acquit D at the end of the prosecution case as he had not 'made off'.

Key Law

It must be proved that D left the spot. In this case the restaurant was identified as the 'spot' and D had not left the premises. Walking towards the door was not enough to constitute the full offence, although this could constitute an attempt to make off without payment.

14.8.2   *Allen* [1985] 2 All ER 64, (1985) 81 Cr App R 200   HL

Key Facts

D owed £1,286 for his stay at a hotel. He left without paying, but his defence was that he genuinely intended to pay in the near future as he was expecting to receive sufficient money to cover the bill. His conviction was quashed.

Key Law

The phrase 'and with intent to avoid payment of the amount due' means there must be an intention to evade payment altogether. Merely intending to delay or defer payment is not sufficient for the *mens rea* of s 3.

14.9.1

Treacy [1971] 1 All ER 110, (1971) 55 Cr App R 113

HL

Key Facts

D posted a letter containing a demand with menaces in England to someone in Germany.

Key Law

Making the demand is the *actus reus* of the offence. The demand does not have to be received by the victim. When a demand is sent through the post the demand is considered made at the point the letter is posted.

14.9.1

Clear [1968] 1 All ER 74, (1968) 52 Cr App R 58

CA

Key Facts

D was an employee of a company who were making a civil claim against their insurers over a stolen lorry. D was required to give evidence. He demanded money from the managing director on the threat that he would give evidence that would be unfavourable to the company.

Key Law

The menace must be of such a nature and extent that the mind of an ordinary person of ordinary courage and firmness might be influenced or made apprehensive by it so as to unwillingly accede to the demand. It is not necessary to prove that the intended victim of the demand was himself alarmed by it.

14.9.1

Garwood [1987] 1 All ER 1032, (1987) 85 Cr App R 85

CA

Key Facts

D accused V of 'doing over D's house and demanded money and jewellery "to make it quits". V was unusually timid and acceded to the demand.

Key Law

A threat which would not affect a normal person can be menacing if D was aware of the likely effect it would have on the specific victim.

Key Link

Harry [1974] Crim LR 32.

14.9.2   *Bevans* [1988] Crim LR 236, (1987) 87 Cr App R 64   CA

Key Facts

D suffered from osteoarthritis, which caused him severe pain. He called a doctor to his house and then pointed a gun at the doctor and demanded a morphine injection for pain relief. His conviction for blackmail was upheld.

Key Law

The drug involved in the injection was property under s 34 of the Theft Act 1968 which specifies that the gain or loss must be in money or other property.

15 Fraud Act 2006

Fraud by false representation (s 2)

- Dishonestly make a false representation
- Intending to make a gain or cause a loss

A representation is false if it is untrue or misleading

Fraud by failing to disclose information (s 3)

- D is under a legal duty to disclose information
- Fails to disclose that information
- Intending to make a gain or cause a loss

FRAUD ACT 2006

Fraud by abuse of position (s 4)

- D occupies a position in which he is expected to safeguard V's financial interests
- D dishonestly abuses that position
- Intending to make a gain or cause a loss

Obtaining services dishonestly (s 11)

- Obtains services by a dishonest act
- The services are available on the basis that payment will be made for them
- Payment is not made or not made in full
- D knows that the services are or might be available only on the basis of payment
- D intends not to make payment or not to make it in full

▶ 15.1 Fraud Act 2006

1 The Fraud Act 2006 abolished the old offences of deception and created new offences in their place.

2 The Act repealed ss 15, 15A, 15B, 16 and 20(2) of the Theft Act 1968 and also ss 1 and 2 of the Theft Act 1978.

3 Four main offences are created in their place. These are:

● fraud by false representation

● fraud by failure to disclose information

● fraud by abuse of position

● obtaining services dishonestly.

▶ 15.2 Fraud by false representation

1 This is an offence under s 2 Fraud Act 2006. It is committed if D:

● dishonestly makes a false representation; and

● intends, by making the representation:

    i) to make a gain for himself or another, or

    ii) to cause a loss to another or to expose another to the risk of loss.

2 The *actus reus* is the making of the false representation. The full offence is then committed even if D does not make a gain or cause a loss.

15.2.1 False representation

1 A representation is false if:

● it is untrue or misleading, and

● the person making it knows that it is, or might be, untrue or misleading.

2 There is no further definition of 'misleading' in the Act but a government paper stated that it means 'less than wholly true and capable of interpretation to the detriment of the victim'.

3 A representation means any representation as to fact or law, including making a representation as to the state of mind of the person making the representation or any other person (s 2(3)).

4 A representation may be express or implied (s 2(4)). There is no limit on the way in which it can be made, e.g. it can be spoken, written, posted to a website or by conduct.

5   Implied representations include wearing a uniform (*Barnard* (1837)), using a credit card (*Lambie* (1981)) and writing a cheque (*Gilmartin* (1983)).

6   The Act covers representations submitted to an automated system of communication (e.g. to a website) (s 2(5)).

7   There is no requirement that V is deceived by the representation.

15.2.2 Gain or loss

1   The gain or loss must be of property.

2   'Property' is defined as 'any property whether real or personal including things in action and other intangible property' (s 5).

3   'Gain' includes a gain by keeping what one has as well as a gain by getting what one does not have. 'Loss' includes a loss by not getting what one might get as well as a loss by parting with what one has (*Kapitene* (2010)).

4   The gain or loss can be temporary or permanent.

15.2.3 *Mens rea* of s 2

1   The defendant must:
   ● be dishonest; and
   ● know or believe the representation to be untrue or misleading; and
   ● have an intention to make a gain or cause a loss.

2   The explanatory notes issued by the Government with the Act make it clear that the *Ghosh* test for dishonesty used in theft cases (see 13.1.4) applies to this offence.

▶ 15.3 Fraud by failing to disclose information

1   This is an offence under s 3 Fraud Act 2006. It is committed where a person:

   a) dishonestly fails to disclose information to another person which he is under a legal duty to disclose; and

   b) intends by failing to disclose the information:

      i) to make a gain for himself or another, or

      ii) to cause loss to another or to expose another to the risk of loss.

2   The Act does not define legal duty. However, the Explanatory Notes state that such a duty may derive from:

- statute;
- the fact that the transaction in question is one of the utmost good faith;
- the express or implied terms of a contract;
- the custom of a particular trade or market; or
- the existence of a fiduciary relationship between the parties.

3   The *Ghosh* test for dishonesty applies.

4   'Gain' and 'loss' have the same meaning as for s 2 (see 15.2.2).

▌ 15.4 Fraud by abuse of position

1   Under s 4 Fraud Act 2006 this offence is committed where a person:

   a)   occupies a position in which he is expected to safeguard, or not to act against, the financial interests of another person; and

   b)   dishonestly abuses that position; and

   c)   intends by means of abuse of that position:

      i)   to make a gain for himself or another, or

      ii)   to cause loss to another or to expose another to the risk of loss.

2   Subsection 4(2) states that this offence can be committed by an omission as well as by an act.

3   The Explanatory Notes give examples of the necessary relationship required for this offence. These included trustee and beneficiary, director and company, professional person and client, agent and principal, and employee and employer.

4   Cases have included the manager of a care home withdrawing money from a resident's account (*Marshall* (2009)) and an office manager using his position to get goods through customs (*Gale* (2008)).

5   The *Ghosh* test for dishonesty applies.

6   'Gain' and 'loss' have the same meaning as for s 2 (see 15.2.2).

▌ 15.5 Obtaining services dishonestly

1   This is committed under s 11 of the Fraud Act 2006, where D obtains services for himself or another:

- by a dishonest act, and
- in breach of subsection (2).

2   A person obtains services in breach of s 11(2) if:

   a) they are made available on the basis that payment has been or will be made for or in respect of them;

   b) he obtains them without any payment having been made for or in respect of them or without payment having been made in full; and

   c) when he obtains them he knows:

      i) that they are being made available on the basis described in paragraph (a), or

      ii) that they might be,

      but intends that payment will not be made, or will not be made in full.

15.5.1 The *actus reus* of obtaining services dishonestly

1   There must be an act; the offence cannot be committed by omission.

2   The services must actually be obtained.

3   The offence is only committed if the defendant does not pay anything or does not pay in full for the service.

15.5.2 The *mens rea* of obtaining services dishonestly

1   The *mens rea* consists of three parts:

   ● dishonesty (*Ghosh* test);

   ● knowledge that the services are or might be available only on the basis that they have been, or will be, paid for;

   ● an intention not to pay or not to pay in full.

▶ 15.6 Other offences under the Fraud Act 2006

The Act created other offences. These include:

● possession etc of articles for use in frauds (s 6);

● making or supplying articles for use in frauds (s 7);

● participating in fraudulent business carried on by a sole trader (s 9); and

● participating in fraudulent business carried on by a company (s 10).

Key Cases Checklist

Fraud Act 2006 s 2

Fraud by false representation

- Representation can be as to fact or law or state of mind
- It can be express or implied: *Barnard* **(1837)**, *Lamble* **(1981)**, *Gilmartin* **(1983)**
- 'False' means untrue or misleading
- D must know representation is or might be untrue or misleading
- Must be dishonest (*Ghosh* **(1982)**)
- Intend to make a gain or cause a loss

Fraud Act 2006 s 3

Fraud by failing to disclose information

- Must be under a legal duty to disclose information
- Intend to make a gain or cause a loss

Fraud Act 2006 offences

Fraud Act 2006 s 4

Fraud by abuse of position

- Must occupy a position in which he is expected to safeguard the financial interests of another: *Marshall* **(2009)**, *Gale* **(2008)**
- Must dishonestly abuse that position
- Intend to make a gain or cause a loss

Fraud Act 2006 s 11

Obtaining services dishonestly

- Must obtain services: *Sofroniou* **(2003)**
- The services must be available on the basis that payment will be made for them
- D must obtain them without paying or paying in full
- Must know payment is expected and intend not to pay or not to pay in full
- Must be dishonest

Cases decided before the Fraud Act 2007 are not binding but are likely to be considered by the courts.

15.2.1   *Barnard* (1837) C & P 784

Key Facts

D went into a shop in Oxford wearing the cap and gown of a fellow commoner of the university. He also said he was a fellow commoner and as a result the shopkeeper agreed to sell him goods on credit.

Key Law

Saying he was a fellow commoner would be an express representation. In addition, the court said, *obiter*, that he would have been guilty even if he had said nothing. The wearing of the cap and gown was itself a false pretence under the old law and would be an implied representation under s 2 Fraud Act 2006.

15.2.1   *Lambie* [1981] 2 All ER 776

Key Facts

D exceeded her Barclays credit card limit. Barclays wrote asking her to return the card. She agreed that she would return the card on 7 December 1977, but did not do so. On 15 December 1977 she purchased goods using the card. She was convicted of obtaining a pecuniary advantage by deception contrary to s 16(1) Theft Act 1968. The Court of Appeal allowed her appeal but the House of Lords reinstated the conviction.

Key Law

By using the card she was implying that she had the authority of the bank to do so. This is an implied representation. She was dishonest because she knew she did not have authority to use the card.

15.2.1   *Gilmartin* [1983] 1 All ER 829   CA

Key Facts

D, a stationer, paid for supplies with post-dated cheques which he knew would not be met. This was held to be a deception.

Key Law

Writing a cheque and giving it as payment implies that D has sufficient funds in the account to meet the cheque when it is presented.

15.2.2   *Kapitene* [2010] EWCA Crim 2061   CA

Key Facts

D, who was an illegal immigrant, applied for a job at ISS Cleaning Services Ltd. He signed a declaration stating that he was legally entitled to remain in the United Kingdom, and showed them a Congolese passport containing his details, his photograph and an immigration stamp indicating that he had 'indefinite leave' to remain in the United Kingdom. He began work as a cleaner.

Key Law

D's 'gain' was the wages he was paid by ISS Cleaning Services. V's 'loss' was the wages paid out.

15.4   *Marshall* [2009] EWCA Crim 2076   CA

Key Facts

D was the joint manager of a residential care home. V was a resident in the home and had severe learning difficulties. V had a bank account which she could not exercise any proper control over herself. D made several withdrawals and used the money for her own benefit. She pleaded guilty to offences under s 4 of the Fraud Act and was sentenced to 12 months' imprisonment.

15.4   *Gale* [2008] EWCA Crim 1344

Key Facts

D was an office manager for one of DHL's divisions at Heathrow airport. He used that position to send a large crate from Heathrow to New York. He certified the crate as 'known cargo' containing empty plastic pots. D took the crate to the airline's goods reception agents and it was passed through without the usual X-ray screening. In fact the crate contained 500 kilos of khat, a drug that is not illegal in England but is illegal in America. He pleaded guilty to fraud by abuse of position.

16 Criminal damage

Basic offence

- S 1(1) Criminal Damage Act 1971
- Without lawful excuse destroys or damages property
- Includes non-permanent damage (*Roe v Kingerlee*)
- Must intend to do the damage or be reckless as to it

CRIMINAL DAMAGE

Endangering life

- Basic offence

PLUS
- Intending by the damage to endanger another's life

or
- Be reckless as to whether the life of another is endangered

Defence to basic offence

- Belief in consent of owner to the damage is a defence (s 5(2) Criminal Damage Act 1971)
- The belief must be honestly held
- But it is immaterial whether the belief is justified (*Jaggard v Dickinson*)

▶ 16.1 The basic offence

1 This is an offence under s 1(1) Criminal Damage Act 1971.

2 The Act makes it an offence for a person who, without lawful excuse, destroys or damages any property belonging to another intending to destroy or damage any such property or being reckless as to whether any such property would be destroyed or damaged.

16.1.1 *Actus reus* of the basic offence

1   The property must be destroyed or damaged.

2   Property is defined in s 10 Criminal Damage Act 1971 as property of a tangible nature, whether real or personal, and including money.

3   So, land is property which can be damaged although it cannot normally be stolen.

4   However, intangible rights cannot be damaged, though they may be stolen.

5   Wild animals that have not been reduced into possession are not property (*Cresswell and Currie v DPP* (2006)).

6   'Destroy' includes where the property has been made useless even though it is not completely destroyed.

7   'Damage' includes non-permanent damage which can be cleaned off, e.g. water-soluble paint (*Hardman v Chief Constable of Avon and Somerset Constabulary* (1986)), and mud (*Roe v Kingerlee* (1986)).

8   Damage includes temporary impairment of value or usefulness (*Morphitis v Salmon* (1990), *Fiak* (2005)).

9   However, damage was held not to include spit which landed on a policeman's uniform and could be wiped off with very little effort (*A (a juvenile) v R* (1978)).

16.1.2 *Mens rea* of the basic offence

1   The defendant must do the damage or destruction either intentionally or recklessly.

2   The test for recklessness is subjective, that is, did the defendant realise the risk.

3   Prior to the House of Lords' decision in *G and another* (2003) it was held that recklessness meant *Caldwell*-style recklessness, which included both subjective and objective recklessness.

4   The objective test was harsh, as shown in *Elliott v C* (1983) where the defendant was incapable of appreciating the risk but was still guilty under use of the objective test.

5   In *G and another* (2003) the House of Lords overruled the decision in *Caldwell* because the Law Lords had 'adopted an interpretation of s 1 of the 1971 Act which was beyond the range of feasible meanings' and held

that only the subjective test should be used for recklessness in criminal damage.

16.1.3 Section 5 defence

1   Section 5(2) Criminal Damage Act 1971 creates defences to the basic offence.

2   Section 5(2)(a) states that a person will be regarded as having a lawful excuse if at the time of the act or acts alleged to constitute the offence he believed that the person or persons whom he believed to be entitled to consent to the destruction or damage to the property in question had so consented, or would have so consented to it if he or they had known of the destruction or damage and its circumstances.

3   Section 5(3) states that for the purposes of s 5, it is immaterial whether a belief is justified or not if it is honestly held.

4   The combination of s 5(2)(a) and s 5(3) allows a defence of mistake to be used, even where the defendant makes the mistake because they are intoxicated (*Jaggard v Dickinson* (1981)).

5   Section 5(2)(b) states that a person will be regarded as having a lawful excuse if he destroyed, damaged, or threatened to destroy or damage the property in order to protect property belonging to himself or another and he believed that the property was in need of immediate protection and that the means used were reasonable in all the circumstances.

6   If the damage is not in order to protect property, then D cannot use this defence (*Kelleher* (2003)).

7   As wild animals that have not been reduced into possession are not property under the Act, then D cannot rely on the defence in s 5(2)(b) if he damages property in order to protect wild animals from damage or destruction (*Cresswell and Currie v DPP* (2006)).

▶ 16.2 Endangering life

1   This is an aggravated offence of criminal damage under s 1(2) Criminal Damage Act 1971.

2   It is committed where a person who, without lawful excuse, destroys or damages any property, whether belonging to himself or another:

a) intending to destroy or damage any property or being reckless as to whether any property would be destroyed or damaged; and

b) intending by the destruction or damage to endanger the life of another or being reckless as to whether the life of another would be thereby endangered.

3   The danger to life must come from the destruction or damage, not from another source in which damage was caused (*Steer* (1988)).

4   Life does not actually have to be endangered.

5   Section 1(2) applies, even where the property damaged is the defendant's own.

6   The *mens rea* is intending or being reckless both as to whether property would be destroyed or damaged and as to whether life would be endangered thereby.

7   The test for recklessness is subjective in both parts. D must realise that life will be endangered (*Castle* (2004)).

▶ 16.3 Arson

1   Where an offence under s 1 Criminal Damage Act 1971 is committed by destroying or damaging property by fire, the offence becomes arson (s 1(3) Criminal Damage Act 1971).

2   In *Miller* (1983) it was held that arson could be committed by an omission where the defendant accidentally started a fire and failed to do anything to prevent damage from that fire.

Key Cases Checklist

Damage

Hardman v Chief Constable of Avon (1986)

Roe v Kingerlee (1986)
The damage does not need to be permanent. The expense and trouble of removing it can be considered

Endangering Life

Steer (1987)
The danger must come from the damage and not from the act

Castle (2004)
The test for recklessness is subjective

Criminal Damage

Mens Rea

G and another (2003)
D must have been aware of the risk of damage occurring: the test is subjective

S 5 Defences

Kelleher (2003)
To have a defence under s 5(2)(b), the act of damage must be done from the immediate protection of property of another

Jaggard v Dickinson (1980)
S 5(3) requires the court to consider D's actual state of mind: intoxication is irrelevant

Cresswell v DPP (2006)
Defence not available if the item is not property as defined in s 10

16.1.1

***Cresswell v DPP: Currie v DPP* [2006] EWHC 3379 (Admin)**

 DC

Key Facts

Ds were opposed to DEFRA's cull of badgers, which was being carried out in order to determine if there were links between badgers and TB in cows. Ds destroyed traps set by DEFRA for the purpose of trapping badgers. Any badgers trapped would then have been killed in the research. Ds claimed that they had a lawful excuse to protect property (badgers) under s 5(2) Criminal Damage Act 1971. Their convictions were upheld.

Key Law

The defence of lawful excuse was not available as the badgers were not property, as defined in s 10 of the Act, at the time the traps were destroyed. They had not been reduced into possession since they had not yet been caught. The court also held that the badgers did not belong to D or to another as required by the defence in s 5(2). They were not in the custody or control of DEFRA or anyone else.

16.1.1   *Hardman v Chief Constable of Avon and Somerset Constabulary* [1986] Crim LR 330   CrCt

Key Facts

CND protesters, to mark the 40th anniversary of the dropping of the atomic bomb on Hiroshima, painted silhouettes on the pavement with water-soluble paint. The local council paid to have the paintings removed with water jets. Ds argued that it would have washed away with rain. They were convicted.

Key Law

Damage does not have to be permanent. The mischief done to property and the expense and trouble of removing it can be considered.

16.1.1   *Roe v Kingerlee* [1986] Crim LR 735   DC

Key Facts

D had smeared mud on the walls of a police cell. It cost £7 to have it cleaned off.

Key Law

It was held that this could be damage even though it was not permanent.

16.1.2   *G and another* [2003] UKHL 50

Key Facts

Two boys aged 11 and 12 years set fire to some bundles of newspapers in a shop yard. They threw the burning papers under a large wheelie bin and left the yard. The bin caught fire; this spread to the shop and other buildings causing about £1 million damage. The boys were convicted under both ss 1 and 3 Criminal Damage Act 1971. On appeal, the House of Lords quashed their conviction.

Key Law

Recklessness for the purposes of the *mens rea* of criminal damage means D must have been aware of the risk of damage occurring. It is a subjective test.

Key Judgment: Lord Bingham (quoting the Draft Criminal Code):

'A person acts recklessly within the meaning of section 1 of the Criminal Damage Act 1971 with respect to –

(i) a circumstance when he is aware of a risk that it exists or will exist;

(ii) a result when he is aware of a risk that it will occur; and it is in the circumstances known to him, unreasonable to take the risk.'

Key Comment

This decision overruled *Caldwell* [1981] 1 All ER 961. The House of Lords held that in *Caldwell* the Law Lords had 'adopted an interpretation of section 1 of the 1971 Act which was beyond the range of feasible meanings'. They emphasised that when the Criminal Damage Act was drafted, the Law Commission had not intended that the *mens rea* for the offence be changed. They had merely replaced the old-fashioned word 'maliciously' used in previous Acts with the phrase 'intending or being reckless'.

16.1.3   *Jaggard v Dickinson* [1980] 3 All ER 716   (DC)

Key Facts

D, who was drunk, went to what she thought was a friend's house. There was no-one in so she broke a window to get in as she correctly believed her friend would consent to this. In fact, she broke into the wrong house.

Key Law

Section 5(3) requires the court to consider D's actual state of belief. It is irrelevant that D was intoxicated.

16.1.3   *Kelleher* [2003] EWCA Crim 3525   (CA)

Key Facts

D had strong and genuine concerns that the policies of the USA and UK were leading towards the eventual destruction of the world. He believed that Lady Thatcher was one of those responsible for the state of affairs. He knocked off the head of a statue of Lady Thatcher. The trial judge ruled as a matter of law that the defence of lawful excuse under s 5(2)(b) Criminal Damage Act 1971 was not available. D's conviction was upheld.

Key Law

The act of damage must be done in order to protect property belonging to another.

Key Links

- *Blake v DPP* [1993] Crim LR 586;
- *Hill* (1988) 89 Cr App R 74.

16.2

Steer [1987] 2 All ER 833

 HL

Key Facts

D fired three shots at the home of his former business partner, causing damage to the house. The Court of Appeal quashed his conviction as they held that the danger came from the shots, not from any damage done to the house through those shots.

Key Law

The danger to life for an offence under s 1(2) must come from the damage itself.

Key Link

Webster and Warwick [1995] 2 All ER 168.

16.2

Castle [2004] EWCA Crim 2758

CA

Key Facts

D broke into some offices at night to burgle them. He then set fire to the premises. There were two flats above the offices which were damaged by soot and smoke. The occupants of the flats were not at home. He was charged with arson being reckless as to whether life would be endangered. The judge directed the jury according to the objective test of *Caldwell*. The Court of Appeal quashed his conviction.

Key Law

The objective *Caldwell* test was no longer appropriate. The test was whether D was subjectively reckless in respect of the risk of endangering life.

17 Public order offences

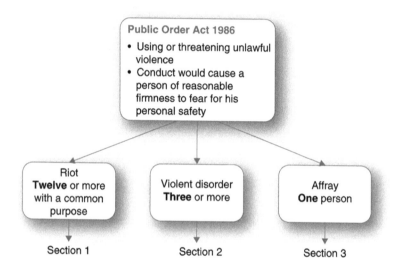

Public Order Act 1986
- Using or threatening unlawful violence
- Conduct would cause a person of reasonable firmness to fear for his personal safety

Riot
Twelve or more with a common purpose

Violent disorder
Three or more

Affray
One person

Section 1

Section 2

Section 3

17.1 Riot

1 This is an offence under s 1 Public Order Act 1986.

2 Where 12 or more persons who are present together use or threaten unlawful violence for a common purpose and the conduct of them (taken together) is such as would cause a person of reasonable firmness present at the scene to fear for his personal safety, each of the persons using unlawful violence for the common purpose is guilty of riot.

17.2 Violent disorder

1 This is an offence under s 2 Public Order Act 1986.

2 Where three or more persons who are present together use or threaten unlawful violence and the conduct of them (taken together) is such as

would cause a person of reasonable firmness present at the scene to fear for his personal safety, each of the persons using threatening or unlawful violence is guilty of violent disorder.

3   The words 'present together' mean being in the same place at the same time. There does not have to be a common purpose (*NW* (2010)).

▶ 17.3 Affray

1   This is an offence under s 3 Public Order Act 1986.

2   A person is guilty of affray if he uses or threatens unlawful violence towards another and his conduct is such as would cause a person of reasonable firmness present at the scene to fear for his personal safety.

3   'Conduct' has been held to include encouraging a dog to attack (*Dixon* (1993)).

4   It is not necessary for a person of reasonable firmness to have been at the scene (*Davison* (1992)).

5   However, there must be a threat to someone who is actually present at the scene (*I, M and H v DPP* (2001));

6   Carrying dangerous weapons such as petrol bombs would amount to a threat of unlawful violence, even if they were not waved or brandished (*I, M and H v DPP* (2001)).

▶ 17.4 Fear or provocation of violence

1   This is an offence under s 4 Public Order Act 1986.

2   A person is guilty of this offence if he:

   a) uses towards another person threatening, abusive or insulting words or behaviour; or

   b) distributes or displays to another any writing, sign or other visible representation which is threatening, abusive or insulting, with intent to cause that person to believe that immediate unlawful violence will be used against him or another by any person, or to provoke the immediate use of unlawful violence by that person

   c) or another, or whereby that person is likely to believe that such violence will be used or it is likely that such violence will be provoked.

3   The words 'threatening, abusive or insulting words or behaviour' are not defined in the Act. Under the previous Public Order Act they were held to include blowing a whistle and distributing leaflets (*Brutus v Cozens* (1972)).

▶ 17.5 Harassment offences

17.5.1 Intentional harassment, alarm or distress

1   This is an offence under s 4A Public Order Act 1986.

2   A person commits this offence if, with intent to cause a person harassment, alarm or distress, he:

    a) uses threatening, abusive or insulting words or behaviour, or disorderly behaviour, or

    b) displays any writing, sign or other visible representation which is threatening, abusive or insulting, thereby causing that or another person harassment, alarm or distress.

3   It is a defence if D can prove that the words or behaviour etc were used in a private dwelling and he had no reason to believe that they would be seen or heard by a person outside that dwelling (s 4(3)).

4   A police cell has been held not to be a dwelling for the purposes of the defence under s 4(3) (*Francis* (2007)).

5   A communal laundry in a block of flats has been held not to be a dwelling for the purpose of s 4(3) (*Le Vine* (2010)).

17.5.2 Harassment, alarm or distress

1   This is an offence under s 5 Public Order Act 1986.

2   A person commits this offence if he:

    a) uses threatening, abusive or insulting words or behaviour, or disorderly behaviour, or

    b) displays any writing, sign or other visible representation which is threatening, abusive or insulting, within the hearing or sight of a person likely to be caused harassment, alarm or distress thereby.

3   It must be proved both that D intended to cause a person harassment, alarm or distress and that D's behaviour did, in fact, cause someone harassment, alarm or distress (*R v DPP* (2006)).

4   The offence is committed if D harasses V. There is no need to prove V was also caused alarm or distress (*Southard* (2006)).

5   It is sufficient that there was someone near enough to hear the words: it is not necessary to prove that any person actually heard them (*Taylor v DPP* (2006)).

▶ 17.6 Racially aggravated offences

1   If a defendant uses words identifying specific nationalities or races or ethnic background then this can make the offence an aggravated one within the definition of s 28 Crime and Disorder Act 1998.

2   More general words such as 'foreigners' or 'immigrants' also come within the scope of s 28, as in *Rogers (Philip)* (2006) where D used the words 'bloody foreigners', or *Attorney-General's Reference (No 4 of 2004)* (2005) where D used the words 'immigrant doctor'.

Key Cases Checklist

Affray

***Dixon* (1993)**
An act such as encouraging a dog to attack can be conduct for the purpose of affray

***Davison* (1992)**
(1) An affray can be committed on private property
(2) It is not necessary for a person of reasonable firmness to have been at the scene

***I, M and H v DPP* (2001)**
(1) Carrying dangerous weapons can be the threat of unlawful violence for affray (2) There must be someone present at the scene who was threatened with unlawful violence for affray

Violent Disorder

***NW* (2010)**
'present together' means being in the same place at the same time

Public Order Offences

Insulting Behaviour

***Brutus v Cozens* (1972)**
Whether words, behaviour or writing etc are 'threatening, abusive or insulting' under s 5 is a question of fact

Intentionally Causing Harassment etc

***R v DPP* (2006)**
There must be evidence that someone had been harassed, alarmed or distressed by the behaviour

***Taylor v DPP* (2006)**
It is enough to prove someone was near enough to hear the racist language. It is not necessary to prove anyone had actually heard

Racially Aggravated Offences

***Rogers (Philip)* (2006)**
A phrase such as 'bloody foreigners' comes within the definition of racial group

17.2   *NW* [2010] EWCA Crim 404   CA

Key Facts

D intervened when a police officer tried to make a friend of D's pick up litter she had just dropped. The incident escalated into a scuffle between NW and the officer. A crowd gathered, some of whom became involved. D and two others were convicted of violent disorder.

Key Law

The words 'present together' in s 2 Public Order Act 1986 mean no more than being in the same place at the same time. There does not have to be a common purpose.

17.3   *Dixon* [1993] Crim LR 579   CA

Key Facts

D ran away from the police following a domestic incident. The officers cornered him and he encouraged his dog to attack them. Two officers were bitten. D's conviction for affray was upheld.

Key Law

An act such as encouraging a dog to attack can be conduct for the purpose of affray.

17.3   *Davison* [1992] Crim LR 31   CA

Key Facts

The police were called to a domestic incident. D threatened a police officer with an eight-inch knife. D's conviction for affray was upheld.

Key Law

1) An affray can be committed on private property.

2) It is not necessary for a person of reasonable firmness to have been at the scene. The test was whether a person of reasonable firmness would have feared for his safety, not whether the police officer actually did fear for his personal safety.

17.3 *I, M and H v DPP* [2001] UKHL 10, [2001] 2 Cr App R 216

HL

Key Facts

The defendants had armed themselves with petrol bombs to use against a rival gang. The police arrived before the Ds met up with the rival gang. The moment the police arrived, the Ds threw the petrol bombs away and dispersed. Their convictions for affray were quashed by the House of Lords.

Key Law

1) The carrying of dangerous weapons such as petrol bombs could constitute the threat of unlawful violence for the offence of affray. This was true whether or not the weapons were brandished.
2) There must be someone present at the scene who was threatened with unlawful violence for the offence of affray to be committed.

17.4 *Brutus v Cozens* [1972] 2 All ER 1297, (1972) 56 Cr App R 799

HL

Key Facts

D made a protest about apartheid by running onto the court, blowing a whistle and distributing leaflets during a Wimbledon tennis match. He was acquitted of an offence under s 5 Public Order Act 1936. This offence has since been abolished, but the words 'threatening, abusive or insulting' used in it are contained in s 4 Public Order Act 1986.

Key Law

It is a question of fact whether the words, behaviour or writing etc are 'threatening, abusive or insulting'. In *Brutus,* the House of Lords held that the magistrates' finding of fact that D's behaviour was not 'threatening, abusive or insulting' was not unreasonable and could not be challenged.

17.5.2   *R v DPP* [2006] All ER (D) 250 May   CA

Key Facts

D, aged 12, was with his sister when she was arrested for criminal damage. D made masturbatory gestures towards the police and called them 'wankers'. D was arrested and charged with an offence contrary to s 4 Public Order Act 1986. The arresting officer gave evidence that he was not personally annoyed or distressed by D's behaviour, but that he found it distressing that a boy of 12 was acting in such a manner.

Key Law

D's conviction was quashed because there was no evidence that anyone had been harassed, alarmed or distressed by his behaviour.

17.5.2   *Southard v DPP* [2006] EWHC 3449 (Admin)   DC

Key Facts

D and his brother were stopped by police as they were cycling with poor lighting at midnight. While his brother was being searched, D twice approached the officer and swore at him, interfering with the search process. D was convicted of an offence under s 5 Public Order Act 1986.

Key Law

Harassment is sufficient. It does not need to be proved that V was alarmed or distressed. The words have quite different meanings.

Key Judgment: Fulford J

'Distress by its very nature involves an element of real emotional disturbance or upset but the same is not necessarily true of harassment. You can be harassed, indeed seriously harassed, without experiencing emotional disturbance

*or upset at all. That said, although the harassment does not
have to be grave, it should not be trivial.'*

Key Link

Harvey (2012) 176 JP 265

17.5.2   ***Taylor v DPP* [2006] EWHC 1202 (Admin)**   DC

Key Facts

The police were called to a private house in the early hours
of the morning by the ambulance service. D was on the
premises shouting and intimidating the occupant. While the
police were escorting her from the premises, she shouted
and swore using racist language. The ambulance crew was
still present. In the street, D continued to shout and swear
using racist language. She appeared to be trying to gain
the attention of the neighbours and lights were being turned
on in adjoining houses. D was convicted of the offence of
using threatening and abusive language under s 5(1)(a)
Public Order Act 1986 which was racially aggravated,
contrary to s 31(1)(c) Crime and Disorder Act 1998.

Key Law

It was enough to prove that there was someone near
enough to hear the racist language. It was not necessary to
prove that anyone had actually heard.

17.6   ***Rogers (Philip)* [2006] EWCA Crim 2863**   CA

Key Facts

D, who was disabled and using a motorised 'mobility
scooter', encountered three Spanish women. He called
them 'bloody foreigners', told them to go back to their own
country and then pursued them in an aggressive manner.
He was convicted of the offence of causing fear or provocation of violence (s 4 Public Order Act 1986) which was
racially aggravated under s 31(1)(a) Crime and Disorder Act
1998.

Key Law

It was held that the definition of racial group in s 28(4) Crime and Disorder Act 1998 was wide enough to include 'bloody foreigners'. It was not necessary to use words identifying a particular racial group.

Key Link

Attorney-General's Reference (No 4 of 2004) [2005] EWCA Crim 889.

Index